TIME FOR KIDS

ALMANAC 2011

TIME FOR KIDS ALMANAC 2011

PRODUCED BY

DOWNTOWN BOOKWORKS INC.

PRESIDENT: Julie Merberg
EDITOR AND PHOTO RESEARCHER: Sarah Parvis
ASSISTANT EDITOR: LeeAnn Pemberton
SENIOR CONTRIBUTORS: Kerry Acker, Marge Kennedy, Jeanette Leardi, Mickey Steiner
SPECIAL THANKS: Patty Brown, Pam Abrams, Amanda Culp, Rebecca Freedholm, Mike DeCapite, Brian Michael Thomas, Stephen Callahan, Morris Katz, Nathanael Katz

DESIGNED BY

Georgia Rucker Design

TIME FOR KIDS

MANAGING EDITOR, TIME FOR KIDS MAGAZINE:
Nellie Gonzalez Cutler
EDITOR, TIME LEARNING VENTURES:
Jonathan Rosenbloom

Time Inc.
HOME ENTERTAINMENT

PUBLISHER: Richard Fraiman
GENERAL MANAGER: Steven Sandonato
EXECUTIVE DIRECTOR, MARKETING SERVICES:
Carol Pittard
DIRECTOR, RETAIL & SPECIAL SALES:
Tom Mifsud
DIRECTOR, NEW PRODUCT DEVELOPMENT:
Peter Harper
DIRECTOR, BOOKAZINE DEVELOPMENT AND MARKETING: Laura Adam
PUBLISHING DIRECTOR, BRAND MARKETING: Joy Butts
ASSISTANT GENERAL COUNSEL: Helen Wan
BOOK PRODUCTION MANAGER: Susan Chodakiewicz
DESIGN & PREPRESS MANAGER:
Anne-Michelle Gallero
ASSOCIATE BRAND MANAGER: Jonathan White
ASSOCIATE PREPRESS MANAGER: Alex Voznesenskiy
ASSISTANT PRODUCTION MANAGER:
Brynn Joyce

SPECIAL THANKS

Christine Austin, Jeremy Biloon, Glenn Buonocore, Jim Childs, Rose Cirrincione, Jacqueline Fitzgerald, Carrie Frazier, Lauren Hall, Jennifer Jacobs, Suzanne Janso, Raphael Joa, Rosalie Khan, Mona Li, Robert Marasco, Amy Migliaccio, Kimberly Posa, Richard Prue, Brooke Reger, Dave Rozzelle, Ilene Schreider, Adriana Tierno, Time Imaging, Sydney Webber

For information on TIME FOR KIDS magazine for the classroom or home, go to **WWW.TFKCLASSROOM.COM** or call 1-800-777-8600.

For subscriptions to SPORTS ILLUSTRATED KIDS, go to **WWW.SIKIDS.COM** or call 1-800-889-6007.

PUBLISHED BY

TIME FOR KIDS BOOKS
Time Inc.
1271 Avenue of the Americas
New York, New York 10020

ISBN 13: 978-1-60320-129-2
ISBN 10: 1-60320-129-7
ISSN: 1534-5718

TIME FOR KIDS is a trademark of Time Inc.

We welcome your comments and suggestions about TIME FOR KIDS Books. Please write to us at:

TIME FOR KIDS BOOKS
ATTENTION: BOOK EDITORS
PO BOX 11016
DES MOINES, IA 50336-1016

If you would like to order any of our TIME FOR KIDS OR SPORTS ILLUSTRATED KIDS hardcover Collector's Edition books, please call us at 1-800-327-6388. (Monday through Friday, 7:00 a.m.–8:00 p.m. or Saturday, 7:00 a.m.–6:00 p.m. Central Time).

1 WCT 10

Contents

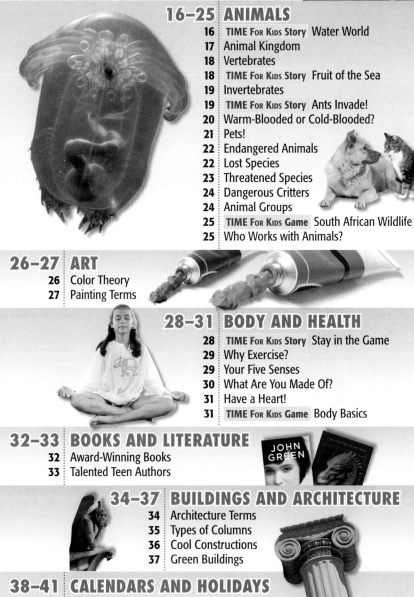

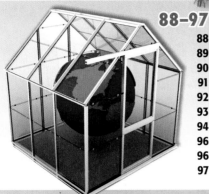

$4.50
$7.00
CHOCOLATE
$8.00
$10.00
$20.00
$4.50

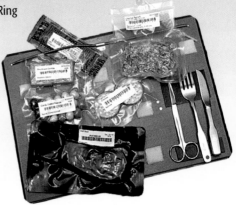

Contents

What's in the News?

Destruction in Haiti

O n January 12, 2010, a devastating earthquake struck the small, poor nation of Haiti, which is on the island of Hispaniola, in the Caribbean Sea. The rest of the island belongs to the Dominican Republic.

The magnitude of earthquakes is measured using the numbers 1 through 10 on the Richter scale. The number 10 indicates the strongest magnitude of an earthquake. Haiti's massive quake registered a 7.0 on the Richter scale, and was the strongest there since 1770. The epicenter of the earthquake was located about 15 miles (24 km) from Haiti's capital, Port-au-Prince. Approximately 20% of the buildings in the capital city collapsed, including the Presidential palace and the National Assembly building. Of the remaining homes and structures, most have suffered some damage.

More than 200,000 Haitians died as a result of the earthquake, and approximately 1.3 million people were left homeless. Following the earthquake, there were more than 50 major aftershocks, which are tremors that follow earthquakes.

Countries around the world quickly sent doctors, peacekeeping troops, specialists, food, medicine, and relief supplies, but because of the extent of the destruction, it may take decades to rebuild Haiti.

guess what? *The Red Cross and other organizations are set up to accept donations sent through cell phones. People around the world posted the information about mobile giving via Facebook and Twitter. It also appeared on the White House blog and in public service announcements on TV. More than $10 million was raised in U.S. text message donations for Haiti in the few days following the disaster.*

Earth-Altering Earthquake

S hortly after the disaster in Haiti, an 8.8-magnitude quake hit Chile. Though the earthquake in Chile was stronger, it did less damage. That is because many of the buildings and structures in Chile were built to withstand earthquakes.

But, the South American quake was still so powerful that it actually shifted the entire planet. This shifting of Earth's axis shortened the length of every day by a few microseconds. One million microseconds make up a second, so this is a small amount of time that won't be noticed. Scientists, though, are interested in any changes to Earth's orbit.

In February 2010, an enormous earthquake struck Chile.

Iran's Green Revolution

Protesters in Iran

On June 12, 2009, voters in Iran went to the polls to cast their ballots for President. The two main candidates were Mahmoud Ahmadinejad, who was supported by the country's Revolutionary Guards and had served as President since 2005, and Mir-Hossein Mousavi, who is supported by many young people who wanted more freedom.

The official results, released a day later, announced that Ahmadinejad had won 63% of the vote. In some cities, the number of votes counted was higher than the number of registered voters. Mousavi and his supporters immediately asked that the results be double-checked and that voter irregularities be investigated.

When the government did not take any action to verify the election results, protesters took to the streets. Many of them wore the color green, which was associated with Mousavi and his political party. For this reason, the unrest in Iran became known as the Green Revolution. As many as 1,000 protesters (the exact figure is unknown) were arrested, and about 20 were killed in clashes with police. The unrest continued for weeks after the election.

Somali Pirates Attack American Ship

In April 2009, young men from Somalia (a country in East Africa) attacked an American ship called the *Maersk Alabama*. At the time, the ship was operated by a crew of 20 people and was carrying food and relief supplies. Most of the crew locked themselves in an engine room and prevented the pirates from being able to steer the ship. Unable to take over completely, the Somali men took Richard Phillips, the ship's captain, hostage. After five days in a lifeboat with the pirates, Phillips was rescued by members of the U.S. Navy.

Richard Phillips

Copenhagen Climate Change Conference

going green

Scientists and government officials around the world have spent years trying to come up with the best ways to battle global warming and protect the environment. And, in December 2009, world leaders from 193 nations met in Copenhagen, Denmark, to try to reach an agreement limiting greenhouse gas emissions (for more on greenhouse gases and global warming, see pages 90–93). The delegates were unable to create a final agreement, but many leaders promised funds to help developing nations curb their emissions, and said they would work to reduce pollution in their home countries.

President Obama addressed world leaders in Copenhagen.

What's in the News

9

What's in the News?

Unemployment Rate Soars

The economic downturn that began in 2008 continued to affect the United States in 2009 and 2010. As a result of the recession, many people spent less money and bought fewer goods. Businesses struggled and laid off employees. Unable to make high monthly loan payments, many people lost their homes or cars. In October 2009, the U.S. unemployment rate hit 10.2%, its highest level in 26 years.

Job seekers flock to a career fair, looking for work.

More Troops for the War on Terror

In a speech delivered in December 2009, President Obama explained that in order to keep the world safe from al-Qaeda, the United States and its allies needed to continue fighting in Afghanistan, resist members of the Taliban that threatened the country's new government, and keep the country safe and stable. The President laid out his plans to send an additional 30,000 troops to Afghanistan, which would bring the total number of military personnel there to more than 100,000. He said he hoped to begin removing servicemen and women in July 2011.

Soldiers patrol a mountainous area of Afghanistan.

guess what?

The U.S. government announced new rules for airlines. The regulations say that airlines must provide food and water to passengers if they have been sitting on a plane, waiting for it to take off for more than two hours. After three hours, the passengers must be allowed off the plane.

Traveling Together

going green

According to a report issued by the American Public Transportation Association, 2008 (the most recent year studied) was a great year for public transportation. More people used buses, trains, subways, and other kinds of mass transportation in 2008 than any year since 1956. At the time, gas prices were extremely high. As the cost of fuel fell, the number of mass-transit users stayed high. Conservationists look forward to next year's report to see if use of energy-saving public transportation continues to grow.

Public transportation in San Francisco includes cable cars.

Sonia Sotomayor meets with President Obama.

Big Changes in U.S. Health Care

On March 23, 2010, President Obama signed an important health care reform bill into law. The new legislation will bring major changes to the nation's health system. This includes extending medical coverage to more than 30 million Americans who did not have health insurance before. "This is what change looks like," Obama said. "We proved that we are still a people capable of doing big things." But not everyone agrees with the new health care plan. Some members of Congress say it will cost too much money and plan to fight to repeal the law.

The push for health care reform played a large part in President Obama's first year in the White House.

Supreme Court Shake-Up

After 19 years on the highest court in the United States, Justice David Souter announced that he would be stepping down from his post. Souter had been selected by President George H.W. Bush in 1990. President Obama chose Sonia Sotomayor, a judge from New York City, as his replacement. Justice Sotomayor is the third woman to serve on the U.S. Supreme Court and the first Hispanic American to hold the post.

Trading Up

going green

To boost the economy and help the environment, the U.S. government came up with a program called Car Allowance Rebate System, or CARS. Known as the Cash for Clunkers program, it offered cash incentives of $3,500 or $4,500 to encourage people to trade in their old automobiles and buy newer, more energy-efficient models. The program was so popular that all of the funding was used up quickly. About two weeks after the initial law took effect, the Senate voted to extend the program. Within a few weeks, vehicle owners had turned in nearly 680,000 older cars and trucks. Many people who had not been planning to buy a new car decided to take advantage of the CARS program. The additional sales helped out the ailing auto industry.

$4,500 FOR THIS CAR CLUNKER

IF YOUR CAR QUALIFIES THIS CAR QUALIFIES

Many car dealers were happy that the CARS program brought in business during the recession.

What's in the News?

HEALTH, SCIENCE, AND TECHNOLOGY

H1N1 Scare

One of the biggest news stories of 2009 was the outbreak of the H1N1 flu pandemic. H1N1 was also known as the swine flu because some scientists thought it might have been transferred from pigs to humans. The first reports of the illness occurred in Mexico. To combat the spread of the infection, Mexican authorities shut down all schools and nonessential services. People around the globe wore face masks, used hand sanitizer, and avoided travel to Mexico and other areas with H1N1 outbreaks.

Because the H1N1 virus passed so quickly from person to person, it quickly spread around the world, reaching the United States by April. On June 11, 2009, the World Health Organization (WHO) declared it a pandemic, which is an epidemic (or rapidly spreading sickness) that infects people on a global scale.

Though the virus traveled quickly, it turned out to be no more dangerous than the regular flu virus. By the end of the year, scientists created a vaccine for that particular strain of the flu.

King Tut in the Papers

Every human has slightly different DNA, and scientists can test that DNA to learn a lot about a person, including information about his or her gender, ancestry, and health conditions. Scientists performed new DNA tests on King Tut and other royal mummies, and unlocked some clues to the ruler's health. King Tut (short for Tutankhamen) was only 9 years old when he took the throne of Egypt in 1333 B.C. Mostly controlled by advisers, he ruled for about 10 years, before dying at age 19. According to new evidence, King Tut suffered from a bone disease that caused his left foot to become deformed. He walked with a cane (several were found in his tomb). The DNA also indicated that he had malaria, a disease spread by mosquitoes that causes fever, chills, sweating, and other flu-like symptoms.

King Tut's mummy was covered with this solid-gold burial mask.

Ardi Unveiled

In October 2009, scientists made an announcement that would change human history. They had identified the oldest fossil remains of a human ancestor. Called "Ardi" for short, the skeleton belonged to a 4-foot-tall (1 m), 110-pound (50 kg) female member of the species *Ardipithecus ramidus*. Found in Ethiopia, Ardi lived approximately 4.4 million years ago—that makes her skeleton the oldest skeleton of a human ancestor ever identified. Scientists worked for 15 years to assemble and analyze the bone fragments that made up parts of Ardi's skeleton.

For years, many scientists believed there was a "missing link" between primates and early humans. The existence of Ardi proves that there is no single missing link, but that there is an entire stage of evolution that scientists know very little about.

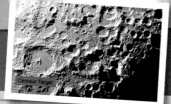
Centaur Target

Water Is Found on the Moon

Though its surface appears dry, gray, and dusty, NASA (National Aeronautics and Space Administration) announced that it found evidence of water on the moon. The Lunar Crater Observation and Sensing Satellite, known as LCROSS, released a rocket that crashed into the surface of the moon going 5,600 miles (9,000 km) per hour. The impact created a huge hole in the moon's surface and kicked up debris and ice, indicating the presence of water at the bottom of the Cabeus crater, where the sun does not shine. According to a statement issued by NASA, "The discovery opens a new chapter in our understanding of the moon."

Books Go Digital

With Amazon.com's release of a new version of the Kindle and Barnes & Noble's introduction of the Nook, more and more readers are using portable, wireless devices for reading books, magazines, newspapers, and other texts. The most recent batch of e-readers has touchscreens and can each hold more than 1,500 full-length books.

A subway rider reads from a Kindle.

Apple's New Device

In early 2010, Apple introduced a new portable flat-screen device called the iPad. Like a small, light computer, the iPad can be used for browsing online, sending e-mail, watching videos, playing games, and even reading e-books. This mini-machine weighs in at 1.5 pounds (.7 kg) and is only .5 inches (1.3 cm) thick. Like an iPhone, it has a color touchscreen and can run countless applications (or apps, as they are popularly known). Also, the images on the screen rotate, adjusting to how you are holding the device.

Apple cofounder Steve Jobs presents the iPad.

Eco-friendly Products

going green

As more people search for ways to combat global warming, consumers are seeing more environmentally friendly products and gadgets on the market. Some of these products actually generate energy, like specially designed rocking chairs and backpacks featuring solar panels that can create enough energy to power cell phones and other handheld devices. Others are made from recycled materials, including furniture made from paper, and building insulation made from used clothing. Scientists have created biodegradable dishes—and even chip bags—that will break apart rather than take up space in landfills.

What's in the News?

ENTERTAINMENT AND SPORTS

There have been many notable names in the world of entertainment. Here are a few of the standouts.

Taylor's Swift Rise to the Top

Taylor Swift's rise from aspiring country singer to household name and pop superstar was incredibly fast. She picked up four awards at the Grammys, five at the American Music Awards, and two at the Teen Choice Awards.

A *Glee*-ful Debut

Lea Michele (left) and Jane Lynch

A fictional high school glee club gets the spotlight in *Glee*, a show that began airing in 2009. This TV hit won the 2010 Golden Globe Award for Best Television Series—Musical or Comedy. Three cast members also received Golden Globe nominations: Lea Michele for Best Actress, Matthew Morrison for Best Actor, and Jane Lynch for Best Supporting Actress.

Lady Gaga's Outrageous Outfits

The years 2009 and 2010 were big ones for pop star Lady Gaga. Known for her crazy costumes and over-the-top performances (like playing a piano that was on fire!), Lady Gaga won a slew of awards, including the 2010 People's Choice Awards for Favorite Pop Artist and Favorite Breakout Artist. She also won Grammy Awards for the Best Dance Recording for her song "Poker Face" and Best Dance/Electronic Album for *The Fame*.

Oprah Says Goodbye

Top talk show host Oprah Winfrey announced that she plans to end her long-running and incredibly popular TV show in 2011. *The Oprah Winfrey Show* has been on CBS for 25 years. She is expected to start a new show on her own TV network.

The *Twilight* Phenomenon

The mega-best-selling book series by author Stephenie Meyer began with *Twilight*, released in 2005. It was followed by *New Moon* in 2006, *Eclipse* in 2007, and *Breaking Dawn* in 2008. The popular books were turned into huge box-office hits, starring Kristen Stewart, Robert Pattinson, and Taylor Lautner.

Lautner (left), Stewart, and Pattinson (right)

Super News for Drew Brees

New Orleans Saints' Quarterback Drew Brees earned the title of Super Bowl MVP after leading his team to victory against the Indianapolis Colts in Super Bowl XLIV.

High-flying Olympic Medalist

Shaun White wowed Olympic fans with his incredible half-pipe runs. Out of 50 possible points, he scored a 46.8 on his first run. Though he was already guaranteed a gold medal, he took a second run, scoring a record 48.4 points.

Vancouver 2010

5

The Yankees Win Again

In November 2009, the Yankees became World Series champs all over again. Led by Andy Pettitte, Mariano Rivera, and Hideki Matsui, the New York team had its 27th World Series win.

FROM
~~TIME~~
FOR KIDS
MAGAZINE

Water World

SCIENTISTS DISCOVER MORE THAN 17,000 SPECIES DEEP IN THE OCEAN

By Andrea Delbanco

An international team of scientists has discovered 17,650 species living more than 656 feet (200 m) beneath the surface of the world's oceans. That is the point where sunlight can no longer be seen. These species survive in the pitch black by feeding on matter that falls down to their depth, including sunken whale bones, oil, and methane gas.

The findings are part of the global Census of Marine Life, set to be completed by October 2010. Oceanographers believe thousands more species are yet to be discovered.

The rare, translucent sea cucumber uses its tentacles to swim very slowly—only about .8 inches (2 cm) per minute.

UNDER THE SEA

More than 2,000 scientists from 80 countries worked together on the census. It was an expensive and difficult process. Research using cameras, sonar, and remotely operated vehicles can cost as much as $50,000 a day.

More than 40 new species of coral were found on deep-sea mountains along with cities of brittle undersea stars and anemone gardens. Other bottom-dwellers include tentacled transparent sea cucumbers and tubeworms that feed on oil deposits.

"The deep sea is the least-explored environment on Earth," said Jesse Ausubel, who works with the Alfred P. Sloan Foundation, a sponsor of the census. "The deep sea was considered a desert until not so long ago," he said. "It's amazing to have documented close to 20,000 forms of life in a zone that was thought to be barren."

The dumbo octopod is one of the largest of the deep-sea creatures. This one is nearly 6 feet (2 m) long!

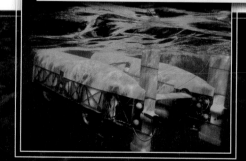

Nereus is an undersea robot used by scientists to explore the bottom of the ocean.

Animal Kingdom

Scientists classify animals according to the following subdivisions:

Phylum

Class

Order

Family

Genus

Species

Each subdivision is smaller than the one preceding it. In this way, scientists are able to assign a name to every creature on the planet, based on its characteristics. This categorization is called taxonomy. The taxonomy for the southern flying squirrel is on the right.

Southern Flying Squirrel

Flying squirrels can't actually fly, but they are able to glide between trees by using the webs of furry skin between their wrists and ankles.

Animalia (an-uh-*may*-lee-uh): All animals belong to this kingdom.

Chordata (kor-*dah*-tuh): The animals in this phylum have backbones.

Mammalia (muh-*may*-lee-uh): Female mammals breast-feed their young. Almost all mammals give birth to live young.

Rodentia (roh-*den*-shee-uh): More than 40% of mammals are rodents. The order includes mice, squirrels, **porcupines, chipmunks,** hamsters, beavers, and prairie dogs. All rodents have a particular kind of teeth called incisors that are good for gnawing. Rodents' teeth grow throughout their lives.

Sciuridae (sigh-*yoor*-uh-dee): Sciurids include 278 species of **squirrels.** They have a jaw shape that is different from that of other rodents. The word *sciuridae* means "shade-tail" and refers to the bushy tails that most squirrels have.

Glaucomys (glo-*koh*-meez): This group includes two types of North American flying squirrel.

Volans (*voh*-lanz): This species is the southern flying squirrel. It is smaller than the northern flying squirrel (*Glaucomys sabrinus*) and has white hair on its belly, unlike the northern flying squirrel.

guess what?

Some people use a **mnemonic** (nih-*mah*-nik) device, or memory aid, to keep track of the order of taxonomy. Each word in this silly sentence begins with a letter of a category used in taxonomy (kingdom, phylum, class, order, family, genus, species):

KING PHILIP CAME OVER FOR GOOD SPAGHETTI.

TOP 5 Longest-Living Animals

Here are the animals that live the longest and the oldest-known age for each.

1. Giant tortoise: up to 200 years
2. Human: up to 122
3. Sturgeon (a type of fish): up to 100
4. Blue whale and golden eagle: up to 80
5. African elephant: up to 77

Vertebrates

There are two basic kinds of animals: vertebrates, which have a backbone, and invertebrates, which don't.

Fish are cold-blooded, live in water, and breathe using gills. Their skin is scaly and, with the exception of sharks (which give birth to live young), they lay eggs. Carp, clown fish, swordfish, tuna, and eels are some examples of fish.

Amphibians are cold-blooded and begin life in the water, breathing through gills. When they are full-grown, they breathe through lungs and can walk on land. They lay eggs. Some examples of amphibians are frogs, toads, newts, and salamanders.

Reptiles are cold-blooded and have lungs. Their skin is scaly. Most reptiles lay eggs. Reptiles include lizards, turtles, snakes, alligators, and crocodiles.

Birds are warm-blooded and have wings and feathers. All birds lay eggs and most can fly (though ostriches and penguins cannot). Other examples of birds are eagles, ducks, parakeets, seagulls, storks, and flamingos.

Mammals are warm-blooded and, with the exception of the platypus and the echidna, give birth to live young. Mammal mothers breast-feed their young. Most mammals have hair or fur and live on land (except for porpoises, dolphins, and whales, which live in the water). Kangaroos, elephants, chimpanzees, bats, lions, raccoons, zebras, otters, and humans are all mammals.

guess what? At birth, a baby kangaroo is so tiny it could fit in a teaspoon.

Fruit of the Sea

By Vickie An

What a *berry* exciting find! On January 5, 2010, scientists in Taiwan announced that they had discovered a new species of crab off the island nation's southern coast. With a bright-red shell and tiny white spots, the little crustacean (kruh-*stay*-shun) looks just like a ripe strawberry.

Taiwanese marine biologist Ho Ping-ho led the research team that made the discovery.

He said the new "strawberry" crab resembles another species that lives in waters near Hawaii, Polynesia, and Mauritius. But this one has a unique clam-shaped shell, measuring about 1 inch (2.5 cm) wide, which makes it distinct.

Ho and his team found two female crabs of the new species in June 2009 off the coast of Taiwan's Kenting National Park, known for its rich marine life. The scientists were there to study the environmental impact of a wrecked cargo ship. The crabs died shortly after being captured, possibly because water in the area had been polluted with oil from the shipwreck.

FROM TIME FOR KIDS MAGAZINE

Invertebrates

Sponges live in water and are immobile. They get their food by filtering tiny organisms that swim by.

Coelenterates (sih-*len*-teh-rates) have stinging tentacles around their mouth. They use their mouth not only to eat with but also to eliminate waste. Examples of coelenterates are corals, hydras, **jellyfish,** and sea anemones.

Echinoderms (ih-*keye*-nuh-derms) live in the sea and have an exoskeleton, which means that their skeleton or supporting structure is located on the outside of their body. Echinoderms include sea urchins, **brittle stars,** and sand dollars.

Worms live in a variety of places, including underwater, in the ground, and even inside other living creatures. Examples of worms include tapeworms, flukes, pinworms, leeches, night crawlers, and **earthworms.**

Mollusks (*mol*-usks) have a soft body. To protect themselves, some have a hard shell. Clams, oysters, mussels, octopuses, scallops, squids, and **snails** are all mollusks.

Arthropods have a body that is divided into different parts, or segments. They also have an exoskeleton. Arthropods include crustaceans (such as lobsters, crabs, shrimps, and barnacles), arachnids (spiders, scorpions, and ticks), centipedes, millipedes, and all insects (such as butterflies, ants, **bees,** dragonflies, and beetles).

Ants Invade!

By Joyce C. Tang

One type of South American ant has been spreading around the world, and living in huge super-colonies. Not only that, but these natural fighters seem to know they are family, and they get along, according to recent scientific findings.

The light-brown Argentine ants are originally from South America. Over the years, the Argentine ant has moved to other parts of the globe, possibly by hiding in people's luggage and in cargo.

Ants are fierce fighters. They protect their territory from invaders, including other types of ants and insects. But Argentine ants, even when they're from separate continents, don't fight when they come together,

scientists say. "Our research found Argentine ants from three continents were rather friendly, and not hostile towards each other," researcher Eiriki Sunamura told the *New Zealand Herald.*

Scientists in Japan and Spain have discovered that the insects in the three super-colonies share similar chemical profiles. This helps them recognize one another. To prove this, the scientists matched ants from each super-colony with ants from a different colony in a similar part of the world. The Mediterranean ant colony couldn't get along with a smaller one from Spain. And members of the colony from the west coast of Japan couldn't get along with ants from another area in Japan. But when Argentine ants from the three super-colonies came together, they got along just fine.

Warm-Blooded or Cold-Blooded?

The temperature of an animal's body depends on whether that animal is warm-blooded or cold-blooded.

WARM-BLOODED ANIMALS (birds, mammals) are able to keep their body temperature constant. In cold weather, they turn the food they eat into energy that creates heat. In hot weather, they sweat, pant, or do other things to help cool their outsides and insides. Most of the food they take in is devoted to maintaining their body temperature.

The temperature of **COLD-BLOODED ANIMALS** (reptiles, fish, amphibians, invertebrates) is the same as that of their surroundings. Because of this, they are able to be very active in hot weather but are sluggish at low temperatures. When it is hot, chemicals in their bodies react quickly to help their muscles move, but these reactions slow down as the outside temperature drops. Most of the food cold-blooded animals take in is devoted to building their body mass.

Keeping Cool in the Desert

Fennec fox

The desert is not the easiest place for animals to live. There is little water for them to drink, and they must deal with extreme temperatures. Many animals in the desert simply stay out of the sunlight. They may spend much of their time underground in burrows, only coming out at night to look for food. Some birds leave the desert during its hottest months, and some mammals, like the round-tailed ground squirrel, estivate. That means they sleep during the hottest months of the year.

Other animals have adapted to the heat. Camels have long legs that keep their body away from the heat of the sand. Some mammals, such as fennec foxes and jackrabbits, have large ears that lose heat. Many desert critters have paler fur or lighter skin than their relatives living in other climates. Lighter colors absorb less heat than darker ones.

Jackrabbit

guess what? A tooth from a fully grown elephant can weigh 11 pounds (5 kg). That is heavier than a brick!

PETS!

TOP 10 Cat Breeds

1. Persian
2. Maine coon
3. Exotic
4. Abyssinian
5. Siamese
6. Ragdoll
7. Sphynx
8. Birman
9. American shorthair
10. Oriental

JUST FIFTH?!

Source: Cat Fanciers' Association

TOP 10 Dog Breeds

	RANK IN 2009	RANK IN 1999
Labrador retriever	1	1
German shepherd	2	3
Yorkshire terrier	3	9
Golden retriever	4	2
Beagle	5	5
Boxer	6	10
Chihuahua	7	7
Dachshund	8	4
Poodle	9	6
Shih tzu	10	11

Source: American Kennel Club

BOXERS RULE!

guess what?

About 25% of mammals are bats. They are the only mammals capable of true flight.

Top Animal Names

DOGS

1. Max
2. Bailey
3. Bella
4. Molly
5. Lucy
6. Buddy
7. Maggie
8. Daisy
9. Sophie
10. Chloe

CATS

1. Max
2. Chloe
3. Tigger
4. Tiger
5. Lucy
6. Smokey
7. Oliver
8. Bella
9. Shadow
10. Charlie

Endangered Animals

In 1973, the Endangered Species Act was passed by the U.S. Congress to protect various plants and animals from vanishing from the United States and its territories. The U.S. Fish and Wildlife Service keeps track of the populations of all known species in the country, adding or removing their names from the list as their survival numbers change. Here are some endangered species on the list.

A member of the U.S. Fish and Wildlife Service prepares to release a black-footed ferret back into the wild in Montana. The black-footed ferret has been on the endangered list in the U.S. since 1967.

- Woodland caribou
- Jaguar
- Black-footed ferret
- Bighorn sheep
- Humpback whale
- Red wolf
- Brown bear
- Whooping crane
- Florida panther
- Ocelot

- Hawaiian coot
- Ivory-billed woodpecker
- Atlantic salmon
- Puerto Rican boa
- Polar bear
- Giant kangaroo rat
- Indiana bat
- Eastern puma

- Hawaiian monk seal
- Blue whale
- Gray wolf
- Giant garter snake
- Green sea turtle
- California condor

Lost Species

SABER-TOOTHED TIGER

If every member of a particular species dies, then that species has become extinct. Once a species is extinct, it is gone forever. The disappearance of one animal can affect the survival and behavior of other animals as well.

Some groups of animals become extinct because they gradually evolve into a different species over time. Other animals become extinct because of human behavior. In the case of the dodo, a flightless bird on the island of Mauritius, European explorers landed on the island and hunted the dodo until none were left. As human populations grow and expand, they move into new areas, often endangering natural habitats. The destruction

DODO

of habitat is another cause of animal extinction.

A major event can lead to the destruction of many species in a short period of time. Throughout the history of Earth, several mass extinctions have occurred. Approximately 65 million years ago, all of the dinosaurs on the planet died out. Many scientists believe that an enormous asteroid collided with Earth, causing an environmental disaster, which led to the extinction of the dinosaurs.

Some of the animals that once roamed North America include the passenger pigeon, ancient bison, Columbian mammoth, giant hutia (a rodent almost as large as a bear), saber-toothed tiger, and glyptodon (an enormous armadillo-like animal). Many scientists, conservationists, and concerned citizens work hard to keep threatened or endangered species from becoming extinct.

TOP 5 Threatened Species

In December 2009, the World Wildlife Fund (WWF) released its annual list of the world's most threatened, or endangered, species. The WWF's list includes mammals, a fish, and the monarch butterfly. Climate change, loss of habitat, hunting, and fishing are putting the species on the list at risk.

1. Javan rhinoceros
2. Tiger
3. Magellanic penguin
4. Pacific walrus
5. Mountain gorilla

1 The Javan rhinoceros is considered the most endangered large mammal in the world. It lives in the wild in Asia. There are fewer than 60 left in the wild.

5 There are about 720 mountain gorillas in the wild in Africa. Conservation efforts have led to an increase in their number.

4 The Pacific walrus lives in the Arctic seas. Walrus rest and give birth on floating ice. Climate change is causing that ice to melt.

2 There may be as few as 3,200 tigers left in the wild, all found in Asia. Illegal hunting and loss of habitat are taking a big toll on the big cats.

3 Magellanic penguins live along the coastal areas of Argentina and Chile in South America. Each year, fewer penguins are born.

going green

Nature has its own way of recycling—and animals help! Insects such as beetles and millipedes break down leaves, grass, and other organic matter into smaller pieces that decompose more easily. Earthworms wriggle through the dirt, which aerates, or lets air into, the soil. These little critters help to enrich the earth, making it fertile ground in which new plants can grow.

Animals

DANGEROUS CRITTERS

One GOLDEN POISON DART FROG has enough poison to kill 2,000 mice—or 10 humans. The 2-inch (5-cm) frogs are found in the rain forests of Colombia. Because of the destruction of their natural habitat, they are now an endangered species.

The highly venomous **BLACK MAMBA SNAKE** is found in southern and eastern Africa. It can move incredibly quickly and strike with precision. Black mambas get their name from the dark color on the inside of their mouth.

MOSQUITOES may look harmless, but they can carry many different diseases, including malaria, yellow fever, dengue fever, and West Nile virus. Mosquitoes are responsible for an estimated 2 to 3 million deaths every year.

Though the body of the **BOX JELLYFISH** is quite small, it can have tentacles up to 15 feet (5 m) long. A sting from a box jellyfish, also known as a sea wasp, is excruciatingly painful and often deadly. Each of its tentacles holds enough poison to kill as many as 50 humans. Box jellyfish are found in the waters north of Australia.

Animal Groups

You've probably heard of a pack of wolves or a herd of cattle, but what about a crash of rhinos? Some animal group names are pretty wacky. Here are a few.

A **shrewdness** of apes
A **colony** of bats
A **sloth** of bears
A **bellowing** of bullfinches
A **murder** of crows
A **gang** of elk
A **tribe** of goats
A **band** of gorillas
A **bloat** of hippopotamuses
A **cackle** of hyenas
A **troop** of kangaroos
A **leap** of leopards
A **pride** of lions
A **labor** of moles
A **romp** of otters
A **streak** of tigers

After a big meal, a **CROCODILE** does not need to feed again for a long while. A large adult can go for nearly two years between meals! This makes it a patient predator. A crocodile will lie motionless in the water and wait for the perfect moment to grab its prey with its enormous jaw. Then the croc will pull its victim into the water and spin around and around in what is known as a "death roll," until the animal has drowned.

One of the world's greatest predators is the **GREAT WHITE SHARK.** While some people have been attacked and killed by great white sharks, humans aren't the sharks' favorite dish. They eat fish, rays, sea lions, seals, and even other sharks. Great white sharks can weigh more than 4,500 pounds (2,000 kg), swim at speeds up to 43 miles (69 km) per hour, and often surprise their prey.

A BLOAT

guess what?

A crocodile cannot move its tongue, which is attached to the bottom of its mouth.

More than 230 types of mammals and at least 900 species of birds live in South Africa. Most live in protected reserves, especially those that wildlife experts call "the big five": buffalo, elephant, leopard, lion, and rhinoceros. Kruger National Park, established in 1898, is the country's largest reserve. This map shows where some of the animals roam.

Look at the map of South Africa and the key, then answer the questions below.

1. How many countries form South Africa's northern border? Name them.

2. In which direction would one travel to get from Johannesburg to Cape Town?

3. What is the name of the landlocked country surrounded on all sides by South Africa?

4. Which game reserve is home to wild dogs?

5. At which reserves can you see giraffes?

Answers on page 244.

KEY
- African buffalo
- African wild dog
- Black rhinoceros
- Elephant
- Giraffe
- Hippopotamus
- Leopard
- Lesser flamingo
- Lion
- Sable antelope
- White rhinoceros
- Zebra

Who Works with Animals?

There are many careers available to animal lovers. Here are just a few.

BREEDERS mate animals to obtain certain characteristics of health, appearance, or longevity.

CONTEST JUDGES award prizes in animal competitions based on behavior and appearance.

FARMERS raise animals as sources of food and clothing.

JOCKEYS ride horses in races.

RESCUERS save animals in danger of abuse or abandonment in domestic environments, or from injury or death during natural disasters.

TRAINERS teach animals to behave properly, become service animals, or perform in entertainment venues (in circuses, at zoos, on TV, and in the movies).

VETERINARIANS vaccinate animals and treat their diseases and injuries.

ZOOKEEPERS feed and maintain animals in zoos.

ZOOLOGISTS study and classify animals. There are different types of zoologists, such as ornithologists, who specialize in birds; ichthyologists, who study fish; herpetologists, who study reptiles and amphibians; and mammalogists, who specialize in mammals.

Animals

25

COLOR THEORY

The three primary colors are red, blue, and yellow. Painters can mix different amounts of these three colors to achieve a wide range of shades in their works of art. On the other hand, no blend of nonprimary colors can result in a primary color.

The secondary colors—violet, green, and orange—are made by combining equal amounts of two primary colors. Blue and red mixed together make violet; blue and yellow make green; and red and yellow make orange.

By arranging the three primary and three secondary colors on a color wheel, we can see how they relate to one another. Colors that are opposite from each other on the wheel are called complementary colors. Complementary colors contrast with each other and appear more vivid when placed side by side.

WARM COLORS

COMPLEMENTARY COLORS

COOL COLORS

Warm colors are found on one side of the color wheel and include orange, yellow, many shades of red, and some yellowish greens. Think about the sun, fire, and other warm things—each has a warm color sense. Cool colors are on the opposite side of the wheel. They include blue, purple, some purplish reds, and some shades of blue-green.

PAINTING TERMS

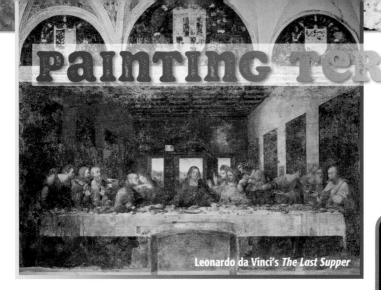

Leonardo da Vinci's *The Last Supper*

A **color palette** is a range of colors used in a painting or in a particular style of art. **Composition** refers to the arrangement of people or items that appear in a painting. A **portrait** features the likeness of a person or group of people. When an artist paints a portrait of himself or herself, this is known as a **self-portrait. Landscape** paintings show land or natural scenery, and **still-life** paintings depict groups of inanimate, or nonmoving, objects.

Visual artists use different kinds of paint to create their work on different surfaces including plaster, wood, canvas, and paper. A **fresco**, such as Leonardo da Vinci's *The Last Supper*, is painted directly onto wet plaster.

Tempera paints are quick-drying paints that are often applied to wood panels. Used for thousands of years and mixed from plants and other things found in nature, tempera paints are often seen in medieval artwork.

Watercolors are usually mixed with water and used on paper. Most watercolor paints are partially transparent, or see-through. Water-based paints have been used since ancient times. The "golden age" of watercolor took place in Great Britain from the mid-18th century to the mid-19th century.

Today, **oil paints** are the most commonly used type of paint. They have been popular with artists since the **Renaissance,** a period of cultural and artistic achievement that took place between the 14th and 16th centuries in Europe. Made by combining a **pigment,** or color, with a natural oil, such as linseed, walnut, or poppy oil, oil paints dry slowly, giving painters the time to blend colors.

Acrylic paints dry more quickly than oil paints and have been used by artists since the mid-20th century.

MYSTERY PERSON

Clue 1: I was born on November 14, 1840, in Paris, France.

Clue 2: The painting style Impressionism was named after my 1873 painting *Impression, Sunrise.*

Clue 3: Throughout my lifetime, I created a series of more than 250 paintings of water lilies based on the flowers found in my own garden at Giverny.

Who am I?

Answer on page 244.

Art

Stay in the Game *By Martha Pickerill,*
with reporting by Christine Gorman and Carolyn Sayre

A dream of pitching in the World Series can drive a kid to do some risky things, and Dr. James Andrews has seen them all. The founder and medical director of the American Sports Medicine Institute, in Birmingham, Alabama, knows of kids who pitch on elite travel teams year-round. Even worse, some kids start working up a curveball. That elbow-mangling pitch spells disaster for anyone whose bones are still growing. "Overspecialization is the problem," said Andrews. "It causes what we call a youth baseball shoulder."

A handful of today's young players may take the mound in the major leagues someday. But far too many will end up with strained elbows and shoulders, stress fractures, even injuries requiring major corrective surgery. More than 3.5 million kids under 15 receive medical treatment for sports injuries each year, most often after collisions or falls. But by the time young athletes are in middle or high school, nearly half of their injuries result from the wear and tear of overuse. To avoid injury, athletes need to give their muscles and bones time to rest between seasons.

BLAME IT ON YOUR BONES

Although injuries are a danger to athletes at any age, young people face special risks because of their growing bones. Young bones generate new tissue at spots called growth plates, located near the ends of most bones. "The growth plate is actually at its most vulnerable in the year before it closes," said Dr. Jon Divine, medical director of the Sports Medicine Biodynamics Center at Cincinnati Children's Hospital, in Ohio. In the teen years, a protective band of tissue that supports the growth plate starts to break down so the bone can completely harden by adulthood. Without that protective band, the plate can be compressed too much or even pulled apart.

IS ANY SPORT SAFE?

Playing any sport year-round is likely to cause an overuse injury. But it's also dangerous to play sports that put stress on the same body parts. For example, swimming, water polo, and volleyball put great strain on the shoulders, so athletes wouldn't get a rest by switching between those sports. A swimmer would be better off switching to biking, which uses different muscles.

Kids may want to try yet another strategy for the off-season: having fun off the field. "We recommend that a young baseball thrower have two to three months off each calendar year to give the throwing arm a period of doing something else," said Andrews.

KEEP YOUR GUARD UP!

Sports are supposed to be fun. Here are some ways to avoid those no-fun injuries.

Take a break. Kids who focus on a single sport need to take two to three months postseason to recover, even if they're uninjured.

Mix it up. Switch from one sport to another during the year. Be sure to choose activities that don't stress the same muscles and joints.

Deal with what you feel. Pain plus tenderness over a joint is often a sign of an overuse injury. Any pain that lingers or interferes with performance should be evaluated by a doctor.

WHY EXERCISE?

Exercising is one of the most important ways to keep your body healthy. When you exercise, you strengthen your bones, muscles, and heart. You also burn off extra fat, improve your balance, regulate your body's metabolism (the process that turns the nutrients in food into energy and heat), and improve your mood.

Today, many kids don't get enough exercise. In fact, the average kid spends about three hours each day watching television and another two and a half hours sitting down using other kinds of media, such as video games or the Internet. Does that sound like you? If it does, it's time to get up and get moving!

Whether you are playing football, swimming, riding your bike, or challenging your neighbor on a homemade obstacle course, you can always find a workout that is fun for you. In addition to organized sports, you can work out alone by doing yoga or stretches or skipping rope. Even doing your chores can help keep you fit! You burn calories by gardening, raking leaves, folding laundry, or vacuuming.

going green Look out for your body's health while looking out for the health of the planet. Instead of taking part in activities that use up energy, like watching TV or playing video games, go outside and work up a sweat! Play tag with a friend, take the dog for a walk, or jump rope. If possible, run errands with your family on foot or on your bike, rather than getting in the car.

YOUR FIVE SENSES

Information about the world around you comes to you through your five senses: sight, hearing, taste, smell, and touch.

- You **SEE** light and dark, as well as color and movement, because of two kinds of eye cells on your retina, which is a membrane at the back of your eye. These two types of cells are rods and cones. Rods detect black, white, and shades of gray, as well as shapes and movement. Cones detect color. Each eye has about 120 million rods and more than 6 million cones.

- You **HEAR** because sound vibrations hit your eardrum, which moves three little bones in your middle ear. These bones move a fluid in your inner ear that flows past tiny hairs, which send signals to your brain.

- Your tongue has about 10,000 **TASTE** buds when you're born and fewer as you get older. Different parts of your tongue can sense sourness, bitterness, sweetness, and saltiness. Some scientists believe that there's a fifth kind of taste called umami, which essentially means "deliciousness."

- It is impossible to truly know the flavor of any food without your sense of **SMELL.** To prove this, pinch your nostrils closed while you eat something.

- Your sense of **TOUCH** tells you all sorts of things about the size, shape, heat, and texture of objects.

WHAT ARE YOU MADE OF?

Bone Up on Bones

BONES HAVE TWO MAJOR PURPOSES: to give shape and structure to your body and to protect internal organs.

At birth, people have more than 300 bones, but by the time you are an adult, you'll have just 206. Where do those additional bones go? Some bones fuse together, making one bone where there had been two.

WHERE ARE YOUR BONES FOUND?

- 27 are in each hand.
- 26 are in each foot.
- 14 are in your face.
- Your funny bone isn't a bone at all. It's a mass of nerves that runs along the long bone in your arm—a bone called the *humerus.*

The **LONGEST BONE** in your body is the thighbone, or femur. It's about one-fourth of your total height. It keeps growing as long as you do. Your spinal cord, however, stops growing when you are about 5 years old.

 Giraffes have the same number of neck bones as humans: seven. Unlike human neck bones, each bone in a giraffe's neck can be as much as 10 inches (25.4 cm) long.

The Skin You're In

Your skin acts as a barrier to protect your soft internal organs and to keep germs and water out.

- An average-size adult has about 20 square feet (1.9 sq m) of skin.
- Skin gets its color from a pigment called *melanin.*
- Skin is the largest organ in the body.
- Three main layers make up your skin: the epidermis (the outer layer that constantly flakes off), the dermis (located beneath the epidermis and containing blood vessels, sweat glands, and hair follicles), and the hypodermis, or subcutaneous tissue (the deepest layer of skin that stores fat and helps keep you warm).

guess what? *The thinnest skin on a person's body is found on the eyelid. The thickest layers of epidermis are found on people's palms and the soles of their feet.*

Muscle Mania

Muscles allow you to move by pulling and pushing your skeleton along. Some muscles, such as your heart, are involuntary. That means they work without your doing anything about it. Other muscle movements are voluntary, like when you move your hand to pick up and clench a ball.

- You have 30 muscles in your face.
- Your largest muscle is called the *gluteus maximus* (another name for buttocks).
- Your eye muscles move more than 100,000 times a day.
- Your heart muscle beats about 70 times a minute.

Have a HEART!

The heart is the main organ of the cardiovascular, or circulatory, system. The heart's main job—and it is an important one—is to pump blood through your arteries to all the parts of the body. Oxygen, digested food, hormones, and nutrients are carried by the blood to the cells that need them. The blood also carries waste materials and carbon dioxide away from the cells.

The human heart has four chambers. The upper chambers, which receive the blood that enters the heart, are the right atrium and the left atrium. The bottom chambers, which pump blood out of the heart, are the right ventricle and the left ventricle.

Blood is carried to and from the heart in three kinds of tubes, or blood vessels: arteries, veins, and capillaries. Arteries carry blood away from the heart. Veins carry blood to the heart. Capillaries connect arteries and veins.

The heart has two main arteries: the aorta and the pulmonary artery. The aorta is the body's largest artery. It carries oxygen-rich blood from the heart to the abdomen, where it separates into branches that supply blood to many organs (but not the lungs).

The heart pumps oxygen-poor blood through the pulmonary artery to the lungs. The lungs remove the carbon dioxide from the blood as you exhale. As you inhale, your lungs replenish the oxygen in the blood.

guess what? The heart beats more slowly when you are resting or sleeping. It beats faster when you are frightened or exercising. On average, the heart beats about 100,000 times a day, more than 30 million times a year, and about 2.5 billion times during a 70-year lifetime.

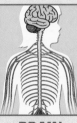

TIME FOR KIDS GAME — Body Basics

To be healthy, it helps to know your own body. Match each riddle to the part or parts of the body that it describes.

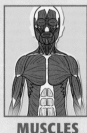
LUNGS

MUSCLES

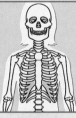
BRAIN

BONES

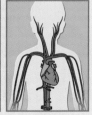
HEART

A I am a muscle. I am the size of your fist. I beat, and I pump your blood.

B We are inside your chest. We get bigger when you inhale. You use us to talk and laugh.

C We are busy. We are often attached to bones. We help you lift, push, and stretch.

D I am the boss. I am awake when you are sleeping. I can think, feel, and remember.

E We hold you up. We protect your inner organs. We can help you to sit, stand, walk, and wave.

Answers on page 244.

Body and Health

Books and Literature

2010 NEWBERY MEDAL
When You Reach Me by Rebecca Stead

2010 CALDECOTT MEDAL
The Lion & the Mouse written and illustrated by Jerry Pinkney

2010 CORETTA SCOTT KING AUTHOR AWARD
Bad News for Outlaws: The Remarkable Life of Bass Reeves, Deputy U.S. Marshal by Vaunda Micheaux Nelson, illustrated by R. Gregory Christie

2010 MICHAEL L. PRINTZ AWARD
Going Bovine by Libba Bray

2010 ROBERT F. SIBERT INFORMATIONAL BOOK MEDAL
Almost Astronauts: 13 Women Who Dared to Dream by Tanya Lee Stone

2010 PURA BELPRÉ AWARD
Return to Sender by Julia Alvarez

2010 MARGARET A. EDWARDS AWARD
An American Plague: The True and Terrifying Story of the Yellow Fever Epidemic of 1793 by Jim Murphy

2010 SCOTT O'DELL HISTORICAL FICTION AWARD
The Storm in the Barn by Matt Phelan

2010 ODYSSEY AWARD FOR EXCELLENCE IN AUDIOBOOK PRODUCTION
Louise, The Adventures of a Chicken by Kate DiCamillo, produced by Live Oak Media, and narrated by Barbara Rosenblat

THE 2010 YALSA EXCELLENCE IN NONFICTION AWARD
Charles and Emma: The Darwins' Leap of Faith by Deborah Heiligman

2009 NATIONAL BOOK AWARD FOR YOUNG PEOPLE'S LITERATURE
Claudette Colvin: Twice Toward Justice by Phillip Hoose

2009 INDIES CHOICE AWARD FOR BEST INDIE YOUNG ADULT BUZZ BOOK (FICTION)
The Graveyard Book by Neil Gaiman

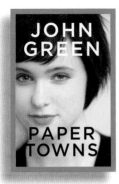

2009 EDGAR ALLAN POE AWARD FOR BEST YOUNG ADULT BOOK
Paper Towns by John Green

2009 BOSTON GLOBE-HORN BOOK AWARD FOR NONFICTION
The Lincolns: A Scrapbook Look at Abraham and Mary by Candace Fleming

2009 BOSTON GLOBE-HORN BOOK AWARD FOR FICTION AND POETRY
Nation by Terry Pratchett

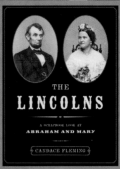

Talented Teen Authors

Want to be a published novelist? You don't even have to wait until you're an adult to become one. Start writing now—and follow in the footsteps of these successful young authors.

AMELIA ATWATER-RHODES

Atwater-Rhodes counts Stephen King among her favorite authors, and his influence shows in her popular teen novels. She wrote her first one—*In the Forests of the Night*, the first in her Den of Shadows series—when she was just 13 years old. Some other books by Atwater-Rhodes include *Demon in My View*, *Shattered Mirror*, and *Midnight Predator* (all in her Den of Shadows series), as well as five volumes of The Kiesha'ra series.

guess what? *The novel* Shattered Mirror *was inspired by Sarah McLachlan's song "Adia," from the album* Surfacing.

CHRISTOPHER PAOLINI

Christopher Paolini was 15 years old when he wrote his original draft of *Eragon*, the first book in his enormously successful The Inheritance Cycle (which also includes *Eldest* and *Brisingr*).

NANCY YI FAN
New York Times best-selling author Yi Fan was 11 when she penned *Swordbird*. Both of her novels (the other one is *Sword Quest*) were informed and inspired by Nancy's lifelong love of birds.

guess what? *Before writing an important scene, Nancy Yi Fan often created a pencil sketch of what she wanted to happen. This helped her to describe the action more vividly.*

MYSTERY PERSON

Clue 1: I am an author who was born in Dublin, Ireland, in 1847. I wrote my first horror story in 1875.

Clue 2: I am best known for writing a spooky tale about Count Dracula, a Transylvanian vampire.

Clue 3: The bloodsucking count has been the subject of plays and movies for decades.

Who am I?

Answer on page 244.

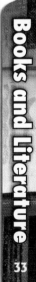

Books and Literature

Buildings and Architecture

ARCHITECTURE TERMS: WHAT'S THAT?

Architects—people who design buildings—have figured out many ways to use windows, walls, doorways, roofs, and other features to make buildings both strong and beautiful.

ARCH A curved or pointed ceiling that bridges a gap. An arch can bear more weight than a flat roof or a bridge can. Before 1100 A.D., arches were always shaped like rounded curves. In the Gothic period, architects first used pointed arches, which they found could support even more weight than rounded arches. This allowed them to use heavier materials and to design and build taller structures.

Washington Square Park Arch, New York City

St. George's Chapel, Windsor Castle, Windsor, England

BUTTRESS A stone support that projects outward from a wall

COLUMN A pillar made of stone or concrete that supports an arch or roof, or that stands alone

The Parthenon, Athens, Greece

DOME A rounded roof of a building

British Columbia Parliament building, Victoria, Canada

FLYING BUTTRESS A buttress that forms an arch, connecting a main wall with another structure

Notre Dame, Paris, France

Westminster Abbey, London, England

GARGOYLE A carved figure of a person or animal that is usually made of stone and is placed on the gutters of a building. Sometimes gargoyles are placed just for ornamentation. Other gargoyles are actually spouts. Rainwater flowing from the roof can escape through the mouths of these decorative beasts.

PORTICO An entrance porch, usually supported by columns

The north portico of the White House, Washington, D.C.

SPIRE A tower shaped like a cone that was developed in Europe and is usually the top of a place of worship

VAULT An arched ceiling; the inside of a dome

The Duomo, Milan, Italy

St. Peter's Basilica, Vatican City

Types of Columns

Doric

This is the most common type of column. It is also the simplest. It has a smooth, rounded top (also called its capital). Doric columns do not have a base at the bottom. The Parthenon in Athens features Doric columns.

Ionic

Ionic columns are known for the scroll-like decorations on their capitals. They have grooves cut into them from the top to the bottom, so they appear fluted. The base of an Ionic column often looks like it is made up of a stack of rings.

Corinthian

These columns are fluted like Ionic columns and rest on similar bases, but they feature more intricate designs on the capital. Inspired by Egyptian architecture, these columns often feature olive, laurel, or acanthus leaves on their capitals.

Buildings and Architecture

35

COOL CONSTRUCTIONS

The Guggenheim Museum in New York City,
designed by Frank Lloyd Wright; completed in 1959

Fascinating Features

- Most of the building's exterior was created without corners.
- Visitors never need to retrace their steps. They can take an elevator to the top floor and walk down a circular path, seeing each object of art just once.
- When it first opened, some artists criticized the building, saying that it was more exciting than the artwork inside.

Temple of the Holy Family (La Sagrada Familia) in Barcelona, Spain,
designed by Antoni Gaudí; construction began in 1882

Fascinating Features

- Gaudí believed that buildings should resemble nature. He designed homes and churches without straight lines or perfect corners.
- Twenty-two different kinds of stone were used to construct Holy Family.
- Many people believe the unfinished stone church resembles a sand castle, a warped Gothic cathedral, or a building melting in the sun.
- The church's towers are topped with bright, colorful mosaics.
- Gaudí died before the building was completed. Based on the drawings he left behind, construction has continued on the church. It is supposed to be completed in 2026, 100 years after the architect's death.

The Burj Khalifa in Dubai, United Arab Emirates,
designed by Adrian Smith; completed in 2010

Fascinating Features

- At 2,684 feet (818 m), the Burj Khalifa is the world's tallest building—and the tallest human-made object ever. Its 78th-floor swimming pool is also the highest swimming pool in the world.
- More than 5,000 workers took part in the construction of the tower. Designed to house more than 35,000 people, the construction features hotel rooms, apartments, offices, and other spaces.

The Palace of Versailles in Versailles, France,
designed by architect Louis Le Vau, interior decorator Charles Le Brun, and landscape architect André Le Nôtre (among others); completed in 1710

Fascinating Features

- Beginning in 1682, it was the official residence of Louis XIV. At different times, 3,000 to 10,000 noblemen and noblewomen lived in Versailles' hundreds of rooms.
- Versailles is an excellent example of Baroque architecture. It is an enormous building filled with flowery details and flashy decorations.
- Inside the palace, the Hall of Mirrors features 17 huge mirrors along one side of the hall and 17 large windows on the other, looking over the garden. With high vaulted ceilings, glittering glass chandeliers, and bronze details, the 240-foot-long (73 m) hallway is considered one of the most impressive in Europe.

Green Buildings

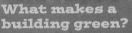
Solar panels

Buildings old and new

Green buildings are not new. For thousands of years, humans have built structures with local natural materials. These structures did not use energy or damage the planet. When the people who lived in them moved on, the structures usually collapsed, and their materials returned to the earth.

Before the 1930s, most buildings used far less energy than today's buildings. Instead of air-conditioning, they had windows that opened to let in breezes. They weren't quite green, however. Coal-burning furnaces were used for heating. As a result, many buildings spewed dirty smoke into the air. Beginning in the 1970s, in the United States and much of the world, air-pollution laws were passed to reduce or eliminate pollution given off by buildings.

Awnings or shades help keep buildings cool—without using energy.

Interior stairs encourage people to skip the elevator and walk instead.

Bamboo

What makes a building green?

going green

From the materials used in its construction to the placement of its windows, there are a number of things that make a building green. Ideally, it is built with materials that don't harm the people inside or the environment. Also, an ecofriendly building is only as big as it needs to be, so it doesn't use a lot of energy for heating or cooling.

- Green buildings use power made by sustainable resources such as sunlight and wind rather than relying on energy supplied by burning fossil fuels, which creates pollution. (For more information on energy sources, see pages 90–93.)

- To avoid using energy for air-conditioning systems, architects take advantage of natural cooling. Windows are placed in such a way that they can be opened to create indoor breezes, and designers include awnings or shades to keep sunlight from making buildings too warm.

- Ecofriendly buildings are built from materials that are plentiful. For example, they are not made with wood or other materials from endangered forests. Bamboo is one great option for builders. It grows quickly and is not an endangered plant.

- Green builders avoid (or limit) the use of chemicals that can create indoor air pollution or harm occupants. To encourage healthy living, some buildings are designed with easy-to-use interior staircases and ramps so that people use elevators or escalators less.

Buildings and Architecture

JANUARY

S	M	T	W	T	F	S
						1
2	3	4	5	6	7	8
9	10	11	12	13	14	15
16	17	18	19	20	21	22
23	24	25	26	27	28	29
30	31					

FEBRUARY

S	M	T	W	T	F	S
		1	2	3	4	5
6	7	8	9	10	11	12
13	14	15	16	17	18	19
20	21	22	23	24	25	26
27	28					

MARCH

S	M	T	W	T	F	S
		1	2	3	4	5
6	7	8	9	10	11	12
13	14	15	16	17	18	19
20	21	22	23	24	25	26
27	28	29	30	31		

APRIL

S	M	T	W	T	F	S
					1	2
3	4	5	6	7	8	9
10	11	12	13	14	15	16
17	18	19	20	21	22	23
24	25	26	27	28	29	30

MAY

S	M	T	W	T	F	S
1	2	3	4	5	6	7
8	9	10	11	12	13	14
15	16	17	18	19	20	21
22	23	24	25	26	27	28
29	30	31				

JUNE

S	M	T	W	T	F	S
			1	2	3	4
5	6	7	8	9	10	11
12	13	14	15	16	17	18
19	20	21	22	23	24	25
26	27	28	29	30		

JULY

S	M	T	W	T	F	S
					1	2
3	4	5	6	7	8	9
10	11	12	13	14	15	16
17	18	19	20	21	22	23
24	25	26	27	28	29	30
31						

AUGUST

S	M	T	W	T	F	S
	1	2	3	4	5	6
7	8	9	10	11	12	13
14	15	16	17	18	19	20
21	22	23	24	25	26	27
28	29	30	31			

SEPTEMBER

S	M	T	W	T	F	S
				1	2	3
4	5	6	7	8	9	10
11	12	13	14	15	16	17
18	19	20	21	22	23	24
25	26	27	28	29	30	

OCTOBER

S	M	T	W	T	F	S
						1
2	3	4	5	6	7	8
9	10	11	12	13	14	15
16	17	18	19	20	21	22
23	24	25	26	27	28	29
30	31					

NOVEMBER

S	M	T	W	T	F	S
		1	2	3	4	5
6	7	8	9	10	11	12
13	14	15	16	17	18	19
20	21	22	23	24	25	26
27	28	29	30			

DECEMBER

S	M	T	W	T	F	S
				1	2	3
4	5	6	7	8	9	10
11	12	13	14	15	16	17
18	19	20	21	22	23	24
25	26	27	28	29	30	31

guess what?

The original Roman calendar featured 10 months, not 12. Some months get their names from the order in which they fell on that calendar. For example, *September* comes from *septem*, meaning seven, and *October* comes from *octo*, meaning eight. Some of the other months were named for gods and goddesses. The word *March* refers to Mars, the Roman god of war, and the name *June* refers to Juno, the Roman name for the queen of the gods.

Calendars and Holidays

39

HOLIDAYS in 2011

JANUARY 1: NEW YEAR'S DAY

JANUARY 17: MARTIN LUTHER KING DAY

FEBRUARY 2: GROUNDHOG DAY

FEBRUARY 3: CHINESE NEW YEAR

FEBRUARY 14: VALENTINE'S DAY

FEBRUARY 21: PRESIDENTS' DAY

MARCH 8: MARDI GRAS

MARCH 13: DAYLIGHT SAVING TIME BEGINS

MARCH 17: ST. PATRICK'S DAY

APRIL 1: APRIL FOOLS' DAY

APRIL 19-26*: PASSOVER

APRIL 22: EARTH DAY

APRIL 24: EASTER

MAY 5: CINCO DE MAYO

MAY 8: MOTHER'S DAY

MAY 30: MEMORIAL DAY

JUNE 19: FATHER'S DAY

JULY 4: INDEPENDENCE DAY

SEPTEMBER 5: LABOR DAY

SEPTEMBER 29-30*: ROSH HASHANAH

OCTOBER 8*: YOM KIPPUR

OCTOBER 10: COLUMBUS DAY CELEBRATED

OCTOBER 31: HALLOWEEN

NOVEMBER 6: DAYLIGHT SAVING TIME ENDS

NOVEMBER 11: VETERANS DAY

NOVEMBER 24: THANKSGIVING

DECEMBER 21-28*: HANUKKAH

DECEMBER 25: CHRISTMAS

DECEMBER 26-JANUARY 1: KWANZAA

*All Jewish holidays begin at sundown the evening before.

Arrr, Matey!

Ever heard of International Talk Like a Pirate Day? It is one of many wacky holidays celebrated throughout the year. In 2011, International Talk Like a Pirate Day falls on Monday, September 19, so put it on your calendar, get your eye patch ready, and be sure to work "ahoy" and "aye" into conversation with your friends. Here are some other wacky holidays.

JANUARY 16: International Hot and Spicy Food Day
FEBRUARY 11: Make a Friend Day
MARCH 2: National Banana Cream Pie Day
MAY 14: Dance Like a Chicken Day
JUNE 6: National Yo-Yo Day
AUGUST 6: Wiggle Your Toes Day

TIME FOR KIDS GAME

LANTERN LOOK-ALIKES

At the end of the 15-day Chinese New Year celebration, some people take part in the Lantern Festival. They fill the streets with lanterns shaped like dragons, birds, and more. Here are six dragon lanterns for the festival. There are three matching pairs. Match each lantern with the one showing the same dragon.

Answers on page 244.

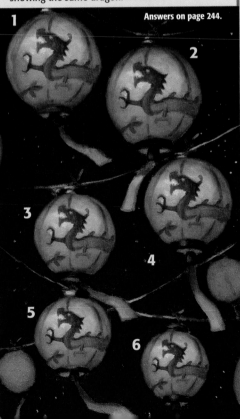

1
2
3
4
5
6

MYSTERY PERSON

Clue 1: I was a general and a politician who was born in Rome in 100 B.C.

Clue 2: In 45 B.C., I introduced the Julian calendar. It had an extra day every fourth year—a leap year.

Clue 3: Changes were made to create the modern calendar. But leap year still happens every four years, with an extra day at the end of February.

Who am I? _____

Answer on page 244.

Calendars and Holidays

FROM
TIME
FOR KIDS
MAGAZINE

Taking It to the Web

IN IRAN, PROTESTERS USE THE INTERNET TO SPREAD NEWS AND COMMUNICATE

By Joyce C. Tang

The presidential elections in Iran caused chaos and violence in the streets, beginning in the summer of 2009. Many Iranians were upset by the reelection of President Mahmoud Ahmedinejad (ma-*mood* ah-mah-*dih*-nah-zhad) on June 12, 2009. They began protesting every day after the election. They claimed that the election results were wrong and that opposition leader Mir-Hossein Mousavi was the real winner.

The Internet provided Iranians and others with at least one relatively safe place to voice their views. Supporters of Mousavi used social-networking websites like Facebook and Twitter to show their support and spread information. Up until a few years ago, most people would have turned to television and print sources, such as magazines and newspapers, to get information. Professional journalists and reporters would have gathered the information. But now, regular citizens can watch and participate online. Internet sources are especially important because Iran has detained or sent out of the country many journalists.

A newscaster in the Netherlands reads news about Iran, gathered from Facebook posts and text messages sent from Iran.

AN ONLINE REVOLUTION

Many people have been communicating using Twitter, a popular website where people can post short comments or stories. The stories are about the length of one sentence. The service is easy to use from cell phones. It is a quick way for people in the streets to spread messages to one another.

Mousavi supporters also created a page on Facebook for their candidate. It was used to organize protests and post pictures, videos, and messages. By midsummer, the page already had nearly 89,000 members. Facebook and Google also made their services available in Farsi, the language most Iranians speak. The Iranian government tried to stop the online revolution by censoring, or blocking, some websites. In response, people outside of Iran set up websites so that Iranians could still access information. Many tried to confuse the censors by changing their location and time zone to Tehran, the capital of Iran.

GOING GREEN

Green was the color displayed by Mousavi supporters. Many wore green and waved green flags and banners. Many Twitter users showed their support by using a green tint on their profile pictures. These protests are now known as the Green Revolution. During the summer of 2009, eight members of Iran's national soccer team wore green wristbands during a game to show their support for Mousavi. After the first half, they were ordered to take off their wristbands. "We will protest until they change the results," an Iranian from Tehran wrote in an e-mail. He didn't give his name because he was afraid of getting in trouble with the government.

WEBBY AWARDS

Every year since 1996 (when the Internet was still quite new), the International Academy of Digital Arts and Sciences has given out awards to recognize excellence on the Internet. The most recent Webby Awards were held on June 8, 2009, in New York City.

EDUCATION
Smarthistory
smarthistory.org

MUSIC
NPR Music
npr.org/music

WEBBY BREAKOUT OF THE YEAR
Twitter

Tim Berners-Lee received the Lifetime Achievement Award for his huge contribution to Internet technology and communications. He is one of the inventors of the World Wide Web.

WEBBY LIFETIME ACHIEVEMENT
Sir Tim Berners-Lee

guess what?

Winners of Webby Awards deliver five-word speeches. When Biz Stone, cocreator of Twitter, accepted the award for Webby Breakout of the Year, he delivered this short speech: "Creativity is a renewable resource."

NEWS
BBC News Website
bbc.com/news

PERSONAL WEBSITE
My Star Wars Collection—Joshua Budich
joshuabudich.com/SWCollection

LIFESTYLE
BBC Climate Change: Bloom
bbc.co.uk/bloom

YOUTH
Tate Kids
kids.tate.org.uk

NEWSPAPER
The Guardian
guardian.co.uk

FAMILY/PARENTING
Disney Family.com
family.com

BEST USE OF ANIMATION OR MOTION GRAPHICS
Coraline Website
coraline.com

SPORTS
ESPN.com
espn.com

GAMES
Club Penguin
clubpenguin.com

CULTURAL INSTITUTIONS
Guggenheim Museum
guggenheim.org

SCIENCE
Cassini Equinox Mission Website
saturn.jpl.nasa.gov

WEBBY PERSON OF THE YEAR
Jimmy Fallon

43

Internet Resource Sites for Kids

General

TIME For Kids **timeforkids.com**
4Kids.org **4kids.org**
Smithsonian Education **smithsonianeducation.org/students**
Brain Pop **brainpop.com**
Homework Help Yahoo! Kids **kids.yahoo.com/learn**
Internet Public Library **ipl.org/div/kidspace; ipl.org/div/teen**

Art

The Artist's Toolkit **artsconnected.org/toolkit**
MuseumKids **metmuseum.org/explore/museumkids.htm**
NGA (National Gallery of Art) Kids **nga.gov/kids**
The Renaissance Connection **renaissanceconnection.org**

Biography

Bio **biography.com**
Academy of Achievement **achievement.org/galleryachieve.html**

Environment

EPA Environmental Kids Club **epa.gov/kids**
National Institute of Environmental Health Sciences
   (NIEHS) Kids' Pages **kids.niehs.nih.gov**
Rainforest Heroes **ran.org/rainforestheroes**
EcoKids **ecokids.ca/pub/kids_home.cfm**
EekoWorld **pbskids.org/eekoworld**

> "Scientists estimate that there are more than 50 million different species of invertebrates living in rain forests. One scientist found 50 different species of ants on a single tree in Peru!" Find facts like this at Rainforest Heroes.

Geography

The CIA World Factbook **cia.gov/library/publications/the-world-factbook/index.html**
State Facts for Students **census.gov/schools/facts**
50states.com **50states.com**
National Geographic Kids **kids.nationalgeographic.com**

> Can you match U.S. states or countries around the world to their locations on a map? Test your skills by playing USA States Map Match or Asia Map Match at kidsgeo.com.

Government and Politics

Congress for Kids **congressforkids.net**
Kidsgeo.com **kidsgeo.com**
Kids.gov **kids.gov**
White House 101 **whitehouse.gov/kids**

Health

KidsHealth **kidshealth.org/kid; kidshealth.org/teen**
BAM! Body and Mind **bam.gov**
Kidnetic.com **kidnetic.com**

> Former slave Harriet Tubman was a leader of the Underground Railroad, which was a network of people who helped escaped slaves travel to safety and freedom in the North. She aided 300 slaves, including her own sister, brother, and parents. Learn about Harriet Tubman and other African-American heroes at African American World for Kids.

History

History.com: This Day in History **history.com/this-day-in-history.do**
Women in World History **womeninworldhistory.com**
America's Story **americaslibrary.gov**
African American World for Kids **pbskids.org/aaworld**
NativeWeb **nativeweb.org/resources/history**

Literature, Language, and Communication

FCC Kids Zone fcc.gov/cgb/kidszone
Aaron Shepard's Home Page aaronshep.com/index.html
Sylvan Book Adventure bookadventure.org/ki/bs/ki_bs_helpfind.asp
ABC's of the Writing Process angelfire.com/wi/writingprocess/index.html
RIF Reading Planet rif.org/readingplanet
The Blue Book of Grammar and Punctuation grammarbook.com

Music, Games, and Entertainment

Zoom: By Kids for Kids pbskids.org/zoom/games/index.html
Dallas Symphony Orchestra (DSO) Kids dsokids.com
San Francisco Symphony (SFS) Kids sfskids.org
AgameAday.com agameaday.com
PBS Kids Games pbskids.org/games/index.html
FunBrain.com funbrain.com/kidscenter.html
Club Penguin clubpenguin.com

Nature

Animal Corner animalcorner.co.uk
Field Trip Earth fieldtripearth.org
Kids' Planet kidsplanet.org
National Wildlife Federation nwf.org/kids

News and Current Events

TIME For Kids News timeforkids.com/TFK/kids/news

Science, Technology, and Mathematics

The Exploratorium exploratorium.edu
The Yuckiest Site on the Internet yucky.discovery.com/flash
Discovery Kids kids.discovery.com
Coolmath.com coolmath.com
Webmath.com webmath.com
Ask Dr. Math mathforum.org/dr.math

> What is a perfect number? Find out at Ask Dr. Math.

Sports

Sports Illustrated Kids sikids.com
Major League Baseball mlb.com
Major League Soccer mlsnet.com
National Basketball Association nba.com
Women's National Basketball Association wnba.com
National Football League nfl.com
National Hockey League nhl.com

Computers and Communication

Emote-i-what?

Sometimes it is difficult to make your tone clear in an e-mail, IM, or text message. One way to share how you are feeling is to use an emoticon, or a symbol that shows a facial expression or an emotion. Smiley faces :) or frowns : (are two examples of emoticons, but there are many wackier faces available to computer users.

Web Address Endings

There are five main endings for Web addresses in the United States: *.com*, *.gov*, *.edu*, *.org*, and *.net*. These endings tell you something about a website before you even visit the home page. For example, addresses ending in *.edu* are for the websites of educational institutions. Those ending in *.gov* are sites for government agencies, and those ending in *.org* are created for and by nonprofit organizations.

IM Dictionary

Sending messages back and forth over computers or cell phones can take a lot more time than having a quick conversation out loud. To save time, many people use acronyms (words formed from the first letter of each word in a phrase or name) and Internet shorthand.

?4U	question for you
2nite	tonight
AFC	away from computer
B4	before
BBS	be back soon
BFN	bye for now
BRB	be right back
CU	see you
DUST	did you see that
EOD	end of discussion
F2F	face to face
FOAF	friend of a friend
FYEO	for your eyes only
G2G	got 2 go
GBH	great big hug
GFETE	grinning from ear to ear
GFU	good for you
GL	good luck
HAGD	have a good day
HB	hurry back
IDK	I don't know
IMO	in my opinion
J/C	just checking
L8R	later
LOL	laugh out loud
N2M	not too much
NP	no problem
OIC	oh I see
OTP	on the phone
SYS	see you soon
U2	you too
VBS	very big smile
W8	wait
WU	what's up
YATB	you are the best

GBH!!

L8R

guess what? In 2009, the average American spent approximately 200 minutes watching videos online each month. That was a 12.5% increase from the year before.

SNAZZY SOFTWARE

Shape Up Your Photos with Special Software

Computer programs like Adobe Photoshop are used to change digital photos, either to fix problems or to make the photos look different. Here are some of the basic things that can be done with a photo-editing program.

Make yourself look like a famous astronaut!

- Cropping, or cutting, a picture down to a different size or shape

- Making the photo darker or lighter

Use special software to become a slam-dunking superstar!

- Reducing that annoying red-eye effect that sometimes happens when you use a flash

You can also do more interesting things—say, taking your cat from one picture and placing her in front of the Eiffel Tower in another photo. Special effects are also possible. You can make your photos look like they were painted with a brush or even carved out of stone!

Where the Wild Things Are

Battle of the Smithsonian

Using Computers for Making Movies

Two exciting things that computers are used for today are animation and special effects in movies. In the old days, moviemakers would create animated films by drawing a picture for each frame by hand. The film would then be played back at 20 or 24 frames per second. That's a lot of drawing! Today, this work can be done by computers, and the results are amazing. *Toy Story* (1995) was the first completely computer-animated feature film. Since then, computer effects and animation have continued to wow audiences in movies like *Up* (2009).

Computer-generated effects aren't just for animated movies. Sometimes what looks like a crazy costume is really the result of computer special effects, like the octopus-faced Davy Jones in the Pirates of the Caribbean series. Many movies have used effects and animation to create characters who aren't really there. Advances in special effects have made it possible to have realistic-looking animals or monsters interacting with actual people in movies like *Night at the Museum: Battle of the Smithsonian* (2009) and *Where the Wild Things Are* (2009).

CELLULAR TECHNOLOGY

CELL PHONES

are much more than portable telephones. Depending on the model you use, a cell phone can do many kinds of tasks, including sending and receiving e-mail and text messages, surfing the Internet, taking photographs, keeping track of appointments, flashing reminders, transmitting TV programs, navigating with global positioning, and downloading music. How can a small handheld device do so much? It's all in the technology that supports it. Here are the basics.

Cell Phones

These are sophisticated radios that tune in to frequencies transmitted by towers that are located everywhere and cover a range of about 10 square miles (26 sq km) each.

SMART PHONES 12:00

More than 223 million people in the United States over the age of 13 use cellular telephones. About 18% of them use smart phones, such as BlackBerries or iPhones, which allow them to make phone calls, access the Internet, play videos, and run all sorts of applications.

go to

MENU   internet

Towers

These are usually made of steel and are hundreds of feet tall. Sometimes they are disguised to look like other things, such as flagpoles, bell towers, and even trees. The towers have antennas and transmitters that are often shared by several different phone companies. As a cell phone user moves from place to place, a different tower picks up the phone's signal and transmits to it.

Some cell-phone towers are disguised to look like palm trees.

This Arizona cell-phone tower is made to look like a saguaro cactus.

Technology

Unlike a walkie-talkie or CB radio, with which only one person can speak at a time, cell phones have a dual-frequency capacity. They can send signals and receive them at the same time. Inside the phone is a microprocessor similar to one inside a computer. This is what enables the phone to act like a computer and do such a wide variety of tasks.

SATELLITE PHONES
use a different technology. They bypass landlines and cellular networks by relying on "low Earth-orbiting" satellites to receive and relay phone messages. This technology is especially valuable during weather disasters, which can break land wires and topple cellular towers. The signal of a satellite call is sent to the satellites of the caller's phone company. The satellites receive the call and send it back to Earth using a ground station, or gateway. The gateway then uses regular landlines or cellular networks to send the call to the recipient.

Satellite phones are often used in remote places, during wartime, or during natural disasters when cell service does not exist or may be damaged.

WIRELESS FIDELITY (Wi-Fi), or BROADBAND SERVICE
is a means of communication that uses low-power microwave radio signals to connect computers to other computers or websites using wireless network cards and hubs. The advantage of this system is that a computer need not be connected to an electrical or telephone outlet or cable line. Instead, a laptop can be carried from room to room without being plugged in.

TOP 5 Wi-Fi-friendly American Cities

1. Seattle, Washington
2. San Francisco, California
3. Austin, Texas
4. Portland, Oregon
5. Atlanta, Georgia

Source: Microsoft Small Business Center

Technology and Teens

More girls than boys own cell phones, according to a recent study.

	CELL PHONE	DESKTOP OR LAPTOP COMPUTER
ALL TEENS	71%	59%
GIRLS	75%	64%
BOYS	66%	55%
AGE		
12–14	61%	54%
15–17	81%	65%

Source: Pew Internet & American Life Project Teen/Parent Survey on Writing

Computers and Communication

Countries

FROM TIME FOR KIDS MAGAZINE

World Wonders in Danger

By Jonathan Rosenbloom

What do rocks in Pakistan, homes in the United States, and a park in Mexico have in common? All are in danger of disappearing. That serious news was made public in October 2009 in a report by the World Monuments Fund (WMF). WMF is an organization that identifies and helps preserve historic structures and land areas. Bonnie Burnham, president of WMF, said the sites need to be preserved because they are part of the world's cultural heritage. She urged governments, environmentalists, and others to save the monuments.

The 2010 World Monuments Watch List named 93 sites in 47 countries. The list, which comes out every two years, turns a spotlight on threatened places. According to WMF, there are several reasons why sites become endangered. Governments may not have the money or the interest to keep them up. War, such as the one in Iraq, can threaten a site. Sometimes, popularity can create a problem. Too many visitors could spoil Peru's Machu Picchu and the Native American structures in Taos, New Mexico. Development projects such as building dams and making way for new homes may destroy sites. And natural disasters such as earthquakes and floods can harm treasured places.

SPAIN The city of Avila, Spain, is known for its thick stone walls and towers, built 900 years ago. They protected Avila from invaders. Today, thousands of tourists come to see the medieval town. Buildings are being constructed around Avila to house a growing population. WMF wants to make sure that new buildings don't ruin the town and its surroundings.

UGANDA The Wamala King's tombs are where some rulers of the African nation of Uganda are buried. Today, this is an important place for the kings' families to gather, as well as for visitors to learn about the history of Uganda. The thatched roofs need to be repaired often, but there is not enough government or private money to care for this historic treasure.

UNITED STATES These Native American adobe dwellings, built by the Pueblo in New Mexico, have been in use for more than 1,000 years. They are now home to about 150 people, but tourists are changing the character of the place. A balance has to be found between the badly needed money that visitors spend and the need to preserve the site.

On the following pages, you will find information about the world's nations. Here's an example.

This tells the main languages and the official languages (if any) spoken in a nation.

This is the type of currency, or money, used in the nation.

Life expectancy is the number of years a person can expect to live. It's affected by heredity, a person's health and nutrition, the health care and wealth of a nation, and a person's occupation.

This tells the percentage of people who can read and write.

This is an interesting fact about the country.

ITALY
LOCATION: Europe
CAPITAL: Rome
AREA: 116,348 sq mi (301,340 sq km)
POPULATION ESTIMATE (2009): 58,126,212
GOVERNMENT: Republic
LANGUAGES: Italian (official), German, French, Slovene
MONEY: Euro (formerly lira)
LIFE EXPECTANCY: 80.2
LITERACY RATE: 98%

Guess what? *San Marino and Vatican City, two of Europe's smallest countries, are found within Italy's borders.*

AFGHANISTAN
LOCATION: Asia
CAPITAL: Kabul
AREA: 251,737 sq mi (652,230 sq km)
POPULATION ESTIMATE (2009): 28,395,716
GOVERNMENT: Islamic republic
LANGUAGES: Pashto and Dari (both official), others
MONEY: Afghani
LIFE EXPECTANCY: 44.4
LITERACY RATE: 28%

Guess what? *Kite-fighting and kite-running are popular sports in Afghanistan that involve flying kites, cutting them loose with glass-coated wire strings, and racing to retrieve them.*

ALBANIA
LOCATION: Europe
CAPITAL: Tirana
AREA: 11,100 sq mi (28,748 sq km)
POPULATION ESTIMATE (2009): 3,639,453
GOVERNMENT: Emerging democracy
LANGUAGES: Albanian (Tosk is the official dialect), Greek, others
MONEY: Lek
LIFE EXPECTANCY: 78
LITERACY RATE: 99%

Guess what? *Albania covers an area of Eastern Europe slightly smaller than the state of Maryland.*

ALGERIA
LOCATION: Africa
CAPITAL: Algiers
AREA: 919,590 sq mi (2,381,741 sq km)
POPULATION ESTIMATE (2009): 34,178,188
GOVERNMENT: Republic
LANGUAGES: Arabic (official), French, Berber dialects
MONEY: Dinar
LIFE EXPECTANCY: 74
LITERACY RATE: 70%

Guess what? *Nobel Prize–winner Albert Camus was born in Algeria. His classic, The Stranger, takes place in Algiers, the nation's capital.*

ANDORRA
LOCATION: Europe
CAPITAL: Andorra la Vella
AREA: 181 sq mi (468 sq km)
POPULATION ESTIMATE (2009): 83,888
GOVERNMENT: Parliamentary democracy
LANGUAGES: Catalán (official), French, Castilian, Portuguese
MONEY: Euro (formerly French franc and Spanish peseta)
LIFE EXPECTANCY: 82.5
LITERACY RATE: 100%

Guess what? *According to legend, Andorra was founded by Charlemagne in 805 as a thank-you gift to the local population for helping him win a battle.*

Countries

ANGOLA

LOCATION: Africa
CAPITAL: Luanda
AREA: 481,350 sq mi (1,246,700 sq km)
POPULATION ESTIMATE (2009): 12,799,293
GOVERNMENT: Republic
LANGUAGES: Portuguese (official), Bantu, others
MONEY: Kwanza
LIFE EXPECTANCY: 38.2
LITERACY RATE: 67%

guess what? *Angola is the only country in the world where the black palanca, a variety of antelope, can be found.*

ANTIGUA AND BARBUDA

LOCATION: Caribbean
CAPITAL: Saint John's
AREA: 171 sq mi (443 sq km)
POPULATION ESTIMATE (2009): 85,632
GOVERNMENT: Constitutional monarchy
LANGUAGE: English
MONEY: East Caribbean dollar
LIFE EXPECTANCY: 74.8
LITERACY RATE: 86%

guess what? *Every year, Antiguans celebrate Carnival, a 10-day festival commemorating the end of slavery in Antigua. Slavery ended in 1834, the earliest of any colony in the British Caribbean.*

ARGENTINA

LOCATION: South America
CAPITAL: Buenos Aires
AREA: 1,073,518 sq mi (2,780,400 sq km)
POPULATION ESTIMATE (2009): 40,913,584
GOVERNMENT: Republic
LANGUAGES: Spanish (official), Italian, English, German, French
MONEY: Argentine peso
LIFE EXPECTANCY: 76.6
LITERACY RATE: 97%

guess what? *The word Argentina comes from the Latin word for silver, argentum. It means "land of silver."*

ARMENIA

LOCATION: Asia
CAPITAL: Yerevan
AREA: 11,484 sq mi (29,743 sq km)
POPULATION ESTIMATE (2009): 2,967,004
GOVERNMENT: Republic
LANGUAGE: Armenian
MONEY: Dram
LIFE EXPECTANCY: 72.7
LITERACY RATE: 99%

guess what? *The Great Silk Road, an important early trade route, once passed through Armenia, linking it with developing empires in both Asia and Europe.*

AUSTRALIA

LOCATION: Oceania
CAPITAL: Canberra
AREA: 2,988,902 sq mi (7,741,220 sq km)
POPULATION ESTIMATE (2009): 21,262,641
GOVERNMENT: Democracy
LANGUAGE: English
MONEY: Australian dollar
LIFE EXPECTANCY: 81.6
LITERACY RATE: 99%

guess what? *The didgeridoo—perhaps the world's oldest instrument—originated in northern Australia. The instrument is generally made from the limbs and trunks of trees that have been hollowed out by insects. It makes a unique low-pitched sound.*

AUSTRIA

LOCATION: Europe
CAPITAL: Vienna
AREA: 32,382 sq mi (83,871 sq km)
POPULATION ESTIMATE (2009): 8,210,281
GOVERNMENT: Federal republic
LANGUAGES: German (official), Croation (official in Burgenland), Turkish, Serbian, others
MONEY: Euro (formerly schilling)
LIFE EXPECTANCY: 79.5
LITERACY RATE: 98%

guess what? *One of the most well-known organizations in Austria is the Vienna Boys' Choir. It was founded in 1498 by Maximilian I.*

AZERBAIJAN

LOCATION: Asia
CAPITAL: Baku
AREA: 33,400 sq mi
(86,600 sq km)
POPULATION ESTIMATE (2009):
8,238,672
GOVERNMENT: Republic
LANGUAGES: Azerbaijani, Lezgi,
Russian, Armenian, others
MONEY: Azerbaijani manat
LIFE EXPECTANCY: 66.7
LITERACY RATE: 99%

guess what? *Azerbaijan has an ongoing conflict with its neighbor Armenia over the Nagorno-Karabakh region. Armenia has occupied almost 20% of Azerbaijan since the early 1990s.*

BAHAMAS

LOCATION: Caribbean
CAPITAL: Nassau
AREA: 5,359 sq mi
(13,880 sq km)
POPULATION ESTIMATE (2009): 307,552
GOVERNMENT: Parliamentary
democracy
LANGUAGES: English, Creole
MONEY: Bahamian dollar
LIFE EXPECTANCY: 69.9
LITERACY RATE: 96%

guess what? *The Bahamas is made up of approximately 700 islands. Only 30 of the islands are inhabited.*

BAHRAIN

LOCATION: Middle East
CAPITAL: Manama
AREA: 286 sq mi (741 sq km)
POPULATION ESTIMATE (2009):
728,709
GOVERNMENT: Constitutional
monarchy
LANGUAGES: Arabic, English,
Farsi, Urdu
MONEY: Bahraini dinar
LIFE EXPECTANCY: 75.2
LITERACY RATE: 87%

guess what? *Bahrain is a small archipelago, or chain of islands, in the Persian Gulf. Its name means "two seas" in Arabic.*

BANGLADESH

LOCATION: Asia
CAPITAL: Dhaka
AREA: 55,598 sq mi
(143,998 sq km)
POPULATION ESTIMATE (2009):
156,050,883
GOVERNMENT: Parliamentary
democracy
LANGUAGES: Bangla (official),
English
MONEY: Taka
LIFE EXPECTANCY: 60.3
LITERACY RATE: 48%

guess what? *The kathal, or jackfruit, is the national fruit of Bangladesh. The fruit can grow to enormous sizes and even weigh hundreds of pounds.*

BARBADOS

LOCATION: Caribbean
CAPITAL: Bridgetown
AREA: 166 sq mi (430 sq km)
POPULATION ESTIMATE (2009): 284,589
GOVERNMENT: Parliamentary
democracy
LANGUAGE: English
MONEY: Barbadian dollar
LIFE EXPECTANCY: 73.9
LITERACY RATE: 100%

guess what? *Pop singer Rihanna was born and raised in Barbados.*

BELARUS

LOCATION: Europe
CAPITAL: Minsk
AREA: 80,154 sq mi
(207,600 sq km)
POPULATION ESTIMATE (2009):
9,648,533
GOVERNMENT: Republic
LANGUAGES: Belarusian, Russian
MONEY: Belarusian ruble
LIFE EXPECTANCY: 70.6
LITERACY RATE: 100%

guess what? *Belarusian rubles are referred to locally as zaichiki, or rabbits, because the first one-ruble note, issued in 1992, featured a jumping rabbit. The currency exists only in bills; there are no coins.*

BELGIUM

LOCATION: Europe
CAPITAL: Brussels
AREA: 11,787 sq mi (30,528 sq km)
POPULATION ESTIMATE (2009): 10,414,336
GOVERNMENT: Parliamentary democracy under a constitutional monarchy
LANGUAGES: Dutch, French, and German (all official)
MONEY: Euro (formerly Belgian franc)
LIFE EXPECTANCY: 79.2
LITERACY RATE: 99%

guess what? *The word spa, used to describe a luxury resort, comes from the city of Spa in Belgium. The first spa in Spa was visited by wealthy people from across Europe.*

BELIZE

LOCATION: Central America
CAPITAL: Belmopan
AREA: 8,867 sq mi (22,966 sq km)
POPULATION ESTIMATE (2009): 307,899
GOVERNMENT: Parliamentary democracy
LANGUAGES: Spanish, Creole, Mayan dialects, English (official), Garifuna, German
MONEY: Belizean dollar
LIFE EXPECTANCY: 68.2
LITERACY RATE: 77%

guess what? *Belize's flag features the words Sub Umbra Florero, which mean "Under the shade, I flourish" in Latin. It refers to the shade of the mahogany tree, also seen on the flag.*

BENIN

LOCATION: Africa
CAPITAL: Porto-Novo
AREA: 43,483 sq mi (112,622 sq km)
POPULATION ESTIMATE (2009): 8,791,832
GOVERNMENT: Republic
LANGUAGES: French (official), Fon, Yoruba, other African languages
MONEY: CFA franc
LIFE EXPECTANCY: 59
LITERACY RATE: 35%

guess what? *Benin has two rainy and two dry seasons each year.*

BHUTAN

LOCATION: Asia
CAPITAL: Thimphu
AREA: 14,824 sq mi (38,394 sq km)
POPULATION ESTIMATE (2009): 691,141
GOVERNMENT: Constitutional monarchy
LANGUAGES: Dzongkha (official), various Tibetan and Nepalese dialects
MONEY: Ngultrum
LIFE EXPECTANCY: 66.1
LITERACY RATE: 47%

guess what? *Most of Bhutan is mountainous, and 70% of the mountainous area is covered by wild, untouched forests.*

BOLIVIA

LOCATION: South America
CAPITALS: La Paz (seat of government), Sucre (legal capital)
AREA: 424,162 sq mi (1,098,581 sq km)
POPULATION ESTIMATE (2009): 9,775,246
GOVERNMENT: Republic
LANGUAGES: Spanish, Quechua, and Aymara (all official)
MONEY: Boliviano
LIFE EXPECTANCY: 66.9
LITERACY RATE: 87%

guess what? *Bolivia is home to the Yungas Road, which might be the most dangerous road in the world. Connecting La Paz to the Yungas Valley, the narrow, curvy cliffside road claims the lives of more than 100 people per year.*

BOSNIA AND HERZEGOVINA

LOCATION: Europe
CAPITAL: Sarajevo
AREA: 19,767 sq mi (51,197 sq km)
POPULATION ESTIMATE (2009): 4,613,414
GOVERNMENT: Emerging democratic republic
LANGUAGES: Bosnian, Croatian, Serbian
MONEY: Convertible mark
LIFE EXPECTANCY: 78.5
LITERACY RATE: 96.7%

guess what? *Bosnia and Herzegovina is part of the Balkan Peninsula in southeastern Europe, along with Greece, Albania, Bulgaria, Kosovo, Macedonia, Montenegro, and Serbia.*

BOTSWANA

LOCATION: Africa
CAPITAL: Gaborone
AREA: 224,607 sq mi
(581,730 sq km)
POPULATION ESTIMATE (2009):
1,990,876
GOVERNMENT: Parliamentary
republic
LANGUAGES: English (official),
Setswana, Kalanga, Sekgalagadi
MONEY: Pula
LIFE EXPECTANCY: 61.9
LITERACY RATE: 81%

guess what? *Protected wildlife areas make up almost 17% of Botswana.*

BRAZIL

LOCATION: South America
CAPITAL: Brasília
AREA: 3,287,612 sq mi
(8,514,877 sq km)
POPULATION ESTIMATE (2009):
198,739,269
GOVERNMENT: Federal republic
LANGUAGES: Portuguese (official),
Spanish, German, Italian,
Japanese, English, various
Amerindian languages
MONEY: Real
LIFE EXPECTANCY: 72
LITERACY RATE: 88.6%

guess what? *Brazil is one of the world's largest producers of commercial beef, with more than 165 million head of cattle.*

BRUNEI

LOCATION: Asia
CAPITAL: Bandar Seri Begawan
AREA: 2,226 sq mi (5,765 sq km)
POPULATION ESTIMATE (2009): 388,190
GOVERNMENT: Constitutional
sultanate
LANGUAGES: Malay (official),
Chinese, English
MONEY: Bruneian dollar
LIFE EXPECTANCY: 75.7
LITERACY RATE: 93%

guess what? *Brunei is located on the island of Borneo—the third-largest island in the world. Parts of Indonesia and Malaysia are also found on Borneo.*

BULGARIA

LOCATION: Europe
CAPITAL: Sofia
AREA: 42,811 sq mi
(110,879 sq km)
POPULATION ESTIMATE (2009):
7,204,687
GOVERNMENT: Parliamentary
democracy
LANGUAGES: Bulgarian, Turkish
MONEY: Lev
LIFE EXPECTANCY: 73.1
LITERACY RATE: 98%

guess what? *Bulgarians celebrate the coming of spring with a holiday called Baba Marta (Grandmother March) on March 1. They give one another red and white tassels or dolls called martenitsa.*

BURKINA FASO

LOCATION: Africa
CAPITAL: Ouagadougou
AREA: 105,870 sq mi
(274,200 sq km)
POPULATION ESTIMATE (2009):
15,746,232
GOVERNMENT: Parliamentary
republic
LANGUAGES: French (official),
tribal languages
MONEY: CFA franc
LIFE EXPECTANCY: 53
LITERACY RATE: 22%

guess what? *The Pan-African Film and Television Festival (FESPACO), which is the largest festival of African films, is held in Ouagadougou every other year.*

BURUNDI

LOCATION: Africa
CAPITAL: Bujumbura
AREA: 10,745 sq mi
(27,830 sq km)
POPULATION ESTIMATE (2009):
9,511,330
GOVERNMENT: Republic
LANGUAGES: Kirundi and French
(both official), Swahili
MONEY: Burundi franc
LIFE EXPECTANCY: 57.8
LITERACY RATE: 59%

guess what? *In ancient Burundi, drums were considered sacred objects and used only on special occasions. Today drums are still central to the cultural life of Burundi.*

Countries

CAMBODIA

LOCATION: Asia
CAPITAL: Phnom Penh
AREA: 69,900 sq mi
(181,035 sq km)
POPULATION ESTIMATE (2009):
14,494,293
GOVERNMENT: Multiparty
democracy under a
constitutional monarchy
LANGUAGES: Khmer (official),
French, English
MONEY: Riel
LIFE EXPECTANCY: 62.1
LITERACY RATE: 74%

Guess what? *There are two main types of traditional music in Cambodia: pinpeath, which uses percussion and stringed instruments, and mohory, which uses only stringed instruments.*

CAMEROON

LOCATION: Africa
CAPITAL: Yaoundé
AREA: 183,567 sq mi
(475,440 sq km)
POPULATION ESTIMATE (2009):
18,879,301
GOVERNMENT: Republic
LANGUAGES: French and
English (both official),
various African languages
MONEY: CFA franc
LIFE EXPECTANCY: 53.7
LITERACY RATE: 68%

Guess what? *The second-wettest place on Earth is Debuncha, Cameroon. Located at the base of Mount Cameroon, Debuncha's annual rainfall is around 400 inches (10 m).*

CANADA

LOCATION: North America
CAPITAL: Ottawa
AREA: 3,855,081 sq mi
(9,984,670 sq km)
POPULATION ESTIMATE (2009):
33,487,208
GOVERNMENT: Parliamentary
democracy
LANGUAGES: English and French
(both official)
MONEY: Canadian dollar
LIFE EXPECTANCY: 81.2
LITERACY RATE: 99%

Guess what? *Much of Canada is snowy and cold, but the country is home to a hot desert, too. Located in the Okanagan Valley, Canada's "pocket desert" is part of a desert system that stretches all the way to Mexico.*

CAPE VERDE

LOCATION: Africa
CAPITAL: Praia
AREA: 1,557 sq mi (4,033 sq km)
POPULATION ESTIMATE (2009): 429,474
GOVERNMENT: Republic
LANGUAGES: Portuguese, Crioulo
MONEY: Cape Verdean escudo
LIFE EXPECTANCY: 71.6
LITERACY RATE: 77%

Guess what? *Cape Verde is home to the Baia das Gatas Music Festival. It takes place on the first weekend in August each year. The festival features mostly bands from tropical countries, and more than 35,000 visitors come annually to camp out on the beach and hear the music.*

CENTRAL AFRICAN REPUBLIC

LOCATION: Africa
CAPITAL: Bangui
AREA: 240,534 sq mi
(622,984 sq km)
POPULATION ESTIMATE (2009):
4,511,488
GOVERNMENT: Republic
LANGUAGES: French (official),
Sangho, other African
languages
MONEY: CFA franc
LIFE EXPECTANCY: 44.5
LITERACY RATE: 49%

Guess what? *Forest elephants are found in the Central African Republic. They are smaller than savanna elephants. Their tusks are made of a harder type of ivory that has a distinctive color.*

CHAD

LOCATION: Africa
CAPITAL: N'Djamena
AREA: 495,752 sq mi
(1,284,000 sq km)
POPULATION ESTIMATE (2009):
10,329,208
GOVERNMENT: Republic
LANGUAGES: French and Arabic
(both official), Sara, others
MONEY: CFA franc
LIFE EXPECTANCY: 47.7
LITERACY RATE: 26%

Guess what? *In the early 20th century, Chad became a territory of France. It remained under French control until declaring independence in 1960.*

CHILE

LOCATION: South America
CAPITAL: Santiago
AREA: 291,933 sq mi
(756,102 sq km)
POPULATION ESTIMATE (2009):
16,601,707
GOVERNMENT: Republic
LANGUAGES: Spanish (official),
Mapudungun, German, English
MONEY: Chilean peso
LIFE EXPECTANCY: 77.3
LITERACY RATE: 96%

guess what? *Chilean poet Gabriela Mistral was the first Latin American to win the Nobel Prize for Literature.*

CHINA

LOCATION: Asia
CAPITAL: Beijing
AREA: 3,705,386 sq mi
(9,596,961 sq km)
POPULATION ESTIMATE (2009):
1,338,612,968
GOVERNMENT: Communist state
LANGUAGES: Chinese (Mandarin),
Yue (Cantonese), local dialects
MONEY: Renminbi yuan
LIFE EXPECTANCY: 73.5
LITERACY RATE: 91%

guess what? *China is home to the world's oldest continuously used written language system. This system includes more than 47,000 known characters.*

COLOMBIA

LOCATION: South America
CAPITAL: Bogotá
AREA: 439,733 sq mi
(1,138,914 sq km)
POPULATION ESTIMATE (2009):
43,677,372
GOVERNMENT: Republic
LANGUAGE: Spanish
MONEY: Colombian peso
LIFE EXPECTANCY: 74.1
LITERACY RATE: 90.4%

guess what? *According to legend, there is a land in South America full of gold and precious gemstones. Some thought this land, known as "El Dorado," could be found in Colombia, prompting Spanish explorers to travel to the country in the 1500s in search of land and fortune.*

COMOROS

LOCATION: Africa
CAPITAL: Moroni
AREA: 863 sq mi (2,235 sq km)
POPULATION ESTIMATE (2009): 752,438
GOVERNMENT: Republic
LANGUAGES: French and Arabic
(both official), Shikomoro
MONEY: Comoran franc
LIFE EXPECTANCY: 63.5
LITERACY RATE: 57%

guess what? *Comoros is sometimes referred to as the "Perfume Islands" because of the exotic flowers that grow there. These flowers have long been used to make expensive French perfumes.*

CONGO, DEMOCRATIC REPUBLIC OF THE

LOCATION: Africa
CAPITAL: Kinshasa
AREA: 905,355 sq mi
(2,344,858 sq km)
POPULATION ESTIMATE (2009):
68,692,542
GOVERNMENT: Republic
LANGUAGES: French (official),
Lingala, Kingwana, others
MONEY: Congolese franc
LIFE EXPECTANCY: 54.4
LITERACY RATE: 67%

guess what? *The Democratic Republic of the Congo in Central Africa is about the size of Western Europe.*

CONGO, REPUBLIC OF THE

LOCATION: Africa
CAPITAL: Brazzaville
AREA: 132,046 sq mi
(342,000 sq km)
POPULATION ESTIMATE (2009):
4,012,809
GOVERNMENT: Republic
LANGUAGES: French (official),
Lingala, Monokutuba,
Kikongo, others
MONEY: CFA franc
LIFE EXPECTANCY: 54.2
LITERACY RATE: 84%

guess what? *The Republic of Congo is home to one of the world's largest populations of chimpanzees.*

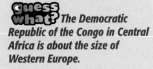

Countries

COSTA RICA

LOCATION: Central America
CAPITAL: San José
AREA: 19,730 sq mi
(51,100 sq km)
POPULATION ESTIMATE (2009):
4,253,877
GOVERNMENT: Democratic republic
LANGUAGES: Spanish (official),
English
MONEY: Colon
LIFE EXPECTANCY: 77.6
LITERACY RATE: 95%

guess what? *There are several active volcanoes in Costa Rica. Located in the northwest of the country, the Arenal volcano is one of the world's most active volcanoes.*

CÔTE D'IVOIRE (IVORY COAST)

LOCATION: Africa
CAPITAL: Yamoussoukro
AREA: 124,502 sq mi
(322,463 sq km)
POPULATION ESTIMATE (2009):
20,617,068
GOVERNMENT: Republic
LANGUAGES: French (official),
various African languages
MONEY: CFA franc
LIFE EXPECTANCY: 55.5
LITERACY RATE: 49%

guess what? *Yamoussoukro is home to the Basilica of Our Lady of Peace. Modeled after St. Peter's Basilica in Vatican City, Our Lady of Peace is one of the largest churches in the world.*

CROATIA

LOCATION: Europe
CAPITAL: Zagreb
AREA: 21,851 sq mi
(56,594 sq km)
POPULATION ESTIMATE (2009):
4,489,409
GOVERNMENT: Presidential
parliamentary democracy
LANGUAGES: Croatian, Serbian
MONEY: Kuna
LIFE EXPECTANCY: 75.4
LITERACY RATE: 98%

guess what? *The Dalmatian dog breed is named after the mountainous Dalmatian Coast, which runs along the west coast of Croatia on the Adriatic Sea.*

CUBA

LOCATION: Caribbean
CAPITAL: Havana
AREA: 42,803 sq mi
(110,860 sq km)
POPULATION ESTIMATE (2009):
11,451,652
GOVERNMENT: Communist state
LANGUAGE: Spanish
MONEY: Peso
LIFE EXPECTANCY: 77.5
LITERACY RATE: 100%

guess what? *None of the species of plants or animals native to Cuba (including snakes) are deadly to humans.*

CYPRUS

LOCATION: Europe
CAPITAL: Nicosia
AREA: 3,571 sq mi (9,250 sq km)
POPULATION ESTIMATE (2009): 108,748
GOVERNMENT: Republic
LANGUAGES: Greek, Turkish,
English
MONEY: Euro (formerly Cyprus
pound), Turkish new lira
LIFE EXPECTANCY: 77.5
LITERACY RATE: 98%

guess what? *The island of Cyprus is divided into a Greek area and a Turkish area.*

CZECH REPUBLIC

LOCATION: Europe
CAPITAL: Prague
AREA: 30,450 sq mi
(78,866 sq km)
POPULATION ESTIMATE (2009):
10,221,904
GOVERNMENT: Parliamentary
democracy
LANGUAGES: Czech, Slovak
MONEY: Koruna
LIFE EXPECTANCY: 76.8
LITERACY RATE: 99%

guess what? *Otto Wichterle, a Czech chemist, invented soft contact lenses, which were later developed in the 1960s.*

DENMARK

LOCATION: Europe
CAPITAL: Copenhagen
AREA: 16,639 sq mi
(43,094 sq km)
POPULATION ESTIMATE (2009):
5,500,510
GOVERNMENT: Constitutional
monarchy
LANGUAGES: Danish, Faroese,
Greenlandic, German
MONEY: Krone
LIFE EXPECTANCY: 78.3
LITERACY RATE: 99%

guess what? *Denmark is the oldest monarchy in Western Europe, tracing its roots back to 958.*

DJIBOUTI

LOCATION: Africa
CAPITAL: Djibouti
AREA: 8,958 sq mi
(23,200 sq km)
POPULATION ESTIMATE (2009): 724,622
GOVERNMENT: Republic
LANGUAGES: Arabic and French
(both official), Somali, Afar
MONEY: Djiboutian franc
LIFE EXPECTANCY: 60.3
LITERACY RATE: 68%

guess what? *Many residents of Djibouti are nomadic animal herders.*

DOMINICA

LOCATION: Caribbean
CAPITAL: Roseau
AREA: 291 sq mi (754 sq km)
POPULATION ESTIMATE (2009): 72,660
GOVERNMENT: Parliamentary
democracy
LANGUAGES: English (official),
French patois
MONEY: East Caribbean dollar
LIFE EXPECTANCY: 75.5
LITERACY RATE: 94%

guess what? *The world's second-largest boiling lake is located in Dominica. The boiling is caused by hot gases escaping from a crack in Earth's crust.*

DOMINICAN REPUBLIC

LOCATION: Caribbean
CAPITAL: Santo Domingo
AREA: 18,792 sq mi
(48,670 sq km)
POPULATION ESTIMATE (2009):
9,650,054
GOVERNMENT: Democratic republic
LANGUAGE: Spanish
MONEY: Dominican peso
LIFE EXPECTANCY: 73.7
LITERACY RATE: 87%

guess what? *Dominican Republic takes up the eastern two-thirds of the island of Hispaniola. Haiti takes up the rest of the island. Christopher Columbus explored Hispaniola in 1492.*

EAST TIMOR
(TIMOR-LESTE)

LOCATION: Asia
CAPITAL: Dili
AREA: 5,743 sq mi (14,874 sq km)
POPULATION ESTIMATE (2009):
1,131,612
GOVERNMENT: Republic
LANGUAGES: Tetum and
Portuguese (both official),
Indonesian, English
MONEY: U.S. dollar
LIFE EXPECTANCY: 67
LITERACY RATE: 59%

guess what? *Until 1975, most East Timorese practiced animism, a belief in the presence of a soul in all things—not only humans and animals but rocks, plants, and rivers. Today, more than 80% of the population is Catholic.*

ECUADOR

LOCATION: South America
CAPITAL: Quito
AREA: 109,483 sq mi
(283,560 sq km)
POPULATION ESTIMATE (2009):
14,573,101
GOVERNMENT: Republic
LANGUAGES: Spanish (official),
Quechua
MONEY: U.S. dollar
LIFE EXPECTANCY: 75.3
LITERACY RATE: 91%

guess what? *Ecuador means "equator" in Spanish. The equator (the line that circles Earth halfway between the North and South Poles) runs through the country.*

EGYPT

LOCATION: Africa
CAPITAL: Cairo
AREA: 386,660 sq mi
(1,001,450 sq km)
POPULATION ESTIMATE (2009):
78,866,635
GOVERNMENT: Republic
LANGUAGE: Arabic
MONEY: Egyptian pound
LIFE EXPECTANCY: 72.2
LITERACY RATE: 71%

guess what? *The iconic Pyramids of Giza are the only Wonder of the Ancient World that still exists.*

EL SALVADOR

LOCATION: Central America
CAPITAL: San Salvador
AREA: 8,124 sq mi (21,040 sq km)
POPULATION ESTIMATE (2009):
7,185,218
GOVERNMENT: Republic
LANGUAGES: Spanish, Nahua
MONEY: U.S. dollar
LIFE EXPECTANCY: 72.3
LITERACY RATE: 80%

guess what? *Just outside the towns of Corinto and Cacaopera in El Salvador, archaeologists have discovered cave paintings dating back to 8000 B.C. The images reveal details about the lives of people who lived more than 10,000 years ago.*

EQUATORIAL GUINEA

LOCATION: Africa
CAPITAL: Malabo
AREA: 10,830 sq mi
(28,051 sq km)
POPULATION ESTIMATE (2009): 633,441
GOVERNMENT: Republic
LANGUAGES: Spanish and French
(both official), Fang, Bubi
MONEY: CFA franc
LIFE EXPECTANCY: 61.6
LITERACY RATE: 87%

guess what? *Equatorial Guinea was under Spanish colonial rule for 190 years. It has been an independent nation since 1968.*

ERITREA

LOCATION: Africa
CAPITAL: Asmara
AREA: 45,406 sq mi
(117,600 sq km)
POPULATION ESTIMATE (2009):
5,647,168
GOVERNMENT: Transitional
LANGUAGES: Afar, Arabic, Tigre, Kunama, Tigrinya, others
MONEY: Nakfa
LIFE EXPECTANCY: 61.8
LITERACY RATE: 59%

guess what? *The Danakil Depression, the lowest point in Eritrea, is one of the hottest places on Earth, with high temperatures around 131°F (55°C) during the dry season.*

ESTONIA

LOCATION: Europe
CAPITAL: Tallinn
AREA: 17,462 sq mi
(45,226 sq km)
POPULATION ESTIMATE (2009):
1,299,371
GOVERNMENT: Parliamentary republic
LANGUAGES: Estonian (official), Russian
MONEY: Kroon
LIFE EXPECTANCY: 72.8
LITERACY RATE: 100%

guess what? *Tallinn's Old Town is one of the best-preserved medieval towns in Europe. Buildings from the 13th through the 16th centuries still stand.*

ETHIOPIA

LOCATION: Africa
CAPITAL: Addis Ababa
AREA: 426,373 sq mi
(1,104,300 sq km)
POPULATION ESTIMATE (2009):
85,237,338
GOVERNMENT: Federal republic
LANGUAGES: Amarigna (official), Oromigna, Tigrigna, Somaligna, others
MONEY: Birr
LIFE EXPECTANCY: 55.4
LITERACY RATE: 43%

guess what? *Some of the oldest human skeletons found to date have been unearthed in Ethiopia. Lucy, found in 1974, is about 3.2 million years old, while Selam, found in 2001, is more than 3.3 million years old.*

FIJI

LOCATION: Oceania
CAPITAL: Suva
AREA: 7,054 sq mi (18,270 sq km)
POPULATION ESTIMATE (2009): 944,720
GOVERNMENT: Republic
LANGUAGES: Fijian and English (both official), Hindustani
MONEY: Fijian dollar
LIFE EXPECTANCY: 70.7
LITERACY RATE: 94%

guess what? *The line of longitude known as the international date line (180°) used to fall across the Fijian island of Taveuni, in the Pacific Ocean. There, a person could stand with one foot in today and one foot in yesterday. The dateline has been moved, so it no longer bisects the island.*

FINLAND

LOCATION: Europe
CAPITAL: Helsinki
AREA: 130,559 sq mi (338,145 sq km)
POPULATION ESTIMATE (2009): 5,250,275
GOVERNMENT: Republic
LANGUAGES: Finnish and Swedish (both official)
MONEY: Euro (formerly markka)
LIFE EXPECTANCY: 79
LITERACY RATE: 100%

guess what? *One-quarter of Finland's land mass exists north of the Arctic Circle, which is the region surrounding the North Pole. Within the Arctic Circle, there is at least one 24-hour period of complete darkness every year.*

FRANCE

LOCATION: Europe
CAPITAL: Paris
AREA: 248,429 sq mi (643,427 sq km)
POPULATION ESTIMATE (2009): 64,057,792
GOVERNMENT: Republic
LANGUAGE: French
MONEY: Euro (formerly franc)
LIFE EXPECTANCY: 81
LITERACY RATE: 99%

guess what? *Many traditional French foods are made with heavy cream, butter, and saturated fats, yet France has a lower percentage of cardiac deaths and health complications than many other countries, including the United States.*

GABON

LOCATION: Africa
CAPITAL: Libreville
AREA: 103,346 sq mi (267,667 sq km)
POPULATION ESTIMATE (2009): 1,514,993
GOVERNMENT: Republic
LANGUAGES: French (official), Fang, Myene, Nzebi, Bapounou/Eschira, Bandjabi
MONEY: CFA franc
LIFE EXPECTANCY: 53.1
LITERACY RATE: 63%

guess what? *Ten percent of Gabon's land has recently been designated as national parkland, making Gabon a popular destination for ecotourists in Africa.*

THE GAMBIA

LOCATION: Africa
CAPITAL: Banjul
AREA: 4,363 sq mi (11,300 sq km)
POPULATION ESTIMATE (2009): 1,778,081
GOVERNMENT: Republic
LANGUAGES: English (official), Mandinka, Wolof, Fula, others
MONEY: Dalasi
LIFE EXPECTANCY: 53.8
LITERACY RATE: 40%

guess what? *The Gambia is split into nearly equal halves by the Gambia River, which flows through the country and into the Atlantic Ocean.*

GEORGIA

LOCATION: Asia
CAPITAL: Tbilisi
AREA: 26,911 sq mi (69,700 sq km)
POPULATION ESTIMATE (2009): 4,615,807
GOVERNMENT: Republic
LANGUAGES: Georgian (official), Russian, Armenian, Azeri
MONEY: Lari
LIFE EXPECTANCY: 76.7
LITERACY RATE: 100%

guess what? *Georgia is home to the Voronya Cave (also known as the Krubera-Voronia Cave), the deepest cave in the world. It has a depth of 1.33 miles (2.1 km).*

Countries

GERMANY

LOCATION: Europe
CAPITAL: Berlin
AREA: 137,846 sq mi
(357,021 sq km)
POPULATION ESTIMATE (2009):
82,329,758
GOVERNMENT: Federal republic
LANGUAGE: German
MONEY: Euro (formerly
deutsche mark)
LIFE EXPECTANCY: 79.3
LITERACY RATE: 99%

guess what? *Hundreds of bunkers and tunnels built during World War II still exist beneath the city of Berlin.*

GHANA

LOCATION: Africa
CAPITAL: Accra
AREA: 92,098 sq mi
(238,533 sq km)
POPULATION ESTIMATE (2009):
23,887,812
GOVERNMENT: Constitutional
democracy
LANGUAGES: Asante, Ewe, Fante,
others
MONEY: Cedi
LIFE EXPECTANCY: 60.1
LITERACY RATE: 58%

guess what? *Fufu is a popular food in Ghana. It is made by boiling and then pounding cassava, yams, plantains, or rice into a soft, doughy consistency.*

GREECE

LOCATION: Europe
CAPITAL: Athens
AREA: 50,949 sq mi
(131,957 sq km)
POPULATION ESTIMATE (2009):
10,737,428
GOVERNMENT: Parliamentary
republic
LANGUAGE: Greek
MONEY: Euro (formerly drachma)
LIFE EXPECTANCY: 79.7
LITERACY RATE: 96%

guess what? *Greeks have used olive oil in many different ways for thousands of years. Today, more olive oil is consumed per person in Greece than in any other country.*

GRENADA

LOCATION: Caribbean
CAPITAL: Saint George's
AREA: 133 sq mi (344 sq km)
POPULATION ESTIMATE (2009): 90,739
GOVERNMENT: Parliamentary
democracy
LANGUAGES: English (official),
French patois
MONEY: East Caribbean dollar
LIFE EXPECTANCY: 66
LITERACY RATE: 96%

guess what? *Grenada is sometimes referred to as the "Spice Island" because it is a leading producer of many of the world's spices, especially nutmeg.*

GUATEMALA

LOCATION: Central America
CAPITAL: Guatemala City
AREA: 42,042 sq mi
(108,890 sq km)
POPULATION ESTIMATE (2009):
13,276,517
GOVERNMENT: Republic
LANGUAGES: Spanish, Amerindian
languages
MONEY: Quetzal
LIFE EXPECTANCY: 70.3
LITERACY RATE: 69%

guess what? *Approximately 4,000 years ago, Guatemala City was home to one of the first Mayan societies.*

GUINEA

LOCATION: Africa
CAPITAL: Conakry
AREA: 94,925 sq mi
(245,860 sq km)
POPULATION ESTIMATE (2009):
10,057,975
GOVERNMENT: Republic
LANGUAGES: French (official),
native tongues
MONEY: Guinean franc
LIFE EXPECTANCY: 57.1
LITERACY RATE: 30%

guess what? *Guinea's capital, Conakry, is the wettest capital in the world, with more than 12 feet (3.7 m) of rain per year.*

GUINEA-BISSAU

LOCATION: Africa
CAPITAL: Bissau
AREA: 13,946 sq mi
(36,120 sq km)
POPULATION ESTIMATE (2009): 1,533,964
GOVERNMENT: Republic
LANGUAGES: Portuguese (official), Crioulo, African languages
MONEY: CFA franc
LIFE EXPECTANCY: 47.9
LITERACY RATE: 42%

guess what? *Guinea-Bissau is one of the poorest countries in the world.*

GUYANA

LOCATION: South America
CAPITAL: Georgetown
AREA: 83,000 sq mi
(290,712 sq km)
POPULATION ESTIMATE (2009): 752,940
GOVERNMENT: Republic
LANGUAGES: English (official), Amerindian dialects, Creole
MONEY: Guyanese dollar
LIFE EXPECTANCY: 66.3
LITERACY RATE: 99%

guess what? *The national bird of Guyana is the unique hoatzin. These birds rarely fly, and babies of the species learn to swim before they fly. The hoatzin eats mostly leaves, and has a stomach that is similar to that of a cow or a sheep.*

HAITI

LOCATION: Caribbean
CAPITAL: Port-au-Prince
AREA: 10,714 sq mi
(27,750 sq km)
POPULATION ESTIMATE (2009): 9,035,536
GOVERNMENT: Republic
LANGUAGES: Creole and French (both official)
MONEY: Gourde
LIFE EXPECTANCY: 60.8
LITERACY RATE: 53%

guess what? *In the late 1700s, Toussaint L'Ouverture led more than half a million slaves in a revolt that resulted in the country declaring its independence from France in 1804.*

HONDURAS

LOCATION: Central America
CAPITAL: Tegucigalpa
AREA: 43,278 sq mi
(112,090 sq km)
POPULATION ESTIMATE (2009): 7,833,696
GOVERNMENT: Republic
LANGUAGES: Spanish, Amerindian dialects
MONEY: Lempira
LIFE EXPECTANCY: 70.5
LITERACY RATE: 80%

guess what? *In 1962, archaeologists found stone tools 6,000 to 8,000 years old near La Esperanza, Honduras.*

HUNGARY

LOCATION: Europe
CAPITAL: Budapest
AREA: 35,919 sq mi
(93,030 sq km)
POPULATION ESTIMATE (2009): 9,905,596
GOVERNMENT: Parliamentary democracy
LANGUAGE: Magyar (Hungarian)
MONEY: Forint
LIFE EXPECTANCY: 73.4
LITERACY RATE: 99%

guess what? *The Rubik's Cube, the ballpoint pen, and the theory behind the hydrogen bomb were devised by Hungarians.*

ICELAND

LOCATION: Europe
CAPITAL: Reykjavík
AREA: 39,768 sq mi
(103,000 sq km)
POPULATION ESTIMATE (2009): 306,694
GOVERNMENT: Constitutional republic
LANGUAGES: Icelandic, English
MONEY: Icelandic krona
LIFE EXPECTANCY: 80.7
LITERACY RATE: 99%

guess what? *The Icelandic horse is a small, hardy breed of horse brought to Iceland more than 1,000 years ago by Vikings. Icelandic law does not allow other horses to be brought onto the island.*

INDIA

LOCATION: Asia
CAPITAL: New Delhi
AREA: 1,269,219 sq mi
(3,287,263 sq km)
POPULATION ESTIMATE (2009):
1,156,897,766
GOVERNMENT: Federal republic
LANGUAGES: Hindi (national),
English, 14 other official
languages
MONEY: Indian rupee
LIFE EXPECTANCY: 66.1
LITERACY RATE: 61%

guess what? *India takes up only about 2.4% of the world's land area, but it is home to 15% of the world's population.*

INDONESIA

LOCATION: Asia
CAPITAL: Jakarta
AREA: 735,358 sq mi
(1,904,569 sq km)
POPULATION ESTIMATE (2009):
240,271,522
GOVERNMENT: Republic
LANGUAGES: Bahasa Indonesia
(official), Dutch, English,
many local dialects
MONEY: Rupiah
LIFE EXPECTANCY: 70.8
LITERACY RATE: 90%

guess what? *Indonesia is home to the Komodo dragon, the largest lizard in the world. It is also one of the most deadly animals on Earth.*

IRAN

LOCATION: Middle East
CAPITAL: Tehran
AREA: 636,372 sq mi
(1,648,195 sq km)
POPULATION ESTIMATE (2009):
66,429,284
GOVERNMENT: Islamic theocracy
LANGUAGES: Persian, Turkic,
Kurdish
MONEY: Rial
LIFE EXPECTANCY: 71.1
LITERACY RATE: 77%

guess what? *Iran was known as Persia until 1935.*

IRAQ

LOCATION: Middle East
CAPITAL: Baghdad
AREA: 169,235 sq mi
(438,317 sq km)
POPULATION ESTIMATE (2009):
28,945,569
GOVERNMENT: Parliamentary
democracy
LANGUAGES: Arabic, Kurdish
MONEY: Dinar
LIFE EXPECTANCY: 70
LITERACY RATE: 74%

guess what? *Iraq was occupied by the British during World War I.*

IRELAND

LOCATION: Europe
CAPITAL: Dublin
AREA: 27,136 sq mi
(70,280 sq km)
POPULATION ESTIMATE (2009):
4,203,200
GOVERNMENT: Republic
LANGUAGES: Irish (Gaelic) and
English (both official)
MONEY: Euro (formerly Irish
pound, or punt)
LIFE EXPECTANCY: 78.2
LITERACY RATE: 99%

guess what? *The national symbol of Ireland is the harp (not the shamrock), making it the only country in the world with a musical instrument as its national symbol.*

ISRAEL

LOCATION: Middle East
CAPITAL: Jerusalem
AREA: 8,522 sq mi
(22,072 sq km)
POPULATION ESTIMATE (2009):
7,233,701
GOVERNMENT: Parliamentary
democracy
LANGUAGES: Hebrew (official),
Arabic, English
MONEY: New Israeli shekel
LIFE EXPECTANCY: 80.7
LITERACY RATE: 97%

guess what? *Israel's paper money is printed with braille on it, so the blind can identify the different denominations.*

ITALY

LOCATION: Europe
CAPITAL: Rome
AREA: 116,348 sq mi
(301,340 sq km)
POPULATION ESTIMATE (2009):
58,126,212
GOVERNMENT: Republic
LANGUAGES: Italian (official),
German, French, Slovene
MONEY: Euro (formerly lira)
LIFE EXPECTANCY: 80.2
LITERACY RATE: 98%

guess what? *San Marino and Vatican City, two of Europe's smallest countries, are found within Italy's borders.*

JAMAICA

LOCATION: Caribbean
CAPITAL: Kingston
AREA: 4,244 sq mi
(10,991 sq km)
POPULATION ESTIMATE (2009):
2,825,928
GOVERNMENT: Parliamentary
democracy
LANGUAGES: English, English patois
MONEY: Jamaican dollar
LIFE EXPECTANCY: 73.5
LITERACY RATE: 88%

guess what? *Jerk cooking is very popular in Jamaica. Foods prepared in the jerk style are rubbed with spices such as Scotch bonnet pepper, thyme, paprika, and allspice, and slow-cooked in deep pits.*

JAPAN

LOCATION: Asia
CAPITAL: Tokyo
AREA: 145,914 sq mi
(377,915 sq km)
POPULATION ESTIMATE (2009):
127,078,679
GOVERNMENT: Parliamentary
government with a
constitutional monarchy
LANGUAGE: Japanese
MONEY: Yen
LIFE EXPECTANCY: 82.1
LITERACY RATE: 99%

guess what? *Japan does not share a land border with any other country. The country is an island chain made up of more than 3,000 islands.*

JORDAN

LOCATION: Middle East
CAPITAL: Amman
AREA: 34,495 sq mi
(89,342 sq km)
POPULATION ESTIMATE (2009):
6,269,285
GOVERNMENT: Constitutional
monarchy
LANGUAGE: Arabic (official)
MONEY: Jordanian dinar
LIFE EXPECTANCY: 79.9
LITERACY RATE: 90%

guess what? *The ancient capital city of Petra, located in southern Jordan, was carved entirely out of stone more than 2,000 years ago. Petra was used to film scenes for* Indiana Jones and the Last Crusade.

KAZAKHSTAN

LOCATION: Asia
CAPITAL: Astana
AREA: 1,052,090 sq mi
(2,724,900 sq km)
POPULATION ESTIMATE (2009):
15,399,437
GOVERNMENT: Republic
LANGUAGES: Kazakh,
Russian (official)
MONEY: Tenge
LIFE EXPECTANCY: 67.9
LITERACY RATE: 100%

guess what? *Kazakhstan is so wide that to travel from one side to the other would be approximately the same distance as traveling from London, England, to Istanbul, Turkey. That's more than 1,550 miles (2,494 km)!*

KENYA

LOCATION: Africa
CAPITAL: Nairobi
AREA: 224,081 sq mi
(580,367 sq km)
POPULATION ESTIMATE (2009):
39,002,772
GOVERNMENT: Republic
LANGUAGES: English and Kiswahili
(both official), others
MONEY: Kenyan shilling
LIFE EXPECTANCY: 57.8
LITERACY RATE: 85%

guess what? *Kenya is named after Mount Kenya, the second-tallest mountain in Africa.*

Countries

KIRIBATI

LOCATION: Oceania
CAPITAL: Tarawa
AREA: 313 sq mi (811 sq km)
POPULATION ESTIMATE (2009): 112,850
GOVERNMENT: Republic
LANGUAGES: English (official),
I-Kiribati (Gilbertese)
MONEY: Australian dollar
LIFE EXPECTANCY: 63.2
LITERACY RATE: Not available

guess what? *Kiribati is pronounced kee-rih-bass.*

KOREA, NORTH

LOCATION: Asia
CAPITAL: Pyongyang
AREA: 46,540 sq mi
(120,540 sq km)
POPULATION ESTIMATE (2009):
22,665,345
GOVERNMENT: Communist
dictatorship
LANGUAGE: Korean
MONEY: North Korean won
LIFE EXPECTANCY: 63.8
LITERACY RATE: 99%

guess what? *North Korea has one of the largest militaries in the world.*

KOREA, SOUTH

LOCATION: Asia
CAPITAL: Seoul
AREA: 38,541 sq mi
(99,720 sq km)
POPULATION ESTIMATE (2009):
48,508,972
GOVERNMENT: Republic
LANGUAGE: Korean
MONEY: South Korean won
LIFE EXPECTANCY: 78.7
LITERACY RATE: 98%

guess what? *The world's first cloned dog, an Afghan hound named Snuppy, was created in labs at Seoul National University in 2005.*

KOSOVO

LOCATION: Europe
CAPITAL: Pristina
AREA: 4,203 sq mi (10,887 sq km)
POPULATION ESTIMATE (2009):
1,804,838
GOVERNMENT: Republic
LANGUAGES: Albanian and
Serbian (both official),
Bosnian, Turkish, Roma
MONEY: Euro, Serbian dinar
LIFE EXPECTANCY: 75.1
LITERACY RATE: 92%

guess what? *Kosovo is the newest country in the world. It declared its independence from Serbia in February 2008.*

KUWAIT

LOCATION: Middle East
CAPITAL: Kuwait City
AREA: 6,880 sq mi
(17,820 sq km)
POPULATION ESTIMATE (2009):
2,692,526
GOVERNMENT: Constitutional
monarchy (emirate)
LANGUAGES: Arabic (official),
English
MONEY: Kuwaiti dinar
LIFE EXPECTANCY: 77.7
LITERACY RATE: 93%

guess what? *About 8% of the world's oil reserves are in Kuwait.*

KYRGYZSTAN

LOCATION: Asia
CAPITAL: Bishkek
AREA: 77,202 sq mi
(199,951 sq km)
POPULATION ESTIMATE (2009):
5,431,747
GOVERNMENT: Republic
LANGUAGES: Kyrgyz and
Russian (official), Uzbek
MONEY: Som
LIFE EXPECTANCY: 69.4
LITERACY RATE: 99%

guess what? *The Tien Shan (which means "heavenly mountains") mountain range takes up almost 75% of Kyrgyzstan's total territory.*

LAOS

LOCATION: Asia
CAPITAL: Vientiane
AREA: 91,429 sq mi
(236,800 sq km)
POPULATION ESTIMATE (2009):
6,834,345
GOVERNMENT: Communist state
LANGUAGES: Lao (official), French,
English
MONEY: Kip
LIFE EXPECTANCY: 56.6
LITERACY RATE: 69%

guess what? *Laos was a monarchy for six centuries, ending with a Communist takeover in 1975.*

LATVIA

LOCATION: Europe
CAPITAL: Riga
AREA: 24,938 sq mi
(64,589 sq km)
POPULATION ESTIMATE (2009):
2,231,503
GOVERNMENT: Parliamentary
democracy
LANGUAGES: Latvian, Russian
MONEY: Lats
LIFE EXPECTANCY: 72.2
LITERACY RATE: 100%

guess what? *Latvia, Lithuania, and Estonia are known as the Baltic states. The Baltic Sea lies to the west of the Baltic states.*

LEBANON

LOCATION: Middle East
CAPITAL: Beirut
AREA: 4,015 sq mi
(10,400 sq km)
POPULATION ESTIMATE (2009):
4,017,095
GOVERNMENT: Republic
LANGUAGES: Arabic (official),
French, English, Armenian
MONEY: Lebanese pound
LIFE EXPECTANCY: 73.7
LITERACY RATE: 87%

guess what? *Lebanon is the only country in the Middle East that doesn't have a desert.*

LESOTHO

LOCATION: Africa
CAPITAL: Maseru
AREA: 11,720 sq mi
(30,355 sq km)
POPULATION ESTIMATE (2009):
2,130,819
GOVERNMENT: Parliamentary
constitutional monarchy
LANGUAGES: English and Sesotho
(both official), Zulu, Xhosa
MONEY: Maloti
LIFE EXPECTANCY: 40.4
LITERACY RATE: 85%

guess what? *Lesotho is a monarchy. There are only three monarchies in Africa; Morocco and Swaziland are the others.*

LIBERIA

LOCATION: Africa
CAPITAL: Monrovia
AREA: 43,000 sq mi
(111,370 sq km)
POPULATION ESTIMATE (2009):
3,441,790
GOVERNMENT: Republic
LANGUAGES: English (official),
ethnic dialects
MONEY: Liberian dollar
LIFE EXPECTANCY: 41.8
LITERACY RATE: 58%

guess what? *In 1847, Liberia became the first independent republic in Africa.*

LIBYA

LOCATION: Africa
CAPITAL: Tripoli
AREA: 679,358 sq mi
(1,759,540 sq km)
POPULATION ESTIMATE (2009):
6,324,357
GOVERNMENT: Authoritarian
state
LANGUAGES: Arabic, Italian,
English
MONEY: Libyan dinar
LIFE EXPECTANCY: 77.3
LITERACY RATE: 83%

guess what? *Libya was under Italian rule from 1911 until 1947.*

Countries

LIECHTENSTEIN

LOCATION: Europe
CAPITAL: Vaduz
AREA: 62 sq mi (160 sq km)
POPULATION ESTIMATE (2009): 34,761
GOVERNMENT: Constitutional monarchy
LANGUAGES: German (official), Alemannic dialect
MONEY: Swiss franc
LIFE EXPECTANCY: 80.1
LITERACY RATE: 100%

guess what? *Liechtenstein remained neutral during World War II.*

LITHUANIA

LOCATION: Europe
CAPITAL: Vilnius
AREA: 25,212 sq mi (65,300 sq km)
POPULATION ESTIMATE (2009): 3,555,179
GOVERNMENT: Parliamentary democracy
LANGUAGES: Lithuanian (official), Polish, Russian
MONEY: Litas
LIFE EXPECTANCY: 74.9
LITERACY RATE: 100%

guess what? *The most popular sport in Lithuania is basketball.*

LUXEMBOURG

LOCATION: Europe
CAPITAL: Luxembourg
AREA: 998 sq mi (2,586 sq km)
POPULATION ESTIMATE (2009): 491,775
GOVERNMENT: Constitutional monarchy
LANGUAGES: Luxembourgish, German, French
MONEY: Euro (formerly Luxembourg franc)
LIFE EXPECTANCY: 79.3
LITERACY RATE: 100%

guess what? *Luxembourg has the highest minimum wage in the European Union.*

MACEDONIA

LOCATION: Europe
CAPITAL: Skopje
AREA: 9,928 sq mi (25,713 sq km)
POPULATION ESTIMATE (2009): 2,066,718
GOVERNMENT: Parliamentary democracy
LANGUAGES: Macedonian, Albanian
MONEY: Denar
LIFE EXPECTANCY: 74.7
LITERACY RATE: 96%

guess what? *Mother Teresa, a nun who helped the poor, was born in Skopje in 1910. She won the Nobel Peace Prize in 1979.*

MADAGASCAR

LOCATION: Africa
CAPITAL: Antananarivo
AREA: 226,656 sq mi (587,040 sq km)
POPULATION ESTIMATE (2009): 20,653,556
GOVERNMENT: Republic
LANGUAGES: Malagasy, French, and English (all official)
MONEY: Malagasy ariary
LIFE EXPECTANCY: 62.9
LITERACY RATE: 69%

guess what? *Madagascar is one of the only places on Earth where baobab trees grow.*

MALAWI

LOCATION: Africa
CAPITAL: Lilongwe
AREA: 45,745 sq mi (118,480 sq km)
POPULATION ESTIMATE (2009): 15,028,757
GOVERNMENT: Multiparty democracy
LANGUAGES: Chichewa (official), Chinyanja, Chiyao, Chitumbuka
MONEY: Kwacha
LIFE EXPECTANCY: 50
LITERACY RATE: 63%

guess what? *Before independence, Malawi was known as the British protectorate of Nyasaland.*

MALAYSIA

LOCATION: Asia
CAPITAL: Kuala Lumpur
AREA: 127,355 sq mi
(329,847 sq km)
POPULATION ESTIMATE (2009):
25,715,819
GOVERNMENT: Constitutional
monarchy
LANGUAGES: Bahasa Malay
(official), Chinese, Tamil,
English, others
MONEY: Ringgit
LIFE EXPECTANCY: 73.3
LITERACY RATE: 89%

guess what? *The Sarawak Chamber, the largest cave chamber in the world, is found in Malaysia's Gunung Mulu National Park. A Boeing 747 airplane could fly through it.*

MALDIVES

LOCATION: Asia
CAPITAL: Male
AREA: 116 sq mi
(300 sq km)
POPULATION ESTIMATE (2009): 396,334
GOVERNMENT: Republic
LANGUAGES: Dhivehi (official),
English
MONEY: Rufiyaa
LIFE EXPECTANCY: 74
LITERACY RATE: 96%

guess what? *The cargo ship Victory hit a reef and sank off the coast of the Maldives in 1981. The wreck, now inhabited by a variety of marine life, is a popular scuba diving spot.*

MALI

LOCATION: Africa
CAPITAL: Bamako
AREA: 478,841 sq mi
(1,240,192 sq km)
POPULATION ESTIMATE (2009):
13,443,225
GOVERNMENT: Republic
LANGUAGES: French (official),
Bambara, African languages
MONEY: CFA franc
LIFE EXPECTANCY: 51.8
LITERACY RATE: 46%

guess what? *The Dogon people, who live in central Mali, are known for their mythology. They re-create their myths by performing elaborate mask dances at funerals and special festivals.*

MALTA

LOCATION: Europe
CAPITAL: Valletta
AREA: 122 sq mi (316 sq km)
POPULATION ESTIMATE (2009): 405,165
GOVERNMENT: Republic
LANGUAGES: Maltese and English
(both official)
MONEY: Euro (formerly
Maltese lira)
LIFE EXPECTANCY: 79.4
LITERACY RATE: 93%

guess what? *Ancient Greeks and Romans knew Malta as "Melita," the land of honey.*

MARSHALL ISLANDS

LOCATION: Oceania
CAPITAL: Majuro
AREA: 70 sq mi (181.3 sq km)
POPULATION ESTIMATE (2009): 64,522
GOVERNMENT: Constitutional
government
LANGUAGES: Marshallese and
English (both official)
MONEY: U.S. dollar
LIFE EXPECTANCY: 71.2
LITERACY RATE: 94%

guess what? *The Marshall Islands, located almost halfway between Hawaii and Australia, are made up of two parallel island chains: the Ratak, or Sunrise, chain and the Ralik, or Sunset, chain.*

MAURITANIA

LOCATION: Africa
CAPITAL: Nouakchott
AREA: 397,953 sq mi
(1,030,700 sq km)
POPULATION ESTIMATE (2009):
3,129,486
GOVERNMENT: Military junta
LANGUAGES: Arabic (official),
French, Pulaar, Soninke, others
MONEY: Ouguiya
LIFE EXPECTANCY: 60.4
LITERACY RATE: 51%

guess what? *Half of Mauritania's land area is covered by desert sand dunes.*

MAURITIUS

LOCATION: Africa
CAPITAL: Port Louis
AREA: 788 sq mi
(2,040 sq km)
POPULATION ESTIMATE (2009):
1,284,264
GOVERNMENT: Parliamentary
democracy
LANGUAGES: English (official),
Creole, Bhojpuri, French
MONEY: Mauritian rupee
LIFE EXPECTANCY: 74
LITERACY RATE: 84%

guess what? *The dodo, a flightless bird extinct since the 1680s, was found only on the island of Mauritius in the Indian Ocean.*

MEXICO

LOCATION: North America
CAPITAL: Mexico City
AREA: 758,449 sq mi
(1,964,375 sq km)
POPULATION ESTIMATE (2009):
111,211,789
GOVERNMENT: Republic
LANGUAGES: Spanish, indigenous
languages
MONEY: Peso
LIFE EXPECTANCY: 76.1
LITERACY RATE: 91%

guess what? *Mexico's border with the United States, stretching nearly 2,000 miles (3,200 km), is the second-longest international border in the world. Only the border between the United States and Canada is longer.*

MICRONESIA

LOCATION: Oceania
CAPITAL: Palikir
AREA: 271 sq mi (702 sq km)
POPULATION ESTIMATE (2009): 107,434
GOVERNMENT: Constitutional
government
LANGUAGES: English (official),
Chuukese, Kosrean, Pohnpeian,
Yapese, Ulithian, others
MONEY: U.S. dollar
LIFE EXPECTANCY: 70.9
LITERACY RATE: 89%

guess what? *Chuuk Lagoon in Micronesia is popular among divers for its wide variety of marine life and its numerous shipwrecks. The lagoon is full of Japanese ships sunk during World War II.*

MOLDOVA

LOCATION: Europe
CAPITAL: Chisinau
AREA: 13,070 sq mi
(33,851 sq km)
POPULATION ESTIMATE (2009):
4,320,748
GOVERNMENT: Republic
LANGUAGES: Moldovan (official),
Russian, Gagauz
MONEY: Leu
LIFE EXPECTANCY: 70.8
LITERACY RATE: 99%

guess what? *On August 31, Moldovans celebrate a holiday called Limba Noastra, or Our Language Day. To celebrate, people hold events such as play and poetry readings. "Limba Noastra" is also the name of the country's national anthem.*

MONACO

LOCATION: Europe
CAPITAL: Monaco
AREA: 0.75 sq mi (1.95 sq km)
POPULATION ESTIMATE (2009): 32,965
GOVERNMENT: Constitutional
monarchy
LANGUAGES: French (official),
English, Italian, Monégasque
MONEY: Euro (formerly French
franc)
LIFE EXPECTANCY: 80.1
LITERACY RATE: 99%

guess what? *With a few exceptions, there is no income tax for the residents of the tiny country of Monaco.*

MONGOLIA

LOCATION: Asia
CAPITAL: Ulaanbaatar
AREA: 603,909 sq mi
(1,564,116 sq km)
POPULATION ESTIMATE (2009):
3,041,142
GOVERNMENT: Parliamentary
republic
LANGUAGES: Khalkha Mongol,
Turkic, Russian
MONEY: Togrog/tugrik
LIFE EXPECTANCY: 67.7
LITERACY RATE: 98%

guess what? *The Gobi Desert covers much of the southern part of Mongolia. Temperatures in the Gobi region are extreme. It can be 113°F (45°C) in the summer and -40°F (-40°C) in the winter.*

MONTENEGRO

LOCATION: Europe
CAPITAL: Podgorica
AREA: 5,333 sq mi
(13,812 sq km)
POPULATION ESTIMATE (2009): 672,180
GOVERNMENT: Republic
LANGUAGES: Montenegrin (official), Serbian, Bosnian, Albanian
MONEY: Euro (formerly deutsche mark)
LIFE EXPECTANCY: 72.8
LITERACY RATE: 94%

guess what? *Montenegro is a young country. It declared its independence on June 3, 2006.*

MOROCCO

LOCATION: Africa
CAPITAL: Rabat
AREA: 172,413 sq mi
(446,550 sq km)
POPULATION ESTIMATE (2009): 31,285,174
GOVERNMENT: Constitutional monarchy
LANGUAGES: Arabic (official), French, Berber dialects
MONEY: Dirham
LIFE EXPECTANCY: 75.5
LITERACY RATE: 52%

guess what? *The Atlas Mountains protect Morocco's fertile coastal lands from the harsh environment of the Sahara Desert, located to the east and south of the country.*

MOZAMBIQUE

LOCATION: Africa
CAPITAL: Maputo
AREA: 308,642 sq mi
(799,380 sq km)
POPULATION ESTIMATE (2009): 21,669,278
GOVERNMENT: Republic
LANGUAGES: Portuguese (official), Emakhuwa, Xichangana, others
MONEY: Metical
LIFE EXPECTANCY: 41.2
LITERACY RATE: 48%

guess what? *Mozambique's tropical climate can result in dangerous flooding of the nation's rivers. In 2001, flooding of the Zambezi River Valley forced the evacuation of 80,000 people from their homes.*

MYANMAR (BURMA)

LOCATION: Asia
CAPITAL: Nay Pyi Taw
AREA: 261,228 sq mi
(676,578 sq km)
POPULATION ESTIMATE (2009): 48,137,741
GOVERNMENT: Military regime
LANGUAGES: Burmese, minority languages
MONEY: Kyat
LIFE EXPECTANCY: 63
LITERACY RATE: 90%

guess what? *Pagan, a former capital of Myanmar, features thousands of Buddhist pagodas. The pagodas have been restored and the area is now an important pilgrimage site and popular tourist destination.*

NAMIBIA

LOCATION: Africa
CAPITAL: Windhoek
AREA: 318,261 sq mi
(824,292 sq km)
POPULATION ESTIMATE (2009): 2,108,665
GOVERNMENT: Republic
LANGUAGES: English (official), Afrikaans, German, native languages
MONEY: Namibian dollar
LIFE EXPECTANCY: 51.2
LITERACY RATE: 85%

guess what? *The* Welwitschia mirabilis, *a plant native to the Namib Desert, can live to be 2,000 years old.*

NAURU

LOCATION: Oceania
CAPITAL: Yaren District (unofficial)
AREA: 8.11 sq mi (21 sq km)
POPULATION ESTIMATE (2009): 14,019
GOVERNMENT: Republic
LANGUAGES: Nauruan (official), English
MONEY: Australian dollar
LIFE EXPECTANCY: 64.2
LITERACY RATE: Not available

guess what? *Nauru, the world's smallest independent republic, is the only republic in the world without an official capital.*

NEPAL

LOCATION: Asia
CAPITAL: Kathmandu
AREA: 56,827 sq mi (147,181 sq km)
POPULATION ESTIMATE (2009): 28,563,377
GOVERNMENT: Republic
LANGUAGES: Nepali (official), Maithali, Bhojpuri, Tharu, Tamang
MONEY: Nepalese rupee
LIFE EXPECTANCY: 65.5
LITERACY RATE: 49%

guess what? *According to Hindu mythology, Nepal's Himalaya mountain range is home to the god Shiva.*

THE NETHERLANDS

LOCATION: Europe
CAPITAL: Amsterdam
AREA: 16,040 sq mi (41,543 sq km)
POPULATION ESTIMATE (2009): 16,715,999
GOVERNMENT: Constitutional monarchy
LANGUAGES: Dutch and Frisian (both official)
MONEY: Euro (formerly guilder)
LIFE EXPECTANCY: 79.4
LITERACY RATE: 99%

guess what? *A favorite dish in the Netherlands is raw herring (a type of fish) with onions on top.*

NEW ZEALAND

LOCATION: Oceania
CAPITAL: Wellington
AREA: 103,363 sq mi (267,710 sq km)
POPULATION ESTIMATE (2009): 4,213,418
GOVERNMENT: Parliamentary democracy
LANGUAGES: English, Maori, and sign language (all official)
MONEY: New Zealand dollar
LIFE EXPECTANCY: 80.4
LITERACY RATE: 99%

guess what? *In New Zealand, swimsuits are called togs.*

NICARAGUA

LOCATION: Central America
CAPITAL: Managua
AREA: 50,336 sq mi (130,370 sq km)
POPULATION ESTIMATE (2009): 5,891,199
GOVERNMENT: Republic
LANGUAGE: Spanish (official)
MONEY: Cordoba
LIFE EXPECTANCY: 71.5
LITERACY RATE: 68%

guess what? *The Miskito Cays, off the coast of Nicaragua, were often used by pirates as safe places to hide out. Now, the white sand beaches welcome tourists.*

NIGER

LOCATION: Africa
CAPITAL: Niamey
AREA: 489,189 sq mi (1,267,000 sq km)
POPULATION ESTIMATE (2009): 15,306,252
GOVERNMENT: Republic
LANGUAGES: French (official), Hausa, Djerma
MONEY: CFA franc
LIFE EXPECTANCY: 52.6
LITERACY RATE: 29%

guess what? *Niger was a French colony from 1922 to 1960.*

NIGERIA

LOCATION: Africa
CAPITAL: Abuja
AREA: 356,667 sq mi (923,768 sq km)
POPULATION ESTIMATE (2009): 149,229,090
GOVERNMENT: Republic
LANGUAGES: English (official), Hausa, Yoruba, Igbo, Fulani
MONEY: Naira
LIFE EXPECTANCY: 46.9
LITERACY RATE: 68%

guess what? *Though English is Nigeria's national language, more than 300 other languages are spoken in the country.*

NORWAY

LOCATION: Europe
CAPITAL: Oslo
AREA: 125,021 sq mi (323,802 sq km)
POPULATION ESTIMATE (2009): 4,660,539
GOVERNMENT: Constitutional monarchy
LANGUAGES: Two official forms of Norwegian—Bokmal and Nynorsk
MONEY: Krone
LIFE EXPECTANCY: 80
LITERACY RATE: 100%

guess what? *Norway has the world's largest population of Arctic reindeer and Arctic reindeer herders.*

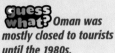

OMAN

LOCATION: Middle East
CAPITAL: Muscat
AREA: 119,499 sq mi (309,500 sq km)
POPULATION ESTIMATE (2009): 3,418,085
GOVERNMENT: Monarchy
LANGUAGES: Arabic (official), English, Baluchi, Urdu, Indian dialects
MONEY: Omani rial
LIFE EXPECTANCY: 74.2
LITERACY RATE: 81%

guess what? *Oman was mostly closed to tourists until the 1980s.*

PAKISTAN

LOCATION: Asia
CAPITAL: Islamabad
AREA: 307,374 sq mi (790,095 sq km)
POPULATION ESTIMATE (2009): 174,578,558
GOVERNMENT: Republic
LANGUAGES: Punjabi, Sindhi, Siraiki, Pashtu, Urdu (official), others
MONEY: Pakistani rupee
LIFE EXPECTANCY: 65.3
LITERACY RATE: 50%

guess what? *In 1988, with the election of Benazir Bhutto as prime minister, Pakistan became the first Muslim nation to elect a woman as its leader.*

PALAU

LOCATION: Oceania
CAPITAL: Melekeok
AREA: 177 sq mi (458 sq km)
POPULATION ESTIMATE (2009): 20,796
GOVERNMENT: Constitutional government
LANGUAGES: Palauan, English, Sonsoralese, Tobi, Anguar, Filipino, Chinese
MONEY: U.S. dollar
LIFE EXPECTANCY: 71.2
LITERACY RATE: 92%

guess what? *Scientists in Palau are leaders in the research on giant clams. One clam found in the country's waters weighed a quarter of a ton (approximately 500 pounds/227 kg)!*

PANAMA

LOCATION: Central America
CAPITAL: Panama City
AREA: 29,120 sq mi (75,420 sq km)
POPULATION ESTIMATE (2009): 3,360,474
GOVERNMENT: Constitutional democracy
LANGUAGES: Spanish (official), English
MONEY: Balboa, U.S. dollar
LIFE EXPECTANCY: 77.3
LITERACY RATE: 92%

guess what? *In 1999, Panama gained sole control over the Panama Canal. It had been controlled by the United States for 85 years.*

PAPUA NEW GUINEA

LOCATION: Oceania
CAPITAL: Port Moresby
AREA: 178,703 sq mi (462,840 sq km)
POPULATION ESTIMATE (2009): 5,940,775
GOVERNMENT: Constitutional parliamentary democracy
LANGUAGES: Tok Pisin, English, and Hiri (all official); about 860 native languages
MONEY: Kina
LIFE EXPECTANCY: 66.3
LITERACY RATE: 57%

guess what? *The Hercules moth, which can have a wingspan of almost 1 foot (31 cm), lives in Papua New Guinea.*

Countries

PARAGUAY

LOCATION: South America
CAPITAL: Asunción
AREA: 157,046 sq mi
(406,750 sq km)
POPULATION ESTIMATE (2009):
6,995,655
GOVERNMENT: Republic
LANGUAGES: Spanish and Guaraní
(both official)
MONEY: Guaraní
LIFE EXPECTANCY: 75.8
LITERACY RATE: 94%

guess what? *Paraguay is one of the most homogeneous nations in South America. Almost 95% of the population are mestizo, which means they come from mixed European and native ancestry.*

PERU

LOCATION: South America
CAPITAL: Lima
AREA: 496,223 sq mi
(1,285,220 sq km)
POPULATION ESTIMATE (2009):
29,546,963
GOVERNMENT: Republic
LANGUAGES: Spanish and Quechua
(both official), Aymara, other
native languages
MONEY: Nuevo sol
LIFE EXPECTANCY: 70.7
LITERACY RATE: 93%

guess what? *Used for producing wool, carrying items, guarding smaller animals, pulling carts, and even kept as pets, llamas were an important part of the ancient Inca empire in Peru and are still found there today.*

THE PHILIPPINES

LOCATION: Asia
CAPITAL: Manila
AREA: 115,830 sq mi
(300,000 sq km)
POPULATION ESTIMATE (2009):
97,976,603
GOVERNMENT: Republic
LANGUAGES: Filipino (based on
Tagalog) and English (both
official), regional languages
MONEY: Philippine peso
LIFE EXPECTANCY: 71.1
LITERACY RATE: 93%

guess what? *The Philippine flag is normally hung with the blue stripe on top. When the country is at war, however, the flag is flipped so the red stripe is above the blue.*

POLAND

LOCATION: Europe
CAPITAL: Warsaw
AREA: 120,728 sq mi
(312,685 sq km)
POPULATION ESTIMATE (2009):
38,482,919
GOVERNMENT: Republic
LANGUAGE: Polish
MONEY: Zloty
LIFE EXPECTANCY: 75.6
LITERACY RATE: 100%

guess what? *At the end of winter, some Polish people participate in a particular tradition. They weave straw or grass dolls that represent winter. After the first big thaw, these dolls are thrown into the river, symbolically killing winter and welcoming spring.*

PORTUGAL

LOCATION: Europe
CAPITAL: Lisbon
AREA: 35,556 sq mi
(92,090 sq km)
POPULATION ESTIMATE (2009):
10,707,924
GOVERNMENT: Republic
LANGUAGES: Portuguese and
Mirandese (both official)
MONEY: Euro (formerly escudo)
LIFE EXPECTANCY: 78.2
LITERACY RATE: 93%

guess what? *The Vasco da Gama Bridge, named for the famed Portuguese explorer, is the longest bridge in Europe. Located in Lisbon, the bridge is 10.7 miles (17 km) long.*

QATAR

LOCATION: Middle East
CAPITAL: Doha
AREA: 4,473 sq mi
(11,586 sq km)
POPULATION ESTIMATE (2009): 833,285
GOVERNMENT: Traditional
monarchy (emirate)
LANGUAGES: Arabic (official),
English
MONEY: Qatari rial
LIFE EXPECTANCY: 75.4
LITERACY RATE: 89%

guess what? *Qatar's Doha Bay offers excellent opportunities for fishing and diving for pearls.*

ROMANIA

LOCATION: Europe
CAPITAL: Bucharest
AREA: 92,043 sq mi
(238,391 sq km)
POPULATION ESTIMATE (2009):
22,215,421
GOVERNMENT: Republic
LANGUAGES: Romanian (official),
Hungarian, Romany
MONEY: Leu
LIFE EXPECTANCY: 72.5
LITERACY RATE: 97%

guess what? *Bram Stoker based his novel* Dracula *on Vlad Tepes, a cruel 15th-century Wallachian prince. Wallachia merged with Moldavia in 1859 to become Romania.*

RUSSIA

LOCATION: Europe and Asia
CAPITAL: Moscow
AREA: 6,601,668 sq mi
(17,098,242 sq km)
POPULATION ESTIMATE (2009):
140,041,247
GOVERNMENT: Federation
LANGUAGES: Russian, others
MONEY: Ruble
LIFE EXPECTANCY: 66
LITERACY RATE: 99%

guess what? *The world's largest cat, the Siberian tiger, can be found in eastern Russia. Now an endangered species, the Siberian tiger can grow to be 10 feet (3 m) long and weigh 600 pounds (272 kg).*

RWANDA

LOCATION: Africa
CAPITAL: Kigali
AREA: 10,169 sq mi
(26,338 sq km)
POPULATION ESTIMATE (2009):
10,746,311
GOVERNMENT: Republic
LANGUAGES: Kinyarwanda,
French, and English
(all official)
MONEY: Rwandan franc
LIFE EXPECTANCY: 56.8
LITERACY RATE: 70%

guess what? *Rwanda was a Belgian colony until 1962.*

SAINT KITTS AND NEVIS

LOCATION: Caribbean
CAPITAL: Basseterre
AREA: 101 sq mi (261 sq km)
POPULATION ESTIMATE (2009): 40,131
GOVERNMENT: Parliamentary
democracy
LANGUAGE: English
MONEY: East Caribbean dollar
LIFE EXPECTANCY: 73.2
LITERACY RATE: 98%

guess what? *Saint Kitts was originally named St. Christopher by Christopher Columbus. The name was later shortened to St. Kitts, which was the explorer's nickname.*

SAINT LUCIA

LOCATION: Caribbean
CAPITAL: Castries
AREA: 238 sq mi (616 sq km)
POPULATION ESTIMATE (2009): 160,267
GOVERNMENT: Parliamentary
democracy
LANGUAGES: English (official),
French patois
MONEY: East Caribbean dollar
LIFE EXPECTANCY: 76.5
LITERACY RATE: 90%

guess what? *Since its founding by the French in the 18th century, Castries has been destroyed by fire four times.*

SAINT VINCENT AND THE GRENADINES

LOCATION: Caribbean
CAPITAL: Kingstown
AREA: 150 sq mi (389 sq km)
POPULATION ESTIMATE (2009): 104,574
GOVERNMENT: Parliamentary
democracy
LANGUAGES: English, French patois
MONEY: East Caribbean dollar
LIFE EXPECTANCY: 73.7
LITERACY RATE: 96%

guess what? *Soufrière, a volcano located on the island of Saint Vincent, last erupted in 1979, the same year the country gained independence from Britain.*

SAMOA

LOCATION: Oceania
CAPITAL: Apia
AREA: 1,093 sq mi (2,831 sq km)
POPULATION ESTIMATE (2009): 219,998
GOVERNMENT: Parliamentary democracy
LANGUAGES: Samoan, English
MONEY: Tala
LIFE EXPECTANCY: 71.9
LITERACY RATE: 100%

guess what? Samoans have practiced the art of the tattoo, or pe'a, for more than 2,000 years. The geometric designs and patterns of their traditional tattoos are based on ancient Samoan designs and usually relate to a person's rank and status in the community.

SAN MARINO

LOCATION: Europe
CAPITAL: San Marino
AREA: 24 sq mi (61 sq km)
POPULATION ESTIMATE (2009): 30,167
GOVERNMENT: Republic
LANGUAGE: Italian
MONEY: Euro (formerly Italian lira)
LIFE EXPECTANCY: 80.8
LITERACY RATE: 96%

guess what? San Marino is one of two microstates found within the borders of Italy. The other is Vatican City.

SÃO TOMÉ AND PRÍNCIPE

LOCATION: Africa
CAPITAL: São Tomé
AREA: 372 sq mi (964 sq km)
POPULATION ESTIMATE (2009): 212,679
GOVERNMENT: Republic
LANGUAGE: Portuguese (official)
MONEY: Dobra
LIFE EXPECTANCY: 68.3
LITERACY RATE: 85%

guess what? During the late 1400s, Portugal settled populations of ex-convicts on São Tomé and Príncipe.

SAUDI ARABIA

LOCATION: Middle East
CAPITAL: Riyadh
AREA: 830,000 sq mi (2,149,690 sq km)
POPULATION ESTIMATE (2009): 28,686,633
GOVERNMENT: Monarchy
LANGUAGE: Arabic
MONEY: Saudi riyal
LIFE EXPECTANCY: 76.3
LITERACY RATE: 79%

guess what? The white script in the center of the Saudi flag is written in Arabic. The phrase is known as the shahada, the Muslim statement of faith. In English, it means, "There is no God but Allah and Muhammad is the Prophet of Allah."

SENEGAL

LOCATION: Africa
CAPITAL: Dakar
AREA: 75,955 sq mi (196,722 sq km)
POPULATION ESTIMATE (2009): 13,711,597
GOVERNMENT: Republic
LANGUAGES: French (official), Wolof, Pulaar, Jola, Mandinka
MONEY: CFA franc
LIFE EXPECTANCY: 59
LITERACY RATE: 39%

guess what? Built in 1776 by the Dutch, the Goree Island Slave House, located just off the coast of Dakar, is now a museum and memorial to the millions of Africans who lost their freedom to the colonial slave trade.

SERBIA

LOCATION: Europe
CAPITAL: Belgrade
AREA: 29,913 sq mi (77,474 sq km)
POPULATION ESTIMATE (2009): 7,379,339
GOVERNMENT: Republic
LANGUAGES: Serbian, Hungarian, others
MONEY: Serbian dinar
LIFE EXPECTANCY: 73.9
LITERACY RATE: 96.4%

guess what? Serbia grows about one-third of the world's raspberries.

SEYCHELLES

LOCATION: Africa
CAPITAL: Victoria
AREA: 176 sq mi (455 sq km)
POPULATION ESTIMATE (2009): 87,476
GOVERNMENT: Republic
LANGUAGES: Creole, English (official), other
MONEY: Seychelles rupee
LIFE EXPECTANCY: 73
LITERACY RATE: 92%

guess what? *Many believe that the lost treasure of pirate Olivier Levasseur, thought to be worth around $160 million, still lies buried at Bel Ombre on the island of North Mahé, which is part of the Seychelles.*

SIERRA LEONE

LOCATION: Africa
CAPITAL: Freetown
AREA: 27,699 sq mi (71,740 sq km)
POPULATION ESTIMATE (2009): 5,132,138
GOVERNMENT: Constitutional democracy
LANGUAGES: English (official), Mende, Temne, Krio
MONEY: Leone
LIFE EXPECTANCY: 55.3
LITERACY RATE: 35%

guess what? *The coast of Sierra Leone is flat, swampy, and prone to flooding.*

SINGAPORE

LOCATION: Asia
CAPITAL: Singapore
AREA: 269 sq mi (697 sq km)
POPULATION ESTIMATE (2009): 4,657,542
GOVERNMENT: Parliamentary republic
LANGUAGES: Chinese (Mandarin), English, Malay, Hokkien, Cantonese, others
MONEY: Singapore dollar
LIFE EXPECTANCY: 82
LITERACY RATE: 93%

guess what? *The world's largest bat, known as the flying fox, lives on Pulau Ubin, an island off of mainland Singapore. The flying fox can have a wingspan of up to 5 feet (152 cm).*

SLOVAKIA

LOCATION: Europe
CAPITAL: Bratislava
AREA: 18,933 sq mi (49,035 sq km)
POPULATION ESTIMATE (2009): 5,463,046
GOVERNMENT: Parliamentary democracy
LANGUAGES: Slovak (official), Hungarian, Roma, Ukranian
MONEY: Koruna
LIFE EXPECTANCY: 75.4
LITERACY RATE: 100%

guess what? *Tennis champion Martina Hingis was born in Slovakia.*

SLOVENIA

LOCATION: Europe
CAPITAL: Ljubljana
AREA: 7,827 sq mi (20,273 sq km)
POPULATION ESTIMATE (2009): 2,005,692
GOVERNMENT: Parliamentary republic
LANGUAGES: Slovenian, Serbo-Croatian
MONEY: Euro (formerly Slovenian tolar)
LIFE EXPECTANCY: 76.9
LITERACY RATE: 100%

guess what? *Slovenia became independent from Yugoslavia in 1991 and joined the European Union in 2004.*

SOLOMON ISLANDS

LOCATION: Oceania
CAPITAL: Honiara
AREA: 111,517 sq mi (28,896 sq km)
POPULATION ESTIMATE (2009): 595,613
GOVERNMENT: Parliamentary democracy
LANGUAGES: Melanesian pidgin, English (official), more than 120 local languages
MONEY: Solomon Islands dollar
LIFE EXPECTANCY: 73.7
LITERACY RATE: Not available

guess what? *Fierce battles took place on the Solomon Islands during World War II.*

SOMALIA

LOCATION: Africa
CAPITAL: Mogadishu
AREA: 246,199 sq mi
(637,657 sq km)
POPULATION ESTIMATE (2009):
9,832,017
GOVERNMENT: Transitional
government
LANGUAGES: Somali (official),
Arabic, English, Italian
MONEY: Somali shilling
LIFE EXPECTANCY: 49.6
LITERACY RATE: 38%

guess what? *Somalia has been without a national government since civil war unseated the country's dictator in 1991. A transitional authority is planning to hold elections in 2011.*

SOUTH AFRICA

LOCATION: Africa
CAPITALS: Pretoria (administrative),
Cape Town (legislative),
Bloemfontein (judicial)
AREA: 471,008 sq mi
(1,219,090 sq km)
POPULATION ESTIMATE (2009):
49,052,489
GOVERNMENT: Republic
LANGUAGES: Zulu, Xhosa, Afrikaans,
Sepedi, English, Setswana,
Sesotho, Tsonga, others
MONEY: Rand
LIFE EXPECTANCY: 49
LITERACY RATE: 86%

guess what? *Nobel prize-winners Nelson Mandela and Archbishop Desmond Tutu both lived on Vilakazi Street in Soweto, South Africa.*

SPAIN

LOCATION: Europe
CAPITAL: Madrid
AREA: 195,124 sq mi
(505,370 sq km)
POPULATION ESTIMATE (2009):
40,525,002
GOVERNMENT: Parliamentary
monarchy
LANGUAGES: Castilian Spanish
(official), Catalan, Galician,
Basque
MONEY: Euro (formerly peseta)
LIFE EXPECTANCY: 80.1
LITERACY RATE: 98%

guess what? *Famous 20th-century artists Pablo Picasso and Salvador Dalí were both Spanish.*

SRI LANKA

LOCATION: Asia
CAPITAL: Colombo
AREA: 25,332 sq mi
(65,610 sq km)
POPULATION ESTIMATE (2009):
21,324,791
GOVERNMENT: Republic
LANGUAGES: Sinhala (official),
Tamil, English
MONEY: Sri Lankan rupee
LIFE EXPECTANCY: 75.1
LITERACY RATE: 91%

guess what? *Sri Lanka's flag is one of the oldest flags in the world. It is meant to symbolize unity and harmony among all peoples of the country.*

SUDAN

LOCATION: Africa
CAPITAL: Khartoum
AREA: 967,493 sq mi
(2,505,810 sq km)
POPULATION ESTIMATE (2009):
41,087,825
GOVERNMENT: Authoritarian
regime
LANGUAGES: Arabic and English
(both official), Nubian, Ta
Bedawie, others
MONEY: Sudanese pound
LIFE EXPECTANCY: 51.4
LITERACY RATE: 61%

guess what? *Egypt isn't the only country in Africa with impressive pyramids. Sudan's pyramids, dating from 592 B.C to 320 A.D., house the remains of the royalty of the ancient kingdom of Kush.*

SURINAME

LOCATION: South America
CAPITAL: Paramaribo
AREA: 63,251 sq mi
(163,820 sq km)
POPULATION ESTIMATE (2009): 481,267
GOVERNMENT: Constitutional
democracy
LANGUAGES: Dutch (official),
Surinamese, English, others
MONEY: Surinamese dollar
LIFE EXPECTANCY: 73.7
LITERACY RATE: 90%

guess what? *Almost 80% of Suriname is made up of tropical rain forest.*

SWAZILAND

LOCATION: Africa
CAPITAL: Mbabane
AREA: 6,704 sq mi
(17,360 sq km)
POPULATION ESTIMATE (2009):
1,337,186
GOVERNMENT: Monarchy
LANGUAGES: Swati and English
(both official)
MONEY: Emalangeni
LIFE EXPECTANCY: 47.9
LITERACY RATE: 82%

guess what? *At the end of every summer, some Swazi women and girls participate in the Umhlanga, or "reed dance," an eight-day festival filled with parades, dancing, and feasts.*

SWEDEN

LOCATION: Europe
CAPITAL: Stockholm
AREA: 173,860 sq mi
(450,295 sq km)
POPULATION ESTIMATE (2009):
9,059,651
GOVERNMENT: Constitutional
monarchy
LANGUAGE: Swedish
MONEY: Krona
LIFE EXPECTANCY: 80.9
LITERACY RATE: 99%

guess what? *Around the summer solstice every year, Sweden celebrates the midnight sun. On this day in many parts of the country, the sun never fully sets.*

SWITZERLAND

LOCATION: Europe
CAPITAL: Bern
AREA: 15,937 sq mi
(41,277 sq km)
POPULATION ESTIMATE (2009):
7,604,467
GOVERNMENT: Federal republic
LANGUAGES: German, French,
Italian, and Romansh (all
official), others
MONEY: Swiss franc
LIFE EXPECTANCY: 80.9
LITERACY RATE: 99%

guess what? *The oldest chocolate factory in Switzerland was founded in 1819 by the François-Louis Cailler family. The factory is still standing and can be visited today.*

SYRIA

LOCATION: Middle East
CAPITAL: Damascus
AREA: 71,498 sq mi (185,180 sq km)
POPULATION ESTIMATE (2009):
21,762,978
GOVERNMENT: Republic under an
authoritarian regime
LANGUAGES: Arabic (official),
Kurdish, Armenian, Aramaic,
Circassian
MONEY: Syrian pound
LIFE EXPECTANCY: 74.2
LITERACY RATE: 80%

guess what? *Palmyra, one of the world's best-preserved ancient ruins, is located in the Syrian desert. Palmyra is believed to have been inhabited since the Neolithic period.*

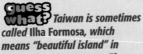

TAIWAN

LOCATION: Asia
CAPITAL: Taipei
AREA: 13,892 sq mi
(35,980 sq km)
POPULATION ESTIMATE (2009):
22,974,347
GOVERNMENT: Multiparty
democracy
LANGUAGES: Chinese (Mandarin),
Taiwanese, Hakka dialects
MONEY: New Taiwan dollar
LIFE EXPECTANCY: 78
LITERACY RATE: 96%

guess what? *Taiwan is sometimes called Ilha Formosa, which means "beautiful island" in Portuguese. The term was coined by Portuguese sailors in the 16th century.*

TAJIKISTAN

LOCATION: Asia
CAPITAL: Dushanbe
AREA: 55,251 sq mi
(143,100 sq km)
POPULATION ESTIMATE (2009):
7,349,145
GOVERNMENT: Republic
LANGUAGES: Tajik (official),
Russian
MONEY: Somoni
LIFE EXPECTANCY: 65.3
LITERACY RATE: 100%

guess what? *Tajikistan is a mountainous country. The majority of the population lives in valleys between the mountains.*

TANZANIA

LOCATION: Africa
CAPITAL: Dar es Salaam
AREA: 365,755 sq mi
(947,300 sq km)
POPULATION ESTIMATE (2009):
41,048,532
GOVERNMENT: Republic
LANGUAGES: Swahili and English
(both official), Arabic, local
languages
MONEY: Tanzanian shilling
LIFE EXPECTANCY: 52
LITERACY RATE: 69%

guess what? *Tanzania's name comes from combining the names of its two main parts: Tanganyika, the mainland, and Zanzibar, a set of islands off the country's eastern coast.*

THAILAND

LOCATION: Asia
CAPITAL: Bangkok
AREA: 198,117 sq mi
(513,120 sq km)
POPULATION ESTIMATE (2009):
65,998,436
GOVERNMENT: Constitutional
monarchy
LANGUAGES: Thai (Siamese),
English, regional dialects
MONEY: Baht
LIFE EXPECTANCY: 73.1
LITERACY RATE: 93%

guess what? *Thailand is the only country in Southeast Asia never to have been taken over by a European power. It was known as Siam until 1939.*

TOGO

LOCATION: Africa
CAPITAL: Lomé
AREA: 21,925 sq mi
(56,785 sq km)
POPULATION ESTIMATE (2009):
6,031,808
GOVERNMENT: Republic, under
transition to multiparty
democratic rule
LANGUAGES: French (official), Ewe,
Mina, Kabye, Dagomba
MONEY: CFA franc
LIFE EXPECTANCY: 59.7
LITERACY RATE: 61%

guess what? *Togo was called French Togoland until it gained independence in 1960.*

TONGA

LOCATION: Oceania
CAPITAL: Nuku'alofa
AREA: 289 sq mi (748 sq km)
POPULATION ESTIMATE (2009): 120,898
GOVERNMENT: Constitutional
monarchy
LANGUAGES: Tongan, English
MONEY: Pa'anga
LIFE EXPECTANCY: 70.7
LITERACY RATE: 99%

guess what? *Located just east of the international date line, Tonga often advertises itself as "the place where time begins."*

TRINIDAD AND TOBAGO

LOCATION: Caribbean
CAPITAL: Port-of-Spain
AREA: 1,980 sq mi (5,128 sq km)
POPULATION ESTIMATE (2009):
1,229,953
GOVERNMENT: Parliamentary
democracy
LANGUAGES: English (official),
Hindi, French, Spanish, Chinese
MONEY: Trinidad and
Tobago dollar
LIFE EXPECTANCY: 70.9
LITERACY RATE: 99%

guess what? *Tobago is the island on which author Daniel Defoe set his novel Robinson Crusoe.*

TUNISIA

LOCATION: Africa
CAPITAL: Tunis
AREA: 63,170 sq mi
(163,610 sq km)
POPULATION ESTIMATE (2009):
10,486,339
GOVERNMENT: Republic
LANGUAGES: Arabic (official),
French
MONEY: Tunisian dinar
LIFE EXPECTANCY: 75.8
LITERACY RATE: 74%

guess what? *The ruins of Carthage, the center of the ancient Phoenician empire, are located about 10 miles (16 km) from Tunis.*

TURKEY

LOCATION: Europe and Asia
CAPITAL: Ankara
AREA: 302,535 sq mi
(783,562 sq km)
POPULATION ESTIMATE (2009):
76,805,524
GOVERNMENT: Parliamentary
democracy
LANGUAGES: Turkish (official),
Kurdish, others
MONEY: Lira
LIFE EXPECTANCY: 72
LITERACY RATE: 87%

guess what? *Ruins of the fabled city of Troy have been found in northwestern Turkey.*

TURKMENISTAN

LOCATION: Asia
CAPITAL: Ashkhabad
AREA: 188,455 sq mi
(488,100 sq km)
POPULATION ESTIMATE (2009):
4,884,887
GOVERNMENT: Republic
LANGUAGES: Turkmen, Russian,
Uzbek, others
MONEY: Manat
LIFE EXPECTANCY: 67.9
LITERACY RATE: 99%

guess what? *Nomadic farmers in Turkmenistan live in yurts, collapsible tents built on wooden frames.*

TUVALU

LOCATION: Oceania
CAPITAL: Funafuti
AREA: 10 sq mi (26 sq km)
POPULATION ESTIMATE (2009): 12,373
GOVERNMENT: Parliamentary
democracy
LANGUAGES: Tuvaluan, English,
Samoan, Kiribati
MONEY: Australian dollar,
Tuvaluan dollar
LIFE EXPECTANCY: 69.3
LITERACY RATE: Not available

guess what? *The pulaka, or swamp taro plant, is Tuvalu's most important plant. Grown in large pits, the plant is valued for its resistance to drought and its salty taste.*

UGANDA

LOCATION: Africa
CAPITAL: Kampala
AREA: 93,065 sq mi
(241,038 sq km)
POPULATION ESTIMATE (2009):
32,369,558
GOVERNMENT: Republic
LANGUAGES: English (official),
Luganda, Swahili, others
MONEY: Ugandan shilling
LIFE EXPECTANCY: 52.7
LITERACY RATE: 67%

guess what? *Uganda's national bird is the crested crane. The colors of the country's flag echo the bird's black, yellow, and red feathers.*

UKRAINE

LOCATION: Europe
CAPITAL: Kiev
AREA: 233,032 sq mi
(603,550 sq km)
POPULATION ESTIMATE (2009):
45,700,395
GOVERNMENT: Republic
LANGUAGES: Ukrainian, Russian
MONEY: Hryvnia
LIFE EXPECTANCY: 68.3
LITERACY RATE: 99%

guess what? *Ukraine is known as the "breadbasket of Europe" because it has a nutrient-rich soil and a climate well suited for growing crops. It produces wheat, barley, rye, oats, beets, and other crops that help feed the entire region.*

UNITED ARAB EMIRATES

LOCATION: Middle East
CAPITAL: Abu Dhabi
AREA: 32,278 sq mi
(83,600 sq km)
POPULATION ESTIMATE (2009):
4,798,491
GOVERNMENT: Federation
LANGUAGES: Arabic (official),
Persian, English, Hindi, Urdu
MONEY: U.A.E. dirham
LIFE EXPECTANCY: 76.1
LITERACY RATE: 78%

guess what? *The Dubai Emirates Mall features an indoor ski slope. The slope is more than 1,300 feet (396 m) tall. It uses 6,000 tons (5,443 metric tons) of snow.*

UNITED KINGDOM

LOCATION: Europe
CAPITAL: London
AREA: 94,058 sq mi
(243,610 sq km)
POPULATION ESTIMATE (2009):
61,113,205
GOVERNMENT: Constitutional
monarchy
LANGUAGES: English, Welsh,
Scottish (Gaelic)
MONEY: British pound
LIFE EXPECTANCY: 79
LITERACY RATE: 99%

Guess what? *Windsor Castle, in England, is the largest inhabited castle in the world. It has also been continuously occupied longer than any other royal residence.*

UNITED STATES

LOCATION: North America
CAPITAL: Washington, D.C.
AREA: 3,794,100 sq mi
(9,826,675 sq km)
POPULATION ESTIMATE (2009):
307,212,123
GOVERNMENT: Republic
LANGUAGES: English, Spanish
(spoken by a sizable minority)
MONEY: U.S. dollar
LIFE EXPECTANCY: 78.1
LITERACY RATE: 99%

Guess what? *The flag that flew over Ft. McHenry in Baltimore, Maryland, during the War of 1812 and inspired Francis Scott Key to write "The Star-Spangled Banner" is on display at the Smithsonian Museum in Washington, D.C.*

URUGUAY

LOCATION: South America
CAPITAL: Montevideo
AREA: 68,039 sq mi
(176,220 sq km)
POPULATION ESTIMATE (2009):
3,494,382
GOVERNMENT: Republic
LANGUAGES: Spanish, Portunol,
Brazilero
MONEY: Uruguayan peso
LIFE EXPECTANCY: 76.4
LITERACY RATE: 98%

Guess what? *An estimated 88% of Uruguayans are descendants of Europeans. This is a much higher percentage than in most Latin American countries.*

UZBEKISTAN

LOCATION: Asia
CAPITAL: Tashkent
AREA: 172,741 sq mi
(447,400 sq km)
POPULATION ESTIMATE (2009):
27,606,007
GOVERNMENT: Republic
LANGUAGES: Uzbek, Russian,
Tajik, others
MONEY: Uzbekistani soum
LIFE EXPECTANCY: 72
LITERACY RATE: 99%

Guess what? *Samarkind is Uzbekistan's second-largest city. Located on the Silk Road, which was the trade route connecting Asia to Europe, the ancient city is 2,750 years old.*

VANUATU

LOCATION: Oceania
CAPITAL: Port-Vila
AREA: 4,710 sq mi (12,200 sq km)
POPULATION ESTIMATE (2009): 218,519
GOVERNMENT: Republic
LANGUAGES: Most people speak
one of more than 100 local
languages; Bislama, English
MONEY: Vatu
LIFE EXPECTANCY: 64
LITERACY RATE: 74%

Guess what? *During World War II, the United States used Vanuatu as a base from which to attack Japanese troops, which inspired author James Michener to write* Tales of the South Pacific. *These stories were eventually adapted into the musical* South Pacific.

VATICAN CITY (HOLY SEE)

LOCATION: Europe
CAPITAL: Vatican City
AREA: 0.17 sq mi (0.44 sq km)
POPULATION ESTIMATE (2009): 826
GOVERNMENT: Ecclesiastical
LANGUAGES: Italian, Latin, French
MONEY: Euro
LIFE EXPECTANCY: 77.5
LITERACY RATE: 100%

Guess what? *Though it is the smallest independent nation in the world, Vatican City has its own radio station.*

VENEZUELA

LOCATION: South America
CAPITAL: Caracas
AREA: 352,143 sq mi
(912,050 sq km)
POPULATION ESTIMATE (2009):
26,814,843
GOVERNMENT: Republic
LANGUAGES: Spanish (official),
native languages
MONEY: Bolivar
LIFE EXPECTANCY: 73.6
LITERACY RATE: 93%

guess what? *European explorers gave Venezuela its name in the 15th century. They named the country after the Italian city of Venice.*

VIETNAM

LOCATION: Asia
CAPITAL: Hanoi
AREA: 127,881 sq mi
(331,210 sq km)
POPULATION ESTIMATE (2009):
88,576,758
GOVERNMENT: Communist state
LANGUAGES: Vietnamese (official),
French, English, Khmer, Chinese
MONEY: Dong
LIFE EXPECTANCY: 71.7
LITERACY RATE: 90%

guess what? *More than 1,000 years old, the Vietnamese art of water puppetry uses a tank of waist-deep water in place of a traditional stage.*

YEMEN

LOCATION: Middle East
CAPITAL: Sanaa
AREA: 203,849 sq mi
(527,970 sq km)
POPULATION ESTIMATE (2009):
22,858,238
GOVERNMENT: Republic
LANGUAGE: Arabic
MONEY: Yemeni rial
LIFE EXPECTANCY: 63.3
LITERACY RATE: 50%

guess what? *When North and South Yemen reunited in 1990, Yemen became the first and only democratic republic on the Arabian Peninsula.*

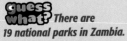

ZAMBIA

LOCATION: Africa
CAPITAL: Lusaka
AREA: 290,584 sq mi
(752,614 sq km)
POPULATION ESTIMATE (2009):
11,862,740
GOVERNMENT: Republic
LANGUAGES: Bemba, Nyanja,
Tonga, Lozi, Lunda, Kaonde,
Luvale, and English (all official),
others
MONEY: Kwacha
LIFE EXPECTANCY: 38.6
LITERACY RATE: 81%

guess what? *There are 19 national parks in Zambia.*

ZIMBABWE

LOCATION: Africa
CAPITAL: Harare
AREA: 150,872 sq mi
(390,757 sq km)
POPULATION ESTIMATE (2009):
11,392,629
GOVERNMENT: Parliamentary
democracy
LANGUAGES: English (official),
Shona, Ndebele (Sindebele)
MONEY: Zimbabwean dollar
LIFE EXPECTANCY: 45.8
LITERACY RATE: 91%

guess what? *Victoria Falls is an enormous waterfall in the Zambezi River on the boundary between Zambia and Zimbabwe. The local name for the waterfall in Zimbabwe is Mosi-oa-Tunya, or "the smoke that thunders."*

MYSTERY PERSON

Clue 1: I am a lawyer, a politician, and a human rights activist. I was born in Ireland in 1944.

Clue 2: In 1990, I became the first woman president of Ireland. At the time, I was one of only three female heads of state in the world.

Clue 3: I served as the president of Ireland for almost seven years. I stepped down to work for the United Nations.

Who am I?

Answer on page 244.

Countries

COOL LANDMARKS AROUND THE WORLD

Eiffel Tower, France

Big Ben, United Kingdom

Chichén Itzá, Mexico

Machu Picchu, Peru

Christ the Redeemer, Brazil

Petra, Jordan

Alhambra, Spain

Great Wall of China

Himeji Castle, Japan

Colosseum, Italy

Taj Mahal, India

Sydney Opera House, Australia

Dome of the Rock, Israel

Countries

85

Dance

Step Right Up!

There's a dance step for just about every time in history, every age group, and every level of physical strength. Here are a few types of dance that have stood the test of time.

BREAK DANCING A cross between acrobatics and dancing, this style began in U.S. cities in the late 1970s and early 1980s.

CHA-CHA A Latin-rhythm dance that includes hip and foot movements done to the beat of "one-two-cha-cha-cha!"

FOX-TROT A ballroom dance that consists of two slow steps followed by two quick movements.

PASO DOBLE Created in Spain, its movements resemble those of a bullfighter. The name means "double step" in Spanish.

RUMBA Created in Cuba, this dance is a mix of Spanish and African moves.

TANGO A ballroom dance that originated in Buenos Aires, Argentina, tango includes sweeping movements and abrupt stops.

WALTZ A dance in which partners follow steps to work their way entirely around the dance floor.

Big-Screen Dance Moves

Mad Hot Ballroom

To see cool dance steps, get a parent's okay, and check out these Hollywood hits.

GENRE	FILM (YEAR)	SUMMARY
Ballet	*Billy Elliot* (2000)	The 11-year-old son of a British coal miner discovers a talent for dancing in spite of his family's disapproval.
Ballroom	*Mad Hot Ballroom* (2005)	This documentary follows the lives and dance steps of New York City school kids in their quest to win a dance competition.
Salsa	*Dance with Me* (1998)	This love story, set in Texas, shows off the Latin beat.
Step Dancing	*Lord of the Dance* (1997) and *Riverdance* (1995)	These videos feature Irish dancing with both traditional and modern steps.

Dancing with the Stars

Donny Osmond and Kym Johnson

Since it premiered on June 1, 2005, *Dancing with the Stars* has been a toe-tapping hit! Based on the British show *Strictly Come Dancing,* it captivates huge TV audiences—as many as many as 22 million people have tuned in to see which dancing duo would take top honors. Here are the show's winners and runners-up.

SEASON	WINNERS	RUNNERS-UP
Season 1: Summer 2005	Kelly Monaco and Alec Mazo	John O'Hurley and Charlotte Jørgensen
Season 2: Winter 2006	Drew Lachey and Cheryl Burke	Jerry Rice and Anna Trebunskaya
Season 3: Fall 2006	Emmitt Smith and Cheryl Burke	Mario Lopez and Karina Smirnoff
Season 4: Spring 2007	Apolo Anton Ohno and Julianne Hough	Joey Fatone and Kym Johnson
Season 5: Fall 2007	Hélio Castroneves and Julianne Hough	Mel B and Maksim Chmerkovskiy
Season 6: Spring 2008	Kristi Yamaguchi and Mark Ballas	Jason Taylor and Edyta Sliwinska
Season 7: Fall 2008	Brooke Burke and Derek Hough	Warren Sapp and Kym Johnson
Season 8: Spring 2009	Shawn Johnson and Mark Ballas	Gilles Marini and Cheryl Burke
Season 9: Fall 2009	Donny Osmond and Kym Johnson	Mya and Dmitry Chaplin

America's Best Dance Crew

We Are Heroes

America's Best Dance Crew showcases a younger, hipper range of dancers than is often seen on dancing shows. In each episode, hosted by Mario Lopez, groups of dancers, or crews, compete for a chance to win a $100,000 cash prize—and a touring contract. Winners are chosen by the television audience.

SEASON	WINNERS	RUNNERS-UP
Season 1	JabbaWockeeZ	Status Quo
Season 2	Super Cr3w	SoReal Cru
Season 3	Quest Crew	Beat Freaks
Season 4	We Are Heroes	AfroBoriké

Season 4 contestants perform a tribute to musical legend Michael Jackson.

Dance

Energy and the Environment

Water Worries

FROM TIME FOR KIDS MAGAZINE

By Bryan Walsh

Most of the water used by Las Vegas residents comes from a reservoir called Lake Mead. The reservoir is an artificial lake created when the Hoover Dam was built in 1935. Because of increased demand and long periods of drought, Mead's water level is declining.

We live in a watery world, but climate change and population growth are leading the planet toward a water crisis. People will have to find smart ways to avoid wasting water.

There are 326 quintillion gallons of water on Earth. But less than 1% of it is available for humans to drink or use. Most of the world's H_2O is salty ocean water or polar ice.

Everyone needs safe drinking water, but about 1.1 billion people have no access to clean water. By 2050, the world's population could grow from 6.7 billion to more than 9 billion. All of those people will need water for drinking, growing crops, and producing energy.

Because of climate change, some areas of the world are growing drier. The total area of the Earth's surface classified as very dry has doubled since the 1970s. The combination of climate change and increased demand is pushing the world toward a crisis over water.

Water is wasted in both rich and poor countries. The precious resource is misused in industry, in farming, and in homes. Peter Gleick, head of the Pacific Institute, an environmental group in Oakland, California, says it is time for bold steps to be taken to conserve water.

A LONG DRY SPELL

Since 2002, Australia has been in the grip of the worst drought in its recorded history. In the Murray-Darling river basin, in southern Australia, farmers have been hit hard. The Australian government is improving the nation's water-use habits. It has launched a $1.3 billion project to upgrade Australia's irrigation system. "It's extracting the most benefit we can from water we have," says Murray Smith, who heads the project.

Australians have serious water worries, but it could be worse. They don't have to fear that when they turn on the tap, nothing will come out.

That's the case in India. New Delhi, the capital, supplies less water than its citizens require, by about 200 million gallons a day. Many go without clean water for days. "Every morning when I get up, my main worry is water," says one woman. She keeps a locked 265-gallon water-storage tank near her apartment.

FAILURE IS NOT AN OPTION

The 1.9 million people who live in Las Vegas, Nevada, have to watch their water use. The area receives just 4 inches (10 cm) of rain per year. Each resident uses 165 gallons of water a day, on average.

City leaders have put in place tough measures to conserve water. Users pay a steep price for it. Homeowners who waste water are given large fines. The measures are working. Las Vegas has grown by more than 300,000 people since 2002. But it uses less water today than it did seven years ago. "Failure is not an option," said Patricia Mulroy, head of the Southern Nevada Water Authority. The same is true everywhere in the world.

Because of drought, many farmers in Australia are unable to irrigate their fields well enough. Crop production is down.

WHAT IS THE GREENHOUSE EFFECT?

Most of the energy people use to heat buildings and run machines comes from coal, oil, or natural gas. These are called fossil fuels (see page 90), because they are made from the remains of animals and plants that lived long ago.

Burning fossil fuels provides energy for industry (electric power plants, manufacturing plants), transportation (cars, planes, boats), and household fixtures and appliances (lights, computers, televisions, dishwashers). But it also releases carbon dioxide (CO_2) and other gases into Earth's atmosphere. Most scientists believe that we are producing far more CO_2 than the atmosphere needs and, as a result, the planet is getting warmer.

Earth is surrounded by an atmosphere—layers of gases that protect it from extreme heat and cold. Gases such as CO_2 and methane trap the sun's heat in the atmosphere (just like the walls of a greenhouse trap heat and moisture). These gases help to keep the temperature of the planet warm enough for all living things.

In recent years, human activity has increased the concentration of greenhouse gases in the atmosphere. As a result, Earth's temperature is rising, which could spell disaster for the entire planet. From planting trees to decreasing the amount of energy we use every day, there are many things we can do to reduce those greenhouse gases and therefore lessen our carbon footprint.

guess what?

Your carbon footprint is not an actual footprint. It refers to the total amount of greenhouse gas emissions that result from your activities.

Energy and the Environment

nonrenewable ENERGY SOURCES

Nonrenewable energy sources are in limited supply, and will eventually be used up entirely. Coal, petroleum, and natural gas were formed in the Earth over millions of years, and are known as **fossil fuels.**

COAL is a hard rock made of carbon. It started out as decaying plant matter that was covered with many layers of earth. Over the course of millions of years, the pressure of all this dirt, as well as Earth's heat, transformed the matter into coal. Because coal takes so long to form, it cannot be manufactured. Coal is the largest source of fossil fuel in the United States.

PETROLEUM is found deep within the Earth, and has to be drilled and piped to the surface. It is made of decaying plant and animal remains that were trapped or covered with mud. Like coal, it was formed from pressure and heat over millions of years. In its crude state—before it is refined—it is known as petroleum. Petroleum can be refined into **oil, gasoline,** or **diesel fuel,** which are used to power engines in vehicles, machines in factories, and furnaces in homes.

NATURAL GAS was formed in the same way and over the same amount of time as coal and oil, except that it is the odorless by-product of decaying matter. Bubbles of gas are trapped underground and can be piped to the surface. Natural gas is used as a source of home heating as well as for cooking.

NUCLEAR ENERGY was developed in the 20th century. It relies on the heat given off when an atom is split during a process known as **nuclear fission.** In nuclear fission, the nucleus of a uranium-235 atom is hit with an atomic particle called a neutron. The uranium atom splits and gives off a lot of heat, which is used to boil water. The steam from this water powers electrical generators.

guess what?

Coal-burning power plants contribute more to global warming than anything else, producing 2.5 billion tons of CO_2 every year. Cars are the second-worst culprits, emitting 1.5 billion tons of CO_2 yearly.

THE DOWNSIDE OF FOSSIL FUELS

Fossil fuels supply about 85% of the energy used in the United States today, but the pollution they cause has a negative effect on humans, animals, and the environment. The burning of fossil fuels leads to global warming, can cause acid rain, and can make water dirty and air unhealthy. Coal mining damages the land, contaminates water supplies, and destroys the health of miners. Nuclear power plants create nuclear waste that is extremely dangerous and must be stored for thousands of years away from people. When oil spills occur, they harm animals and ecosystems.

ACID RAIN

Today, Earth's air contains many pollutants. Sulfur dioxide (SO_2) and nitrogen dioxide (NO_2) are two of the most common. These gases are released when fossil fuels such as coal and petroleum are burned by factories, vehicles, and power plants. Acid rain is formed when water vapor in the air combines with SO_2 and NO_2 to form sulfuric and nitric acids. Acid rain falls to the ground and causes many problems, such as:

- Breathing difficulties in people with lung illnesses.
- Killing trees and plants and poisoning streams, rivers, and lakes. This, in turn, harms fish and other water-dwellers. The effects of this poisoning travel up the food chain to other water creatures and animals who eat fish, including humans.
- Eating away at stone and slowly destroying old buildings and monuments.

OIL SPILLS

Oil spills are particularly devastating to the oceans because of their widespread effects on marine life. Birds cannot fly when their wings are soaked in oil, so many drown or get poisoned when they try to clean themselves. Oil sticks to furry marine animals such as seals, otters, and walrus. When this happens, they can no longer keep themselves warm and may freeze to death. The blowholes of whales, porpoises, and dolphins can be blocked up with oil, making it so they cannot breathe. Many other animals and sea creatures may be poisoned or blinded by eating, breathing, or coming into contact with the oil.

ReNewaBLe ENERGY SoURCES

Renewable energy sources **are created continually by nature and can be used repeatedly by people.**

BIOMASS is an energy source found in plants and animals. It includes such natural products as wood, corn, sugarcane, manure, and plant and animal fats, and can also be found in organic trash. Biomass energy can be used in three ways:

- When burned, it creates steam that can be converted into electricity or captured to heat homes.
- Sources such as manure and organic trash give off a gas called **methane,** which can be used as fuel.
- Plant crops and plant and animal fats can be made into **ethanol** and **biodiesel,** two fuels used to power cars and trucks.

SUNLIGHT can be converted into heat and electricity.

- Solar cells absorb the heat from the sun and convert it into energy. They are used in calculators, watches, and some highway signs.
- Solar power plants collect the sun's heat on huge **solar panels,** which then heat water to produce steam. The steam, in turn, powers electrical generators. A similar system is used on a smaller scale in solar-powered homes.

WIND has been used as an energy source for centuries. For example, windmills were used to help grind grain. Today, wind towers much taller than those windmills—usually about 20 stories high—are used to capture the power of wind. The wind turns giant blades connected to a long shaft that moves up and down to power electrical generators.

WATER can produce energy called **hydropower.** Water pressure can turn the shafts of powerful electrical generators, making electricity. Waterfalls and fast-running rivers are major sources of hydropower because their natural flow creates pressure. Another way to harness hydropower is the storage method, in which dams are used to trap water in large reservoirs. When power is needed, the dams are opened and the water flows out. The water pressure created is then converted into energy.

GEOTHERMAL ENERGY uses the heat that rises from Earth's core, which is located 3,000 to 4,000 miles (4,800 to 6,400 km) under the planet's surface. The most common way of harnessing geothermal energy involves capturing steam that comes from deep in the Earth and emerges in volcanoes, hot springs, fumaroles (vents in Earth's surface that give off steam), and geysers (fountainlike bursts of water). This steam, heat, or hot water can be trapped in pipes that lead directly to electrical power plants and even to homes.

HYDROGEN is the most common element in the universe. It is everywhere, but it doesn't exist on its own. Instead, hydrogen atoms bind with the atoms of other elements to form such compounds as water (hydrogen and oxygen), methane (hydrogen and carbon), and ammonia (hydrogen and nitrogen). Up-to-date technology is being used to separate hydrogen molecules and turn the hydrogen gas into a liquid that can be used in fuel cells. These fuel cells can power vehicles and electrical generators.

Make a Change

It would be nearly impossible to give up using energy entirely, but take a moment to think of ways you can use less. Here are a few things you and your family can do to cut down on your energy use (and your energy bill).

Tell your parents to lower the thermostat in the winter. Even a few degrees can make a difference.

Cut back on air-conditioning. Switch to a fan whenever you can.

Always turn off lights and appliances when you leave the room.

Take short showers.

Wash laundry in cold water when possible.

Walk or ride your bike. Skip car trips whenever you can.

Pick one night a week to go electronics-free. Read a book, play cards or a board game with your family, or write a letter to a relative or friend.

Energy Use at Home

The average U.S. household produces more than 26,000 pounds (12,000 kg) of carbon dioxide per year. Here's how.

Heating the home **34%**

Appliances and lighting **34%**

Heating water **13%**

Air-conditioning **11%**

Refrigerator **8%**

Source: Energy Data Book

Energy and the Environment

93

Habitats and WILDLIFE

The landmasses on Earth consist of six different kinds of large regions called biomes. The environment of each biome reflects the climate, temperature, and geographical features that exist there. Within a biome are many smaller areas called habitats. Wildlife thrives in its own habitat. For example, thick-furred animals live in the Arctic Circle, and color-changing chameleons thrive in lush forests filled with colorful plants. The relationship between various species of plants, insects, and other animals within a habitat is called an ecosystem.

TROPICAL RAIN FOREST

Tropical rain forests are hot, humid, and rainy. More kinds of trees exist in rain forests than anywhere else in the world. Rain forests are lush, with tall, densely growing trees and thick undergrowth. Rain forests in Africa, Asia, and South America have different species of wildlife, but include monkeys, jaguars, anteaters, toucans, snakes, frogs, and parrots. Many insects thrive in tropical rain forests, including colorful butterflies, ants, and camouflaged stick insects.

DESERT

Deserts, both hot and cold, receive very little rain. The Sahara and Mojave deserts are examples of hot, dry deserts. They are filled with sandy dunes and have little plant life. Cacti, low shrubs, and short woody trees such as sweet acacia can survive in the harsh climate. Snakes, scorpions, and camels are some animals found in hot deserts. The Gobi and Antarctic deserts are examples of cold deserts. Shrubs, sagebrush, gazelles, antelopes, wolves, mice, and jackrabbits are some examples of plants and animals found in cold deserts.

TAIGA Winter in the taiga is long, snowy, and cold. The summers are short and wet. Many evergreen, or coniferous, trees live there. The rocky soil of the taiga is covered with twigs and evergreen needles. Elk, grizzly bears, moose, caribou, lynx, wolverines, rabbits, sparrows, and reindeer are some examples of taiga wildlife.

TEMPERATE FOREST
In temperate forests, also known as deciduous forests, there are four seasons and a moderate amount of rain. Many hardwood trees, such as maple, oak, birch, and hickory, are found in this climate. Mushrooms, shrubs, moss, and lichen grow in temperate forests. Some pine trees and coniferous trees are also found in temperate forests, though they thrive in the taiga. Most trees lose their leaves in winter in temperate forests. Animals include deer, foxes, squirrels, frogs, rabbits, eagles, sparrows, cardinals, and black bears.

TUNDRA It is very cold year-round in the tundra biome. Tundra covers much of the land between the North Pole and the taiga below it. There is hardly any precipitation—rain or snow—in the tundra. Underneath a rocky layer of topsoil is a layer of permafrost, which is permanently frozen soil that never gets soft or warm enough to cultivate plant life. The tundra is a treeless area where moss, lichen, grasses, and low shrubs can be found. During the short, cool summers, some flowering plants flourish. Tundra animals include polar bears, wolves, owls, foxes, falcons, seals, and salmon.

GRASSLAND There are several types of grassland. Savannas are warm year-round, with rainy and dry seasons. They have dusty soil and some scattered trees. Trees and shrubs are largely absent from temperate grassland, like prairies and steppes. In a prairie, there are hot summers and cold winters. The soil is rich and grows wildflowers and grasses, but no trees. In the steppes, the winters are cool and the summers are hot. Steppe soil is dry. Grassland animals include zebras, elephants, lions, tigers, giraffes, buffalo, cattle, sheep, horses, gophers, and coyotes.

What Is a Dead Zone?

A dead zone appeared along the coast of Oregon in 2004, killing crabs and other types of marine life.

Ocean water is a mixture of salt, hydrogen, oxygen, and other elements. The amount of oxygen is vital to supporting sea life, from the tiniest creature to the largest whale. If oxygen disappears from an area of an ocean or sea, all of the life forms in that area will die. When this happens, the area is called a "dead zone."

Dead zones are caused when fertilizers and other types of nitrogen-rich wastes flow or are dumped into a body of water. The nitrogen, combined with sunlight, causes a huge growth in tiny plant-like organisms called phytoplankton. When a bloom of phytoplankton dies, it sinks to the bottom of the body of water. As it decomposes, it removes the oxygen from the water and attracts bacteria, which remove even more oxygen. This lack of oxygen, called a state of hypoxia, begins to kill off all other marine life, resulting in a dead zone.

Phytoplankton

A large dead zone can be found in the Gulf of Mexico. It is located where the Mississippi River flows into the Gulf, because the Mississippi carries huge amounts of nitrogen waste from sewers, industrial plants, and farm fertilizers. Other major dead zones include the large parts of the Baltic Sea and the Kattegat Strait, between Denmark and Sweden, but the conditions of these bodies of water have improved over the last 20 years.

In 1999, runoff produced by Hurricane Floyd flowed into the Pamlico Sound, along the coast of North Carolina, creating a dead zone.

THE STINKY TRUTH ABOUT TRASH!

On average, Americans produce about 1,600 pounds (726 kg) of garbage per person per year. To cut down on all that trash, make sure that you and your family are following the three Rs: *reduce, reuse,* and *recycle.*

What happens to the waste that garbage trucks collect? In the United States, most trash is taken to landfills, which are not very good for the environment. A thick layer of clay or plastic separates the garbage from the ground in order to prevent dangerous waste from escaping into the soil and getting into groundwater. Every day, workers add a layer of soil to cover the trash on top, but many of the items dumped in landfills do not decompose quickly. Other trash is transported to incinerators, where it is burned for energy.

CLEAN UP THE COASTS

For one day each year in mid-September, thousands of volunteers around the world gather at beaches, rivers, lakes, and other waterways to remove trash and other debris. The event is called the International Coastal Cleanup, organized by the Ocean Conservancy (oceanconservancy.org). Since the annual event began, in 1986, more than 6 million volunteers have collected more than 100 million pounds (45 million kg) of debris from beaches and inland waterways around the world. In 2008, helpers collected 26,585 tires from coastal areas—that's enough for 6,646 cars, with one to spare!

Clue 1: I was a conservationist, born in Scotland in 1838. I worked to preserve wildlife and protect forests in the United States.

Clue 2: In 1890, I helped establish Yosemite National Park, in California. I also helped start the Sierra Club, an environmental group.

Clue 3: I'm featured on the quarter released in 2005 that honors California.

Who am I?

Answer on page 244.

Do Your Part!

For ideas about helping the environment, check out some environmental organizations online.

KIDS FOR SAVING EARTH
kidsforsavingearth.org

THE NATURAL RESOURCES DEFENSE COUNCIL'S GREEN SQUAD
nrdc.org/greensquad

GLOBAL RESPONSE'S YOUNG ENVIRONMENTALIST ACTIONS
globalresponse.org/kidsactions.php

FROM
TIME
FOR KIDS
MAGAZINE

A Groundbreaking Event

FIRST LADY MICHELLE OBAMA PLANTS A FRUIT AND VEGETABLE GARDEN ON THE WHITE HOUSE LAWN

By Jaime Joyce

In March 2009, 26 fifth graders from George Bancroft Elementary School, in Washington, D.C., went to the White House. It was an unforgettable field trip. They used shovels, rakes, pitchforks, and wheelbarrows to help First Lady Michelle Obama break ground on a new fruit and vegetable garden.

The garden is an L-shaped patch near the fountain on the South Lawn and includes crops such as butterhead lettuce, sugar snap peas, collard greens, onions, and spinach. The herb garden features garlic, sage, and cilantro (sih-*lon*-tro). Cilantro, which is also called coriander, looks like parsley. It is often used in Mexican food, an Obama family favorite.

White House chefs prepare meals for the First Family using food from the garden. Some of the crops are donated to Miriam's Kitchen, a soup kitchen near the White House. Assistant White House chef Sam Kass is in charge of the garden. He said that the crops will change with the seasons. The garden will also have two

Radishes and lettuce from the White House garden are ingredients in a meal served to congressional spouses.

beehives. "We're going to try to make our own honey here," Mrs. Obama told the students.

EATING RIGHT FOR GOOD HEALTH

Healthy food is important to Mrs. Obama. She said that the purpose of the garden is to make sure that her family, White House staff, and guests eat fresh fruits and vegetables. Mrs. Obama has also said that she hopes the new White House garden will help educate Americans about the importance of fresh, nutritious food at a time when obesity is a national crisis. A diet high in natural, unprocessed foods can help people maintain a healthy weight.

Mrs. Obama said she has found that her daughters, Malia and Sasha, like vegetables more if they taste good. "Especially if they were involved in planting and picking it, they were much more curious about giving it a try," she said.

Michelle Obama and a student help prepare the White House lawn for planting.

guess what?

The current White House garden is the first since World War II. In the 1940s, First Lady Eleanor Roosevelt planted a White House victory garden to encourage Americans to plant gardens at home.

The Food Pyramid

Because 2-year-olds and 80-year-olds have different dietary requirements, the U.S. Department of Agriculture has introduced 12 versions of the food pyramid. Depending on your age, gender, height, weight, and how often you exercise, your dietary needs will be different.

| GRAINS | VEGETABLES | FRUITS | MILK | MEAT & BEANS |

OILS are not a food group, but you need some for good health. Get your oils from fish, nuts, and liquid oils such as corn oil, soybean oil, and canola oil.

Based on the new food pyramid, here are the recommended food amounts for a 9-year-old girl and an 11-year-old boy of average height and weight, who both exercise 30 to 60 minutes per day.

	9-YEAR-OLD GIRL	11-YEAR-OLD BOY
GRAINS	5 ounces	6 ounces
VEGETABLES	2 cups	2½ cups
FRUITS	1½ cups	2 cups
MILK	3 cups	3 cups
MEAT AND BEANS	5 ounces	5½ ounces

Organic Food

The term *organic* usually refers to food that has been grown and processed without the use of any chemicals such as fertilizers, pesticides, or artificial additives. Organic farmers believe that these materials are harmful to the environment and bad for the consumer. Organic foods are more expensive to produce and to buy, but organic food is often safer to eat and more nutritious than food exposed to chemicals—and many people insist it tastes better!

Nutrition Basics

Food provides the human body with the nutrients it needs to grow, repair itself, and keep fit and healthy. These nutrients include proteins, carbohydrates, fats, vitamins, and minerals.

STAY HYDRATED!
Make sure to drink lots of water every day.

CARBOHYDRATES

Carbohydrates are the body's main source of fuel. Your body breaks down carbohydrates into glucose (blood sugar), which travels through your bloodstream and supplies your cells with energy. Simple carbohydrates, which are found in fruits, soda, candy, and table sugar, are digested quickly. Complex carbohydrates (fiber and starches), which are found in rice, bread, whole grains, pasta, and vegetables, take longer for the body to digest.

PROTEINS

Proteins, found in fish, meat, poultry, eggs, nuts, dairy products, and legumes (such as peanuts, lentils, and beans), keep us strong. They help the body build new cells and repair damaged cell tissues. Most Americans eat much more protein than they actually need. Excess protein is often stored in our bodies as fat.

FATS

Not only do fats help your body grow, but they also help protect your internal organs and your skin. They should be eaten only in small quantities. There are different types of fats, and some are better than others. Saturated fats are considered "bad" fats, as they increase your risk for diseases. Saturated fats are most often found in foods that come from animals, including meat, cheese, and butter. Monounsaturated fats and polyunsaturated fats are considered "good" fats. They lower your risk for disease. These fats are found in olive, safflower, and canola oils, among others. They are also found in fish and nuts.

EAT THE RAINBOW
Consuming many different-colored foods in a day helps to ensure that you get lots of different vitamins and minerals.

KEEP MOVING!
In addition to eating healthfully, exercise regularly to stay fit. Playing basketball, tennis, and soccer are great ways to get your heart rate up.

calories
Calories measure how much energy we get from food. You can tell how many calories a food has by looking at the nutrition facts label. Girls ages 9 through 13 need between 1,600 and 2,200 calories a day, while boys of the same age need between 1,800 and 2,600. Eating too many calories can lead to weight gain.

A LITTLE SWEET GOES A LONG WAY
Avoid eating too many sugary sweets or fried foods.

Vitamins and minerals
Vitamins and minerals are micronutrients that help regulate body processes.

VITAMIN A, found in milk, many greens, carrots, and egg yolks, benefits your skin and eyes.

VITAMIN C, found in many fruits and vegetables, is good for skin, teeth, gums, and the immune system.

VITAMIN D, found in fish, eggs, milk, yogurt, and cheese, helps promote strong bones and teeth, and regulates cell growth.

VITAMIN E, found in spinach, nuts, and olives, has great antioxidant properties, and it may lower your risk for heart disease.

MINERALS such as potassium, iron, calcium, and magnesium are necessary for healthy bones, blood, and muscle. Minerals are found naturally in many foods. For example, milk, yogurt, and leafy greens like spinach and broccoli are good sources of calcium, and red meat is high in iron. Minerals are sometimes added to foods to make them more nutritious. For example, you may see calcium-fortified orange juice at the grocery store.

WHAT ARE ANTIOXIDANTS?
Antioxidants are substances in foods that prevent or repair damage to your cells.

An Amazing Harvest
TIME FOR KIDS GAME

Help the kid get out of this corny place. Go from the tractor to the barn. There's one catch, though. You must take the path that spells CORNUCOPIA. Find each letter, or you'll get stuck! Answer on page 244.

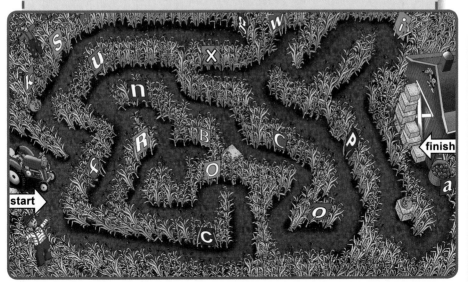

Food and Nutrition

Games

Wii Fit

RANK	GAME	YEAR RELEASED	CONSOLE	GAMES SOLD
1.	Wii Sports	2006	Wii	47 million
2.	Super Mario Bros.	1985	Nintendo	40 million
3.	Pokémon Red/Green/Blue	1998	Nintendo	31 million
4.	Tetris	1989	Game Boy	30 million
5.	Duck Hunt	1985	Nintendo	28 million
6.	Wii Play	2007	Wii	24 million
7.	Pokémon Gold/Silver	2000	Game Boy	23 million
8.	Nintendogs	2005	Nintendo DS	23 million
9.	Wii Fit	2008	Wii	21 million
10.	Super Mario World	1991	Super Nintendo	21 million

TOP 5
Best-Selling Portable Games of 2009, Rated E for Everyone

RANK	TITLE
1.	Wii Sports Resort with Wii Motion Plus
2.	New Super Mario Bros. Wii
3.	Wii Fit with Balance Board
4.	Wii Fit Plus
5.	Mario Kart Wii with Wii Wheel

Source: The NPD Group/Retail Tracking Service

Wii SPORTS RESORT was one of the hottest video games of 2009. At the start of the game, players are whisked away to Wuhu Island, where they can choose from 12 different resort-themed activities such as wakeboarding, cycling, hang gliding, and golf. The Motion Plus accessory attaches to the Wii Remote controller and detects the movements of a player's hand for accurate Frisbee-throwing and archery. Wii Sports Resort offers games for different age and experience levels, and some offer more intense physical workouts than others.

guess what?
Sony PlayStation 2 is the best-selling console. More than 138 million consoles have been sold.

Wii Remote

guess what?
Twenty-five percent of video gamers are under the age of 18. The average age of a video gamer is 35.

PUZZLES

WHAT IS A REBUS? A rebus is a puzzle that uses letters, numbers, symbols, and pictures. Each of these items represents the sound of a syllable or word in the puzzle's answer. An easy example of a rebus (using only letters) is "IOU." Each letter stands for a full word, and the solution is "I owe you."

Rebuses can get pretty tricky, too. Here are a few to puzzle over.

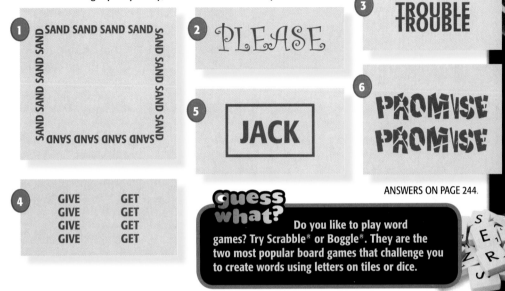

1 SAND SAND SAND SAND (arranged in a square)

2 PLEASE

3 TROUBLE TROUBLE

5 JACK

6 PROMISE PROMISE

4
GIVE	GET
GIVE	GET
GIVE	GET
GIVE	GET

ANSWERS ON PAGE 244.

guess what? Do you like to play word games? Try Scrabble® or Boggle®. They are the two most popular board games that challenge you to create words using letters on tiles or dice.

PICTURE PUZZLES

Think you have a sharp pair of eyes? Check out these picture puzzles to put your peepers to the test. At first—and maybe second—glance, the two pictures seem exactly the same. But when you look closely, you begin to notice differences. Someone's shoes may have changed color, or perhaps a book has appeared. If you're really good, maybe you can find all nine differences in the puzzle below!

ANSWERS ON PAGE 244.

Geography

THE SEVEN CONTINENTS

NORTH AMERICA
(including Central America and the Caribbean)
How big is it? 9,449,460 square miles (24,474,000 sq km)
Highest point Mount McKinley, 20,322 feet (6,194 m)
Lowest point Death Valley, 282 feet (86 m) below sea level

EUROPE
How big is it? 3,837,000 square miles (9,938,000 sq km)
Highest point Mount Elbrus, 18,481 feet (5,642 m)
Lowest point Caspian Sea, 92 feet (28 m) below sea level

ASIA
(including the Middle East)
How big is it? 17,212,000 square miles (44,579,000 sq km)
Highest point Mount Everest, 29,035 feet (8,850 m)
Lowest point Dead Sea, 1,286 feet (392 m) below sea level

SOUTH AMERICA
How big is it? 6,879,000 square miles (17,819,000 sq km)
Highest point Mount Aconcagua, 22,834 feet (6,960 m)
Lowest point Valdes Peninsula, 131 feet (40 m) below sea level

AUSTRALIA/OCEANIA
How big is it? 3,132,000 square miles (8,112,000 sq km)
Highest point Mount Wilhelm, 14,794 feet (4,509 m)
Lowest point Lake Eyre, 52 feet (16 m) below sea level

ANTARCTICA
How big is it? 5,100,000 square miles (13,209,000 sq km)
Highest point Vinson Massif, 16,066 feet (4,897 m)
Lowest point Bentley Subglacial Trench, 8,383 feet (2,555 m) below sea level

AFRICA
How big is it? 11,608,000 square miles (30,065,000 sq km)
Highest point Mount Kilimanjaro, 19,340 feet (5,895 m)
Lowest point Lake Assal, 512 feet (156 m) below sea level

guess what?
Many scientists believe that all the land on Earth was once a single supercontinent, which they call **Pangaea**. They say it broke apart to become the seven continents we have today.

EARTHY VOCABULARY

A group of scattered islands is called an **archipelago.** Many archipelagoes have formed in isolated parts of the ocean. Examples include Hawaii, the Philippines, Indonesia, and Fiji.

This tiny atoll is in the Indian Ocean near the Maldives.

The **equator** is an imaginary line drawn all the way around the world. It is located halfway between the North and South Poles. Above the equator, you will find the Northern Hemisphere, and below, the Southern Hemisphere.

An **atoll** is a coral island or group of coral islands, often made up of a reef surrounding a lagoon.

A **butte** is a flat-topped hill or rock formation with steep sides.

A **canyon** is a deep, narrow valley with steep sides. The Grand Canyon in the United States and the Copper Canyon in Mexico are well-known examples.

An **isthmus** is a narrow piece of land that connects two larger land areas.

An **oasis** is a small green area in a desert region. Water is usually present at an oasis.

The state of Florida is an example of a **peninsula,** which is a piece of land that juts into the water.

A **plateau** is a mountain with a wide, flat top. Plateaus are a common feature in the landscape of the Southwest.

The Grand Canyon is 277 miles (446 km) long and up to 18 miles (29 km) wide in some places.

Panama is an isthmus. It connects Central and South America.

North America

South America

Merrick Butte is located in Monument Valley on the Arizona–Utah border.

Geography

The Five Oceans

More than 70% of the surface of Earth is water. Here are the five oceans that cover much of the planet.

INDIAN OCEAN
Area: 26,469,500 square miles (68,556,000 sq km)
Average depth: 13,002 feet (3,963 m)

A scuba diver explores a reef in the Indian Ocean.

ATLANTIC OCEAN
Area: 29,637,900 square miles (76,762,000 sq km)
Average depth: 12,880 feet (3,926 m)

An iceberg floats in the Southern Ocean.

Sailboats race in the Atlantic Ocean, off the coast of Portugal.

SOUTHERN OCEAN
Area: 7,848,300 square miles (20,327,000 sq km)
Average depth: 13,100–16,400 feet (4,000–5,000 m)*
*Official depths of the Southern Ocean are in dispute.

PACIFIC OCEAN
Area: 60,060,700 square miles (155,557,000 sq km)
Average depth: 15,215 feet (4,638 m)

RECORD BREAKER
The Pacific Ocean covers about one-third of Earth's surface.

A surfer rides a wave in the Pacific Ocean, off the coast of Hawaii.

ARCTIC OCEAN
Area: 5,427,000 square miles (14,056,000 sq km)
Average depth: 3,953 feet (1,205 m)

guess what?
The average depth of Earth's oceans is more than 2.5 miles (4 km). The average temperature of ocean water is 38.3°F (3.5°C).

The Arctic Ocean is bordered by Greenland, Canada, Alaska, Russia, and Norway. Here is a view from Svalbard, an island in Norway.

WATERY WORDS

A **bay** is a section of an ocean or lake that fills an indentation in the coastline. Large bays are usually called **gulfs.** Examples include San Francisco Bay (shown) and the Gulf of Mexico.

A **canal** is a man-made waterway. The Suez and Panama Canals are two well-known examples built to provide shorter passageways for people and goods. Venice, Italy (pictured), is famous for its canals.

At the mouth of a river, water will often branch out into a triangle-shaped area called a **delta.** Known for their diverse wildlife, **estuaries** form in deltas. They are partially separated bodies of water where the salt water from the ocean mixes with freshwater from the river. Rivers with deltas include the Nile and the Mississippi. The Chesapeake Bay and Puget Sound are estuaries.

A **fjord** is a narrow inlet of sea that is bordered by steep cliffs. There are many fjords along the coastline of Norway.

A **geyser** is a naturally occurring hot spring that sometimes sprays water and steam above the ground.

Reefs are found just under the surface of a body of water. They are made up of coral, rock, or sand.

A **sea** is an inland body of water. It is often filled with salt water and is sometimes connected to the ocean. Examples include the Aegean Sea off of Greece and the Dead Sea between Israel and Jordan.

A **strait,** sometimes called a channel, is a narrow strip of water connecting two larger bodies of water. The Bering Strait is between Alaska and Russia. The English Channel separates Great Britain and France.

Geography

going green
Only about 2.5% of the water on Earth is freshwater. The rest is salt water. Only a small amount of the world's freshwater is safe and available for use by people. Water is a valuable natural resource—remember to use it wisely. Take shorter showers and don't leave water running when you are not using it.

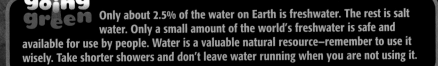

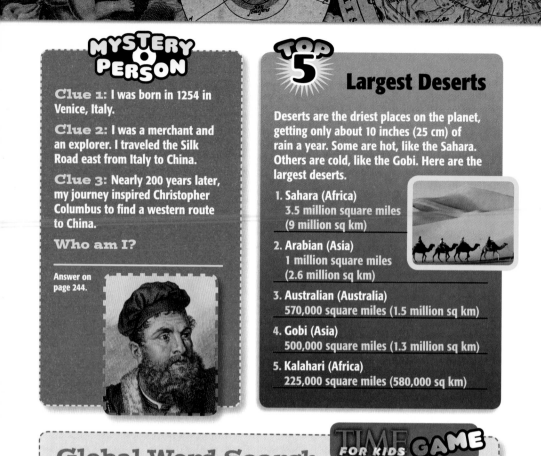

MYSTERY PERSON

Clue 1: I was born in 1254 in Venice, Italy.

Clue 2: I was a merchant and an explorer. I traveled the Silk Road east from Italy to China.

Clue 3: Nearly 200 years later, my journey inspired Christopher Columbus to find a western route to China.

Who am I?

Answer on page 244.

TOP 5 Largest Deserts

Deserts are the driest places on the planet, getting only about 10 inches (25 cm) of rain a year. Some are hot, like the Sahara. Others are cold, like the Gobi. Here are the largest deserts.

1. **Sahara (Africa)**
   3.5 million square miles (9 million sq km)

2. **Arabian (Asia)**
   1 million square miles (2.6 million sq km)

3. **Australian (Australia)**
   570,000 square miles (1.5 million sq km)

4. **Gobi (Asia)**
   500,000 square miles (1.3 million sq km)

5. **Kalahari (Africa)**
   225,000 square miles (580,000 sq km)

Global Word Search

TIME FOR KIDS GAME

Test your geographical vocabulary with this world-wise search-a-word. Find the words below in the puzzle. Words can go up, down, sideways, or diagonally.

Africa
Atlantic
butte
canal
equator
Europe
fjord
geyser
gulf
Pacific
peninsula
reef

Answer on page 244.

P	T	O	A	L	K	W	R	I	T
E	Z	C	E	Q	U	A	T	O	R
N	U	P	T	P	O	A	G	R	M
I	J	R	B	U	T	T	E	B	P
N	X	E	O	F	U	H	Y	W	A
S	B	E	A	P	J	N	S	F	C
U	D	F	S	E	E	O	E	F	I
L	R	P	A	O	C	J	R	S	F
A	F	R	I	C	A	E	N	D	I
U	Z	V	F	Y	N	X	A	S	C
L	E	A	T	L	A	N	T	I	C
H	Y	N	G	U	L	F	N	A	Q

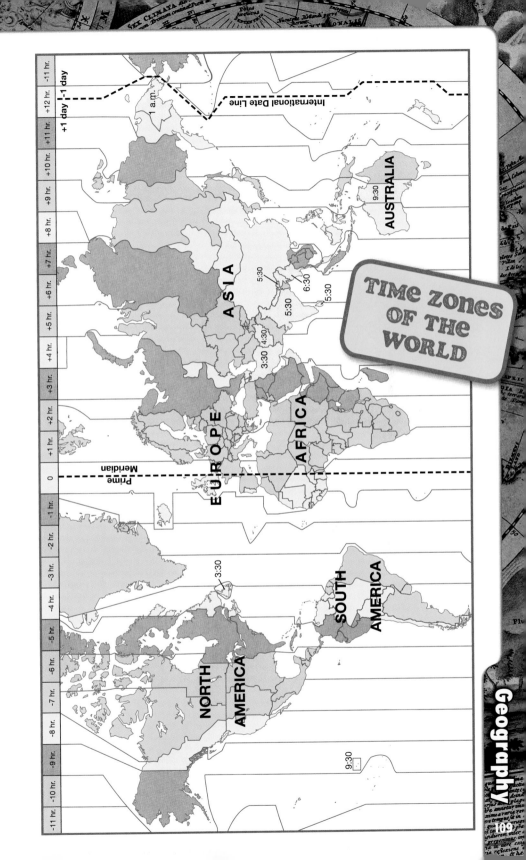

TIME ZONES OF THE WORLD

aFRICA

ATLANTIC OCEAN

BLACK SEA

MEDITERRANEAN SEA

RED SEA

EUROPE

FRANCE
SPAIN
PORTUGAL
MOLDOVA
ROMANIA
BULGARIA
HUNGARY
CROATIA
SLOVENIA
AUSTRIA
SWITZERLAND
BOSNIA AND HERZEGOVINA
MONTENEGRO
KOSOVO
MACEDONIA
ALBANIA
GREECE
ITALY
MALTA

Corsica
Sardinia
Sicily
Crete
Majorca
Madeira Islands
Canary Is.

GEORGIA
ARMENIA
AZERBAIJAN
TURKEY
IRAN
IRAQ
SYRIA
LEBANON
CYPRUS
ISRAEL
JORDAN
KUWAIT
SAUDI ARABIA
BAHRAIN
QATAR
YEMEN

SAHARA

MOROCCO
Tangier
Casablanca
Rabat
Fès
Erfoud
Marrakech

WESTERN SAHARA
Laayoune (El Aaiún)
Nouakchott

MAURITANIA

ALGERIA
Oran
Algiers
Constantine

TUNISIA
Tunis
Qafsah

LIBYA
Tripoli
Banghazi

EGYPT
Alexandria
Cairo
Suez
Luxor
Aswan
Al Jawf

Nile River

SUDAN
Khartoum
Port Sudan

ERITREA
Asmara

DJIBOUTI
Djibouti

ETHIOPIA
Addis Ababa
Harer
Gore
Juba
Hargeysa

SOMALIA
Mogadishu

KENYA
Kampala

UGANDA

CHAD
N'Djamena

NIGER
Agadez
Zinder

CENTRAL AFRICAN REPUBLIC
Bangui

CAMEROON
Yaoundé
Douala

Congo River

THE

NIGERIA
Kano
Abuja
Ibadan
Lagos

Niger River
Benue River

MALI
Timbuktu
Bamako
Gaoua

BURKINA FASO
Ouagadougou

SENEGAL
Dakar

THE GAMBIA
Banjul

GUINEA-BISSAU
Bissau

GUINEA
Conakry

SIERRA LEONE
Freetown

LIBERIA
Monrovia

CÔTE D'IVOIRE
Yamoussoukro
Abidjan

GHANA
Accra

TOGO
Lomé

BENIN
Porto-Novo
Niamey

EQUATORIAL GUINEA
Malabo

INDIAN OCEAN

Antananarivo ✪ MADAGASCAR

Mozambique Channel

Moroni ✪
COMOROS

Mombasa •
Dar es Salaam •
Zanzibar •

Cidade de Nacala •

MOZAMBIQUE

RWANDA
BURUNDI

TANZANIA

Lake Nyasa

MALAWI
Lilongwe ✪
Blantyre •

Kigali ✪
Bukavu •
Bujumbura ✪
Kigoma •

Lake Tanganyika

Beira •

ZIMBABWE
Harare ✪

Maputo •

Lubumbashi •
Kitwe •
ZAMBIA
Lusaka ✪

SWAZILAND
Pretoria ✪
Mbabane ✪

Durban •

DEMOCRATIC REPUBLIC OF THE CONGO

Kananga •

BOTSWANA
Gaborone ✪

LESOTHO
Johannesburg •
Maseru ✪

Port Elizabeth •

ANGOLA

Kinshasa ✪
Brazzaville ✪

NAMIBIA
Windhoek ✪

SOUTH AFRICA

GABON

Pointe-Noire •

Luanda ✪

Lubango •

Namibe •

Walvis Bay •

Cape Town •

Annobon •
(EQUATORIAL GUINEA)

ATLANTIC OCEAN

1,000 mi.

500 mi.

0 mi.

1,000 km

500 km

0 km

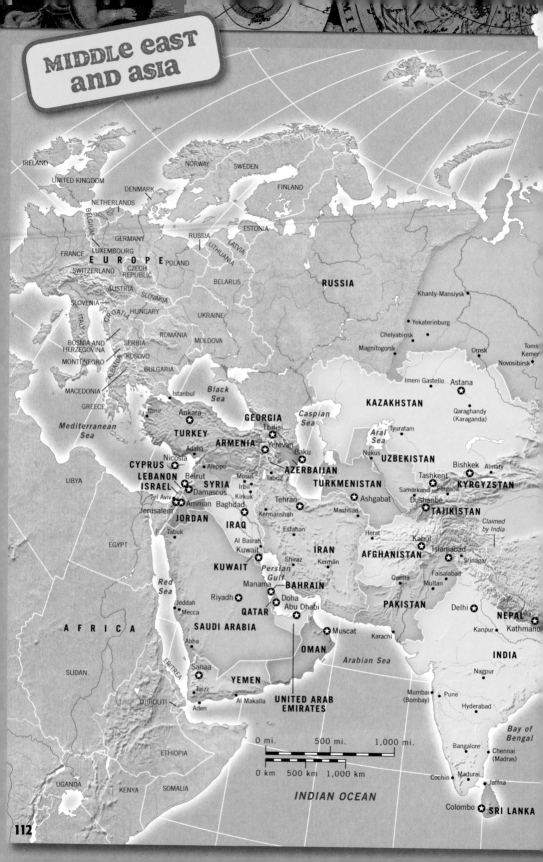

MIDDLE EAST AND ASIA

IRELAND

UNITED KINGDOM

NETHERLANDS
BELGIUM
LUXEMBOURG
FRANCE
SWITZERLAND

NORWAY

DENMARK

GERMANY

POLAND

EUROPE

AUSTRIA
SLOVENIA
ITALY

SLOVAKIA
HUNGARY

CROATIA
BOSNIA AND
HERZEGOVINA
MONTENEGRO
MACEDONIA
GREECE

SERBIA
KOSOVO

ALBANIA

ROMANIA

MOLDOVA

BULGARIA

SWEDEN

FINLAND

ESTONIA
LATVIA
LITHUANIA

RUSSIA

BELARUS

UKRAINE

RUSSIA

CZECH
REPUBLIC

Khanty-Mansiysk

Yekaterinburg

Chelyabinsk
Magnitogorsk

Omsk

Toms
Kemer
Novosibirsk

Mediterranean
Sea

LIBYA

Black
Sea

Istanbul

Izmir

Ankara

TURKEY

Adana

Nicosia
CYPRUS

LEBANON
ISRAEL
Tel Aviv

Jerusalem

Beirut

Aleppo

Mosul

Damascus Irbil

SYRIA

Kirkuk

Amman
JORDAN
Tabuk

Baghdad

IRAQ

Al Basrah
Kuwait
KUWAIT

GEORGIA

Tbilisi

ARMENIA
Yerevan

Baku

AZERBAIJAN

Tabriz

Caspian
Sea

Aral
Sea

Nukus

TURKMENISTAN

KAZAKHSTAN

Tyuratam

Imeni Gastello

Astana

Qaraghandy
(Karaganda)

UZBEKISTAN

Tashkent

Ashgabat

Samarkand Fergana

Bishkek

Almaty

KYRGYZSTAN

Dushanbe
TAJIKISTAN

Claimed
by India

Tehran

Kermanshah

Esfahan

IRAN

Mashhad

Herat

Kabul

AFGHANISTAN

Islamabad

Srinagar

Kermān

Quetta

Faisalabad
Multan

PAKISTAN

Delhi

NEPAL
Kathmandu

Kanpur

INDIA

Shiraz

Persian
Gulf
Manama

Riyadh

Doha
Abu Dhabi

BAHRAIN

QATAR

Muscat

Karachi

Red
Sea

Jeddah
Mecca

SAUDI ARABIA

Abha

AFRICA

EGYPT

SUDAN

Sanaa

Taizz

Aden

Al Makalla

YEMEN

OMAN

UNITED ARAB
EMIRATES

Arabian Sea

Nagpur

Mumbai
(Bombay)
Pune

Hyderabad

Bay of
Bengal

Bangalore

Chennai
(Madras)

Cochin
Madurai
Jaffna

Colombo
SRI LANKA

INDIAN OCEAN

ERITREA

DJIBOUTI

ETHIOPIA

UGANDA

KENYA

SOMALIA

0 mi.   500 mi.   1,000 mi.

0 km   500 km   1,000 km

ARCTIC OCEAN

Bering
Sea

Cherskiy

Tiksi

Verkhoyansk

Noril'sk

RUSSIA

Yakutsk

Magadan

Kamchatka
Peninsula

S I B E R I A

Sea of
Okhotsk

Petropavlovsk-
Kamchatskiy

Krasnoyarsk

Novokuznetsk

Irkutsk

Khabarovsk

Sakhalin

Ulaanbaatar

Harbin

Sapporo

Sea of
Japan

MONGOLIA

Gobi

Changchun

Vladivostok

JAPAN

Urümqi

Shenyang

N. KOREA

Tokyo

Hohhot

Jinxi

P'yongyang

Nagoya

Beijing

Kyoto

Taiyuan

Tianjin

Yellow Sea

Seoul

Kobe Osaka

Jinan

Taegu
Pusan

Hiroshima

Lanzhou

Qingdao

S. KOREA

Fukuoka

Xi'an

Nagasaki

CHINA

Hefei

Shanghai

Chengdu

Wuhan

East
China Sea

Chongqing

Lhasa

PACIFIC
OCEAN

Thimphu

Fuzhou

Naha

BHUTAN

Xiamen

Taipei

BANGLADESH

Liuzhou

Dhaka

Guangzhou

TAIWAN

Mandalay

Nanning

Kao-hsiung

Calcutta Chittagong

Macao

Hong Kong

Nay Pyi Taw

Hanoi

MYANMAR
(BURMA)

LAOS

Luzon

Chiang Mai

Vientiane

South
China Sea

Baguio

Rangoon

Quezon City

THAILAND

Da Nang

Manila

Bangkok

VIETNAM

PHILIPPINES

CAMBODIA

Cebu

Phnom
Penh

Ho Chi Minh City

Davao

Phuket

Songkhla

Borneo

MALAYSIA

MALAYSIA

AUSTRALIA AND THE PACIFIC ISLANDS

JAPAN

CHINA

ASIA

TAIWAN

PHILIPPINE
SEA

Wake

NORTHERN
MARIANA
ISLANDS
Saipan ★ (U.S.)

LAOS

VIETNAM

PHILIPPINES

Agana ★ Guam
(U.S.)

THAILAND

CAMBODIA

Yap Islands

Caroline Islands

Koror
⊛

MICRONESIA

Palikir
⊛

Bandar Seri Begawan

PALAU

BRUNEI
Kota Kinabalu
⊛

Manado

PAPUA NEW GUINEA

Ipoh

M A L A Y S I A

Medan •

Kuala Lumpur
⊛
SINGAPORE

Kuching

Borneo

Pontianak

Sorong

Jayapura

Wewak

Pakanbaru •

Samarinda

Palu •

Palembang •

Banjarmasin

Celebes

New Guinea

Honiara ⊛
Guadalcanal

Sumatra

Ujungpandang •

I N D O N E S I A

Jakarta
⊛ Surabaya
Semarang

Port Moresby

Java

Denpasar (Bali)

Kupang

EAST TIMOR
Timor

West Island •

Ashmore and Cartier Islands
(Australia)

Timor Sea

Darwin •

Gulf of
Carpentaria

CORAL
SEA

Coral Sea Islands (Australia)

Great Barrier Reef

Cairns •

INDIAN OCEAN

Derby •

Townsville •

Mackay •

Alice Springs •

Rockhampton •

Gladstone •

AUSTRALIA

Brisbane •

Tropic of Capricorn

Geraldton •

Kalgoorlie •

Broken Hill •

Lord Howe
Island
(Australia)

Perth •

Whyalla •

Sydney •

Bunbury •

Esperance •

Adelaide •

Canberra
⊛

Melbourne •

TASMAN
SEA

Hobart •

Tasmania

Tropic of Cancer

Honolulu
Hilo
Hawaii
(U.S.)

Johnston Atoll (U.S.)

PACIFIC OCEAN

MARSHALL ISLANDS

Majuro

Kingman Reef (U.S.)
Palmyra Atoll (U.S.)

Tarawa

Howland Island (U.S.)
Baker Island (U.S.)

aren
strict
URU

Gilbert
Islands

K I R I B A T I

Jarvis
Island
(U.S.)

Equator

Phoenix Islands

**SOLOMON
ISLANDS**

Funafuti

TUVALU

TOKELAU (N.Z.)

Mata-Utu

SAMOA

**WALLIS AND
FUTUNA**
(FR.)

Apia

Pago
Pago

COOK ISLANDS
(N.Z.)

Marquesas
Islands

**AMERICAN
SAMOA**

VANUATU

Port-Vila

Suva

TONGA

Alofi

Papeete

Tahiti

Tuamotu Archipelago

Society
Islands

FIJI

Nuku'alofa

NIUE
(N.Z.)

Avarua

FRENCH POLYNESIA (France)

Noumea

**NEW
CALEDONIA**
(France)

Kermadec Islands
(N.Z.)

Adamstown

Norfork Island
Kingston
Australia)

**PITCAIRN
ISLANDS**
(U.K.)

NEW ZEALAND

International Date Line

Auckland

Hastings

Wellington

Christchurch

Chatham Islands

Dunedin
Invercargill

Stewart Island

0 mi.   500 mi.   1,000 mi.

0 km   1,000 km

Geography

europe

Reykjavik
ICELAND

Arctic Circle

FAROE ISLANDS
(Denmark)
Tórshavn

NORWEGIAN
SEA

Trondheim

SHETLAND ISLANDS

ORKNEY
ISLANDS

HEBRIDES

Bergen
NORWAY

Oslo

Gävle

St

0 mi.   300 mi.   600 mi.

0 km   300 km   600 km

Stavanger

SWEDEN

Göteborg

Aberdeen

Glasgow

Edinburgh

Belfast

DENMARK

Ålborg

Copenhagen

Malmö

Ka

IRELAND
Dublin

UNITED
KINGDOM

NORTH
SEA

Liverpool   Leeds

Manchester

Sheffield

Birmingham

London

NETHERLANDS

Amsterdam
The Hague

Hamburg

Bremen

Berlin

Poznan

Gda

GUERNSEY (U.K.)

JERSEY (U.K.)

Calais   Lille

Le Havre

Brussels

Rotterdam

Antwerp

Essen

Dusseldorf

Cologne

GERMANY

Wroclaw

BELGIUM

Bonn

Frankfurt

ATLANTIC OCEAN

LUXEMBOURG

Paris

Luxembourg

Stuttgart

Prague

CZECH
REPUBLIC

Brno

Nantes

Strasbourg

Dijon

LIECHTENSTEIN

Munich

Bratislava

Vienna

Bu

FRANCE

Zürich   Vaduz

AUSTRIA

HUNGARY

BAY OF
BISCAY

Geneva   Bern

SWITZERLAND

Ljubljana

SLOVENIA

Bordeaux

Lyon

Turin

Milan

Trieste

CROATIA

Porto

Bilbao

Toulouse

Genoa

Zagreb

SAN
MARINO

BOSNIA AND
HERZEGOVINA

S

PORTUGAL

Madrid

Andorra
la Vella

Marseille

MONACO

Florence

ITALY

Sarajevo

Lisbon

ANDORRA

Bastia

MONTENEGRO

Faro

SPAIN

Barcelona

Corsica

VATICAN
CITY

Rome

Podgorica

KO

Seville

Valencia

Majorca

ADRIATIC SEA

Tiran

Málaga

Palma

Sardinia

Naples

Bari

Kor

Gibraltar

MEDITERRANEAN SEA

Palermo

Messina

Sicily

AL

Kerkira

MOROCCO

ALGERIA

Cagliari

TUNISIA

Valletta

MALTA

AFRICA

Murmansk

Pechora

ASIA

Arkhangel'sk

FINLAND

Oulu

Tampere

Turku Helsinki

St. Petersburg

ESTONIA Tallinn

RUSSIA

Izhevsk

Riga LATVIA

Nizhniy Novgorod

Kazan

ITHUANIA

Vilnius

Smolensk

Moscow

Samara

Minsk

BELARUS

Lipetsk

Saratov

AND

Hornyel'

Voronezh

KAZAKHSTAN

Brest

Kiev

Kharkiv

L'viv Derazhnya

UKRAINE

Voroshilovgrad

Volgograd

Gorlovka

Makeyevka

Zhdanov Rostov

Chisinau

MOLDOVA

Iasi

Odessa Mykolavia

Kerch'

Groznyy

ROMANIA

Simferopol'

Arad

rade

Bucharest

Sevastopol'

Craiova Constanta

A

Nis

BLACK SEA

istina

Sofia BULGARIA

Varna

VO

Skopje

ACEDONIA

Istanbul

Thessaloniki

IA

Volos

T U R K E Y

REECE

Izmir

Athens

SYRIA

IRAN

Crete

CYPRUS

IRAQ

LEBANON

Green

GREENLAND
(Denmark)

Narsarsuaq

Nuuk (Godthab)

Qaanaaq (Thule)

Davis Strait

Baffin Bay

Baffin Island

Iqaluit

St. John's

Island of Newfoundland

Saint-Pierre

Charlottetown

Labrador Sea

Happy Valley
Goose Bay

CANADA

Quebec

Chisasibi
(Fort George)

HUDSON BAY

Moosonee

Alert

Queen Elizabeth Islands

Kavujitoq (Resolute)

ARCTIC OCEAN

Victoria Island

Banks Island

Arctic Circle

Echo Bay

Yellowknife

Churchill

Saskatoon

Regina

Winnipeg

Beaufort Sea

Inuvik

Bismarck

Prudhoe Bay

Barrow

Edmonton

Calgary

Helena

Whitehorse

Juneau

Alaska (U.S.)

Fairbanks

Anchorage

Valdez

Nome

Bethel

Kodiak

Boise

RUSSIA

Vancouver

Victoria

Seattle

Olympia

Portland

Salem

San Francisco

Sacramento

Carson City

Bering Sea

Aleutian Islands

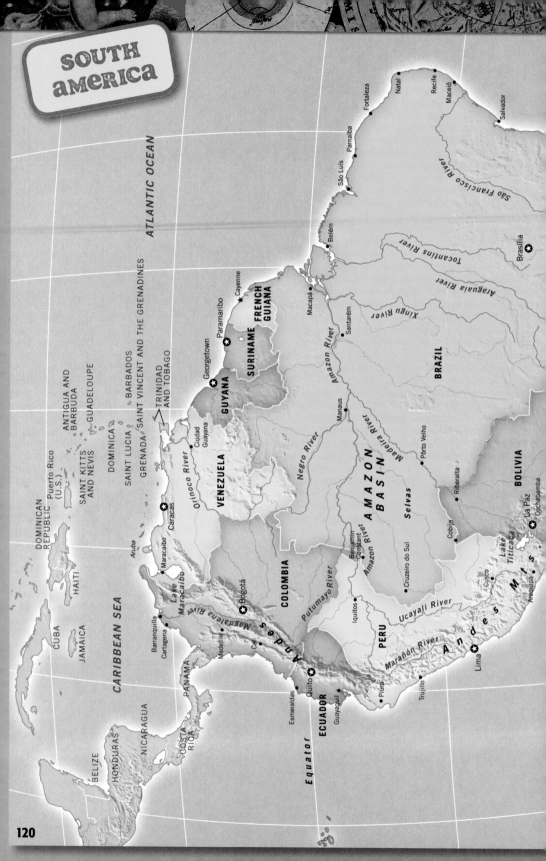

SOUTH AMERICA

ATLANTIC OCEAN

CARIBBEAN SEA

CUBA

JAMAICA

HAITI

DOMINICAN REPUBLIC

Puerto Rico (U.S.)

SAINT KITTS AND NEVIS

ANTIGUA AND BARBUDA

GUADELOUPE

DOMINICA

SAINT LUCIA

BARBADOS

SAINT VINCENT AND THE GRENADINES

GRENADA

TRINIDAD AND TOBAGO

BELIZE

HONDURAS

NICARAGUA

COSTA RICA

PANAMA

Aruba

Barranquilla

Cartagena

Maracaibo

Lake Maracaibo

Medellín

Cali

Caracas

Ciudad Guayana

VENEZUELA

Orinoco River

Magdalena River

COLOMBIA

Bogotá

Putumayo River

Andes

Esmeraldas

Quito

Guayaquil

ECUADOR

Equator

Piura

Trujillo

Iquitos

Marañón River

Ucayali River

PERU

Lima

Cusco

Arequipa

Andes Mts.

BOLIVIA

La Paz

Cochabamba

Lake Titicaca

Cobija

Riberalta

Cruzeiro do Sul

Benjamin Constant

Amazon River

SELVAS

A M A Z O N   B A S I N

Pôrto Velho

Madeira River

Manaus

Negro River

GUYANA

Georgetown

SURINAME

Paramaribo

FRENCH GUIANA

Cayenne

Macapá

Santarém

Amazon River

Belém

São Luís

Parnaíba

Fortaleza

Natal

Recife

Maceió

Salvador

São Francisco River

Tocantins River

Araguaia River

Xingu River

BRAZIL

Brasília

ATLANTIC OCEAN

Belo Horizonte
Rio de Janeiro
São Paulo
Curitiba
Porto Alegre

Brazilian Highlands

Paraná River

Paraguay River

PARAGUAY
Asunción
Ciudad del Este
Encarnación
Formosa
Resistencia
Sucre

San Miguel de Tucumán

Córdoba

Salto
URUGUAY
Montevideo
Río de la Plata
Mar del Plata
La Plata
Buenos Aires
Rosario

Paraná River

ARGENTINA

Bahía Blanca

Comodoro Rivadavia

Andes Mts.

CHILE
Arica
Iquique
Antofagasta
Valparaíso
Santiago
Concepción
Puerto Montt

Río Gallegos
Punta Arenas
Ushuaia

Strait of Magellan
Stanley

Falkland Is.
(Islas Malvinas)
(Administered by U.K.;
claimed by Argentina)

Cape Horn

PACIFIC OCEAN

0 mi.   500 mi.   1,000 mi.
0 km   500 km   1,000 km

Government

The Articles of Confederation

During the Revolutionary War, the people of the 13 American colonies fought to become independent from Great Britain. Mostly written by Thomas Jefferson, the Declaration of Independence was adopted by the Second Continental Congress in Philadelphia on July 4, 1776, officially creating the United States of America.

The first constitution, or set of laws governing the nation, was known as the Articles of Confederation.

Ratified by the 13 states in 1781, the Articles of Confederation established a loosely formed connection among the individual states. It gave a great deal of power to the states and very little to the central government, which was only able to request money from the states and to suggest rules for commerce between one state and another or between a state and a foreign country. It couldn't force the states to obey any federal rules or any treaties made by Congress. It quickly became clear that a new constitution was needed—one that would form a stronger central government.

The Constitution of the United States

The Constitutional Convention

In May 1787, a convention was held in Philadelphia to come up with a new set of rules for the United States. George Washington was unanimously chosen to preside over the gathering of 55 representatives of 12 states. (Rhode Island refused to take part.) James Madison was chiefly responsible for the success of the convention.

Many people with different opinions contributed to the Constitution. Some leaders (Federalists) wanted to have a strong central government, while others (Anti-Federalists) wanted the strongest powers to remain with the states. There were many angry debates and arguments, but on September 17, 1787, the Constitution of the United States was approved unanimously by the convention. By July 1788, it was ratified by three-quarters of the states. On March 4, 1789, the Constitution took its place as the supreme law of the land.

James Madison

The Constitution begins with a passage called the preamble, which states the document's purpose:

"We the people of the United States, in order to form a more perfect union, establish justice, insure domestic tranquility, provide for the common defense, promote the general welfare, and secure the blessings of liberty to ourselves and our posterity, do ordain and establish this Constitution for the United States of America."

Branches of Government

The Constitution divides the basic structure of the U.S. government into three branches: the legislative, executive, and judicial branches. The purpose of this structure is to provide a separation of powers among three equally important branches—one that makes laws, another that carries out those laws, and a third that determines whether those laws are constitutional. In the process of carrying out their responsibilities, the three branches make sure that no single branch becomes too powerful. This system of checks and balances has been a model of democracy for other nations in the world. The arrows below show some of the ways each branch has control over another one.

Checks and Balances

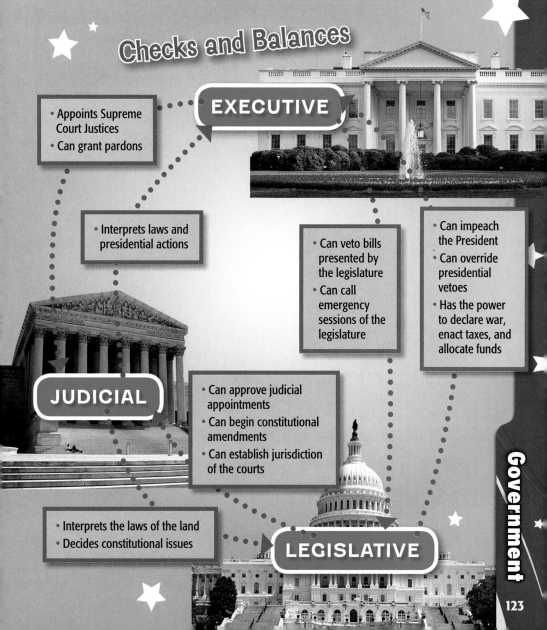

EXECUTIVE

- Appoints Supreme Court Justices
- Can grant pardons

- Interprets laws and presidential actions

- Can veto bills presented by the legislature
- Can call emergency sessions of the legislature

- Can impeach the President
- Can override presidential vetoes
- Has the power to declare war, enact taxes, and allocate funds

JUDICIAL

- Can approve judicial appointments
- Can begin constitutional amendments
- Can establish jurisdiction of the courts

- Interprets the laws of the land
- Decides constitutional issues

LEGISLATIVE

Government

123

The Legislative Branch

The legislative branch was the first of the three branches of government to be created in the Constitution. The founders did this on purpose, because they wanted to set up a government that represented and was accountable to the people of the United States. The legislature is a bicameral structure, which means that it has two chambers: the House of Representatives (often referred to as "the House") and the Senate.

The number of state representatives in the House is determined by a state's population. In contrast, the Senate gives every state the same number of senators: two. In this way, the large states are not able to control political affairs. In general, the Senate determines many national and foreign policies, and the House is in charge of finding ways to carry out these policies in an effective, financially responsible manner. Both chambers have the power to hold hearings to gather information on the bills they are considering and to investigate wrongdoings relating to the issues for which they are responsible. Every bill must be approved by both chambers to become a law.

THE U.S. CAPITOL

The United States Capitol is located in Washington, D.C. Members of the House and the Senate both meet in the Capitol, but they are in different areas of the building.

The SENATE CHAMBER is on the north side of the Capitol Building.

The HOUSE CHAMBER is on the south side of the Capitol Building.

guess what?

The political party with more members in the House of Representatives or the Senate is called the majority party. The party with fewer members is known as the minority party. In each chamber, each party selects a leader, who coordinates party strategy and schedules when bills are introduced, and a whip, who tries to get party members to vote the same way for each bill considered.

The House of Representatives

This chamber includes 435 representatives chosen based on the population of each state, with a minimum of one representative for each state. The larger a state's population, the more representatives it has. For example, California has 53 representatives, and Montana has one. Representatives are elected to two-year terms. Each representative must be at least 25 years old, a U.S. citizen for at least seven years, and must live in the state they represent.

The Speaker of the House presides over the sessions. The House of Representatives has the following special powers and responsibilities:

- Create bills that allow the government to collect taxes.
- Create bills that empower the government to spend money.
- Elect the President in the event that no candidate receives a majority of electoral votes.
- Vote to impeach the President, Vice President, or other elected official, which means to formally charge a public official with wrongdoing.

The leader of the House of Representatives is known as the Speaker of the House. The current speaker of the House is Nancy Pelosi of California. She calls sessions to order, runs debates, and gives the oath of office to new representatives, among other things.

The Senate

This chamber includes 100 senators, two from each state. Senators are elected to six-year terms, with one-third of the Senate being elected every even-numbered year. A Senator must be at least 30 years old, a U.S. citizen for at least nine years, and live in the state they represent. The Vice President (or president pro tempore, in the Vice President's absence) presides over the sessions. The Senate has the following special powers and responsibilities:

- Ratify, or approve, treaties made by the President. This requires a two-thirds vote of all senators.
- Accept or reject (by majority vote of all senators) the President's appointments of Supreme Court Justices and federal judges, ambassadors, Cabinet secretaries, and other high-level executive-branch officials.
- Hold trials of officials impeached by the House of Representatives and convict or acquit them. A two-thirds vote of all senators is needed for conviction.

The Vice President of the United States serves as the president of the Senate. He can only cast a vote in the Senate if there is a tie, but this happens very rarely.

The Executive Branch

President Obama signs a bill into law.

When George Washington became President of the United States on April 30, 1789, it was the beginning of the executive branch of the U.S. government as outlined in Article II of the Constitution. The President, Vice President, and Cabinet make up this branch.

The President

Barack Obama

The President serves a term of four years, with a maximum of two terms. A President must be a native-born U.S. citizen, at least 35 years old, and must have lived in the United States for at least 14 years. The President has the following powers and responsibilities:

• Carry out the laws of the land

• Appoint U.S. ambassadors, Supreme Court justices, federal judges, and Cabinet secretaries (who then must be approved by the Senate)

• Give the annual State of the Union address to Congress

• Receive foreign ambassadors, thus recognizing their governments

• Propose treaties with other nations

• Serve as commander in chief of the armed forces; send troops overseas (he needs congressional approval to declare war)

• Call both houses of Congress to meet in a special session

• Approve or veto bills passed by Congress

• Grant pardons for federal crimes

The Vice President

Joe Biden

Under Article I of the Constitution, the Vice President presides over the Senate and votes only to break a tie. Article XXV allows the Vice President to assume the office of President under certain conditions. The Vice President must also be a native-born U.S. citizen and meet the same age and residential qualifications as the President.

Vice President Biden attends a meeting with the President's national security team in 2009.

The Cabinet

guess what?

The first Cabinet convened in 1789. There were only four members: the attorney general and the secretaries of foreign affairs, treasury, and war.

The Cabinet is made up of 15 department heads who advise the President. Cabinet secretaries are nominated by the President, then each nominee is questioned by the Senate. These interviews are known as confirmation hearings. Each nominee must be confirmed, or approved, by a majority of 51 or more senators.

Here are the 15 members of the Cabinet, along with a brief description of what each department handles.

President Obama and Vice President Biden pose with members of the Cabinet and other trusted advisors.

1. Secretary Robert Gates The **Department of Defense** *is in charge of the U.S. armed forces.* defenselink.mil

2. Secretary Timothy Geithner The **Department of Treasury** *creates U.S. money and handles the collection of taxes.* ustreas.gov

3. Secretary Hillary Clinton The **Department of State** *helps to develop foreign policy and works with other countries.* state.gov

4. Attorney General Eric Holder The **Department of Justice** *enforces laws and makes sure all Americans are treated fairly under the law.* usdoj.gov

5. Secretary Tom Vilsack The **Department of Agriculture** *supports farmers and develops healthful agriculture and food policies.* usda.gov

6. Secretary Steven Chu The **Department of Energy** *develops energy policies and researches cleaner energy sources.* doe.gov

7. Secretary Janet Napolitano The **Department of Homeland Security** *works to keep the country secure and to prevent terrorist attacks.* dhs.gov

8. Secretary Kathleen Sebelius The **Department of Health and Human Services** *works to ensure public health and food safety and provide assistance to low income families.* hhs.gov

9. Secretary Eric Shinseki The **Department of Veterans Affairs** *provides help and services to former soldiers and their families.* va.gov

10. Secretary Arne Duncan The **Department of Education** *develops educational policies and helps with financial aid for schooling.* ed.gov

11. Secretary Ray LaHood The **Department of Transportation** *manages plane travel and the country's highways, shipping ports, and railroads.* dot.gov

12. Secretary Gary Locke The **Department of Commerce** *promotes business and trade within the country and with other nations.* doc.gov

13. Secretary Hilda Solis The **Department of Labor** *looks after the safety and rights of workers.* dol.gov

14. Secretary Ken Salazar The **Department of the Interior** *protects and preserves natural resources and wildlife and oversees national parks.* doi.gov

15. Secretary Shaun Donovan The **Department of Housing and Urban Development** *supports affordable housing and community development.* hud.gov

Government

127

The Judicial Branch

Samuel Alito Jr.

Ruth Bader Ginsburg

Stephen Breyer

Sonia Sotomayor

John Paul Stevens

Antonin Scalia

Anthony Kennedy

Chief Justice John Roberts

Clarence Thomas

On February 1, 1790, the U.S. Supreme Court held its first session. As part of the checks and balances and the separation of powers built into the nation's governmental structure, the main task of the judicial branch, and of the Supreme Court in particular, is to see that the Constitution and the laws formed under its provisions are preserved and followed. The U.S. Supreme Court and federal courts interpret the way an established law must be carried out.

guess what?

In 1789, the Chief Justice of the Supreme Court made $3,500 a year. By 2009, the salary had risen to $217,400.

The Supreme Court also has the power to declare a law unconstitutional. Supreme Court Justices and federal judges are appointed by the President and confirmed by the Senate. They serve for life or until they decide to resign or retire. The Supreme Court consists of eight Associate Justices and a Chief Justice. All decisions are made by a majority vote of the Justices.

guess what?

In 1811, Joseph Story became the youngest judge ever appointed to the U.S. Supreme Court. He was 32 years of age at the time.

A Justice Like No Other

FROM TIME FOR KIDS MAGAZINE

By Brenda Iasevoli

Sonia Sotomayor made history on September 8, 2009, when she was formally sworn in as the 111th U.S. Supreme Court Justice. She is the first Hispanic American to serve on the nation's highest court. Sotomayor took the judicial oath in a packed courtroom. "We wish you a long and happy career," Chief Justice John Roberts said.

Nine Justices make up the Supreme Court. They decide if laws agree with the U.S. Constitution. Sotomayor heard her first case the day after taking the oath.

President Obama speaks with Sotomayor shortly before she is sworn in as a Supreme Court Justice.

FROM THE BRONX TO THE BENCH

President Obama nominated Sotomayor to be a Justice on the Supreme Court in May 2009. She replaced David Souter, who retired. Obama said he was drawn by Sotomayor's "extraordinary" life.

Sotomayor's parents moved from Puerto Rico to New York City in the 1950s. She grew up in a working-class neighborhood in the Bronx. Her father died when she was 9. Her mother raised two kids on her own. "[My mother] taught us that the key to success in America is a good education," Sotomayor said after her nomination.

She and her brother took their studies seriously. Today, Sotomayor's brother is a doctor. Sotomayor has worked as a lawyer and a judge. She says she never dreamed she would one day sit on the Supreme Court.

"It is our nation's faith in a more perfect union that allows a Puerto Rican girl from the Bronx to stand here now," she said. "I am struck again by the wonder of my own life and the life we in America are so privileged to lead."

guess what? Sonia Sotomayor is only the third woman to serve on the U.S. Supreme Court in its 220-year history. The other two are Sandra Day O'Connor and Ruth Bader Ginsburg.

MYSTERY PERSON

Clue 1: I was born in 1743.

Clue 2: I am the author of the Declaration of Independence.

Clue 3: James Madison and I founded the Democratic party in 1792.

Who am I? _____

Answer on page 244.

History

Ancient History

5000–3500 B.C. Sumer, located in what is now Iraq, becomes the earliest known civilization. Among other advancements, Sumerians develop a written alphabet.

3500–2600 B.C. People settle in the Indus River Valley, in what is now India and Pakistan.

2600 B.C. Minoan civilization begins on the island of Crete in the Mediterranean Sea.

circa 2560 B.C. The Egyptian king Khufu finishes building the Great Pyramid at Giza. The Great Sphinx is completed soon after by his son Khaefre.

2000 B.C. Babylonians develop a system of mathematics.
• The kingdom of Kush in Africa becomes a major center of trade and learning.

1792 B.C. Hammurabi becomes the ruler of Babylonia. He creates the first set of laws, now known as Hammurabi's Code.

circa 1600–1050 B.C. The Shang dynasty is the first Chinese dynasty to leave written records.

1200 B.C. The Trojan War is fought between the Greeks and Trojans.

814 B.C. The city of Carthage, located in what is now Tunisia, is founded by the Phoenicians.

753 B.C. According to legend, Rome is founded by Romulus.

563 B.C. Siddhartha Gautama, who becomes the Buddha, or Enlightened One, is born. He will become the founder of the Buddhist religion.

551 B.C. Chinese philosopher Confucius is born. His teachings on honesty, humanity, and how people should treat one another are the foundations of Confucianism.

510 B.C. Democracy is established in Athens, Greece.

431 B.C. The Peloponnesian War breaks out between Sparta and Athens. In 404 B.C., Sparta finally wins the war and takes over Athens.

334 B.C. Alexander the Great invades Persia. He eventually conquers lands from Greece to India. He even crosses into North Africa.

100 B.C. The great city of Teotihuacán flourishes in Mexico.

58 B.C. Julius Caesar leaves Rome for Gaul (France) and spends nine years conquering much of Central Europe. He is murdered in 44 B.C.

27 B.C. Octavian becomes the first Roman emperor, ushering in a long period of peace. He is also known by the title Augustus.

The Great Sphinx

Confucius

Alexander the Great

World History 1–2010 A.D.

circa 1 A.D Jesus Christ is born. He is crucified by the Romans around 30 A.D.

66 Jews rebel against Roman rule. The revolution is put down by the Romans, who destroy Jerusalem, Israel, in 70 A.D. and force many Jews into slavery.

79 Mount Vesuvius erupts, destroying the city of Pompeii (in present-day Italy).

122 Construction on Hadrian's Wall begins. It spans across northern England and offers protection from the barbarian tribes to the north.

circa 250 The classic period of Mayan civilization begins. It lasts until about 900. The Maya erect impressive stone buildings and temples in areas that are now part of Mexico and Central America.

330 Constantine the Great chooses Byzantium as the capital of the Roman Empire, and the city becomes known as Constantinople.

476 The Roman Empire collapses.

622 Muhammad, the founder of Islam, flees from Mecca to Medina in what is called the Hegira. After the death of Muhammad in 632, Muslims conquer much of North Africa and the Middle East. In 711, Muslims also conquer Spain.

800 Charlemagne is crowned the first Holy Roman Emperor by Pope Leo III.

960 The Song dynasty begins in China. This dynasty is known for its advances in art, poetry, and philosophy.

circa 1000–1300 During the classic period of their culture, Anasazi people build homes and other structures in the sides of cliffs in what is now the southwestern United States.

1066 At the Battle of Hastings, the Norman king William the Conqueror invades England and defeats English king Harold II.

1095 Pope Urban II delivers a speech urging Christians to capture the Holy Land from the Muslims. The fighting between 1096 and 1291 is known as the Crusades.

circa 1200 The Inca Empire begins, and elaborate stone structures are eventually built in Cuzco and Machu Picchu, Peru. The Incas flourish until Francisco Pizarro, a Spaniard, conquers them in 1533.

1206 A warrior named Temujin is proclaimed Genghis Khan. He expands his empire so that it includes most of Asia.

1215 A group of barons in England force King John to sign the Magna Carta, a document limiting the power of the king.

1271–95 Marco Polo, a Venetian merchant, travels throughout Asia. His book, *Il Milione* (*The Million*), is a major European source of information about Asia.

1273 The Habsburg dynasty begins in Eastern Europe. It will remain a powerful force in the region until World War I.

1325 Aztecs begin building Tenochtitlán on the site of modern Mexico City.

Mount Vesuvius erupting

The Crusades

Signing the Magna Carta

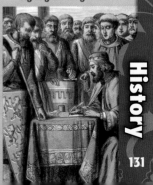

History

1337 The Hundred Years' War starts between the English and French. France finally wins in 1453.

1347 The Black Death, or bubonic plague, breaks out in Europe. It spreads quickly, killing more than one-third of Europe's population.

1368 The Ming dynasty is founded in China by Buddhist monk Zhu Yuanzhang (or Chu Yuan-Chang).

1433 Portuguese explorer Gil Eannes sails past Cape Bojador in western Africa, which was thought to be the end of the world.

1453 Constantinople falls to the Ottoman Turks, ending the Byzantine Empire.

1455 Johannes Gutenberg invents the printing press. The Gutenberg Bible is the first book printed on the press.

1478 The Spanish Inquisition begins.

1487–88 Bartholomeu Dias of Portugal leads the first European expedition around the Cape of Good Hope, at the southern tip of Africa, opening up a sea route to Asia.

1492 Christopher Columbus leaves Spain, hoping to sail to the West Indies. Instead, he and his crew land in the Bahamas and visit Cuba, Hispaniola (which is now Haiti and the Dominican Republic), and other small islands.

1497–99 Vasco da Gama leads the first European expedition to India by sea via the Cape of Good Hope.

1517 Martin Luther protests the abuses of the Catholic Church, which leads to a religious split and the rise of the Protestant faith.

1519 While exploring Mexico, Spanish adventurer Hernán Cortés conquers the Aztec Empire.

1519–22 Ferdinand Magellan's expedition circumnavigates, or sails around, the globe.

1532–33 Francisco Pizarro conquers the Inca Empire in South America.

1543 Copernicus releases his theory that the sun, not the Earth, is the center of the universe.

1547 Ivan the Terrible becomes the first czar, or ruler, of Russia.

1588 The English defeat the Spanish Armada, or fleet of warships, when Spain attempts to invade England.

1618 The Thirty Years' War breaks out between Protestants and Catholics in Europe.

1620 English pilgrims aboard the *Mayflower* land at Plymouth Rock.

1632 The astronomer Galileo, the first person to use a telescope to look into space, confirms Copernicus's theory that Earth revolves around the sun.

1642 The English Civil War, sometimes called the Puritan Revolution, begins in Britain.

1688 The Glorious Revolution, or Bloodless Revolution, takes place in England. James II is removed from the throne, and William and Mary become the heads of the country.

1721 Peter the Great becomes emperor of Russia.

Hundred Years' War

Christopher Columbus

Martin Luther

1789 An angry mob storms the Bastille, a prison in Paris, setting off the French Revolution.

1819 Simón Bolívar crosses the Andes to launch a surprise attack against the Spanish, liberating New Granada (now Colombia, Venezuela, Panama, and Ecuador) from Spain.

1824 Mexico becomes independent from Spain.

1845 A blight ruins the potato crop in Ireland. More than 1 million Irish starve to death, and another million leave for America to escape the famine.

1848 This is known as the year of revolutions in Europe, as there is upheaval in France, Italy, Germany, Hungary, and elsewhere.

1859 Charles Darwin publishes *On the Origin of Species.*

1871 A group of independent states unifies, creating the German Empire.

1876 Alexander Graham Bell invents the telephone.

1884 Representatives of 14 European countries meet at the Berlin West Africa Conference and divide Africa into areas of control.

1892 The diesel engine is invented by Parisian Rudolf Diesel.

1893 New Zealand becomes the first country to extend to women the right to vote.
• The Columbian Exposition, also known as the Chicago World's Fair, is held.

1894 The Sino-Japanese War breaks out between China and Japan, who are fighting for control of Korea. An 1895 treaty declares Korea independent.

1898 The Spanish-American War begins.

1899 During the Boxer Rebellion, the Chinese fight against Christian and foreign influences in their country. American, Japanese, and European forces help stop the fighting by 1901.

1904 Japan declares war on Russia, beginning the Russo-Japanese War. The countries clash over influence in Manchuria and Korea. Japan wins the conflict and becomes a world power.

1909 Robert Peary is credited as the first to reach the North Pole, although recent evidence suggests he might have been as far as 30 to 60 miles (48 to 97 km) away.

1911 Roald Amundsen, the first man to travel the Northwest Passage, reaches the South Pole.

1914 Austro-Hungarian archduke Franz Ferdinand is assassinated, setting off the chain of events that starts World War I.

1917 The United States enters World War I.
• The Russian Revolution begins. The czarist government is overthrown and, in 1922, the Soviet Union is formed.

1918 A flu epidemic spreads quickly around the world, killing more than 20 million people.

1919 The Treaty of Versailles ends World War I.

1927 Philo Farnsworth invents the television.

Galileo   **Storming the Bastille**   **World War I**

1928 Alexander Fleming discovers penicillin accidentally after leaving a dish of staphylococcus bacteria uncovered and finding mold.

1929 The U.S. stock market collapses, beginning the Great Depression.

1933 Adolf Hitler becomes chancellor of Germany.
• Frequency modulation, or FM, radio is developed by Edwin Armstrong.

1936 The Spanish Civil War breaks out.

1939 World War II begins when Germany invades Poland. Britain responds by declaring war on Germany. The United States declares neutrality.

1941 The Japanese launch a surprise attack on the United States, bombing U.S. ships docked in Hawaii's Pearl Harbor. In response, the U.S. declares war on Japan, and both Germany and Italy declare war on the U.S.

1945 Germany surrenders on May 7, ending the war in Europe. In August, the United States drops two atomic bombs on the Japanese cities Hiroshima and Nagasaki. Japan surrenders, ending World War II.

1947 India and Pakistan become free of British colonial rule.

1948 Israel becomes a nation.

1949 Following China's civil war, Mao Zedong sets up the Communist People's Republic of China.
• South Africa enacts apartheid laws, which make discrimination against nonwhite people part of public policy.

1950 North Korean Communist forces invade South Korea, beginning the Korean War. American forces support South Korea. China backs North Korea. The war ends three years later.
• Frank McNamara develops the first credit card, the Diners' Club. It is not made out of plastic but paper stock.

1952 The hydrogen bomb is developed by Edward Teller and a team at Los Alamos, New Mexico.

1953 Edmund Hillary and Tenzing Norgay climb to the top of Mount Everest.

1955 Jonas Salk's polio vaccine is introduced.

1961 A group of Cuban exiles, supported by the United States, invades Cuba at the Bay of Pigs. The invasion fails, and U.S.–Cuban relations worsen.

1962 The Cuban Missile Crisis, a conflict between the United States, the Soviet Union, and Cuba, brings the world to the brink of nuclear war.

1963 U.S. President John F. Kennedy is assassinated. Lyndon B. Johnson is inaugurated.

1964 The United States begins sending troops to Vietnam to aid South Vietnam in its civil war with North Vietnam.

1967 The Six-Day War breaks out between Israel and neighboring Arab nations Egypt, Syria, and Jordan. Israel seizes the Golan Heights, the Gaza Strip, the Sinai Peninsula, and part of the West Bank of the Jordan River.

Adolf Hitler

Robert McNamara, secretary of defense during the Vietnam War

1973 The Paris Peace Accords end the Vietnam War. North Vietnam later violates the terms of the treaty and, in 1975, takes control of Saigon, the capital of South Vietnam.
• Egypt and Syria conduct a surprise attack on Israel, beginning the Yom Kippur War.

1978 U.S. President Jimmy Carter, Israeli President Menachem Begin, and Egyptian President Anwar Sadat sign the Camp David Accords in an attempt to achieve peace in the Middle East.

1979 Religious leader Ayatollah Khomeini returns to Iran and declares it an Islamic republic.

1981 NASA develops the first reusable spacecraft, the space shuttle. The space shuttle *Columbia* is the first to fly.

1989 The Chinese army crushes a demonstration in Tiananmen Square in Beijing, killing hundreds or thousands of students and protesters.
• The Berlin Wall is torn down and the city of Berlin, Germany, is reunified.

1990 Apartheid ends in South Africa. Four years later, Nelson Mandela is elected president in the country's first free, multiracial elections.
• The Persian Gulf War begins when Iraq invades Kuwait.

1991 The Soviet Union dissolves. Croatia, Slovenia, and Macedonia declare independence from Yugoslavia. The next year, Bosnia and Herzegovina also declares independence, but war breaks out and does not end until 1995.
• Tim Berners-Lee develops the World Wide Web.

1994 Conflict between the Hutu majority and the Tutsi minority in the African nation of Rwanda leads to a bloody civil war and genocide, which is the systematic killing of a racial or ethnic group.

1999 Honda releases the two-door Insight, the first hybrid car mass-marketed in the United States. A year later, the Toyota Prius, the first hybrid four-door sedan, is released.

2001 After the September 11 terrorist attacks in New York City and Washington, D.C., the United States declares an international War on Terror, attacking the Taliban government in Afghanistan and searching for Osama Bin Laden and al-Qaeda.

2003 With the aid of Britain and other allies, the United States invades Iraq. Though the government falls quickly, resistance and fighting continue. In 2006, Saddam Hussein is executed for crimes against humanity.
• War in the Darfur region of Sudan begins, leading to a humanitarian crisis.

2004 A powerful tsunami kills nearly 300,000 people in Indonesia, Sri Lanka, India, Thailand, and other Asian countries.

2006 Montenegro becomes independent from Serbia.

2008 Kosovo declares its independence from Serbia.
• Global economic crisis leads to loss of jobs, homes, and credit, and to a downturn in trade worldwide.

2010 A devastating earthquake strikes Haiti.

Asian tsunami damage

Displaced persons in Darfur

MYSTERY PERSON

Clue 1: I was born on September 7, 1533, in England.

Clue 2: I succeeded my half sister, Mary Tudor, on November 17, 1558, to become queen.

Clue 3: During my long reign, England became a major European power.

Who am I? _____

Answer on page 244.

1524 Giovanni da Verrazano is the first European to reach New York Harbor.

1540 In search of gold, Francisco Vásquez de Coronado travels north from Mexico. One of his lieutenants is the first European to spot the Grand Canyon.

1541 Spaniard Hernando de Soto crosses the Mississippi River.

1579 Sir Francis Drake of England explores California's coastline.

1607 English settlers found Jamestown in Virginia. The colony's leader, John Smith, is captured by Indians. According to legend, he is saved by Pocahontas.

1609–11 Henry Hudson visits the Chesapeake, Delaware, and New York bays and becomes the first European to sail up the Hudson River.

1620 Pilgrims land at Plymouth, Massachusetts.

1626 Dutchman Peter Minuit buys the island of Manhattan from the Canarsie Indians.

1692 Accusations of witchcraft lead to the Salem witch trials and executions of 20 people.

1770 Tensions between British soldiers and colonists erupt in the Boston Massacre, when British troops kill five men.

1773 Colonists protest a tax on tea by dressing up as Native Americans, boarding ships, and dumping tea into Boston Harbor.

Known as the Boston Tea Party, the protest angers the British, who pass other harsh laws.

1775 Paul Revere warns the colonists that the British are coming. The Battle of Lexington and Concord is the first fight of the American Revolution. The British surrender at Yorktown, Virginia, in 1781.

1776 Drafted by Thomas Jefferson, the Declaration of Independence is signed, and the United States is formed.

1787 The U.S. Constitution is written and submitted to the states for ratification. By the end of the year, Delaware, Pennsylvania, and New Jersey have accepted it.

1789 George Washington becomes the first President of the United States.

1791 The Bill of Rights, written mostly by James Madison, becomes part of the Constitution.

1803 Thomas Jefferson buys the Louisiana Territory from France.

1804–06 Meriwether Lewis and William Clark explore the Louisiana Territory. They travel from St. Louis up the Missouri River, then over the Rockies on horseback, reaching the Pacific Ocean in November 1805.

1812 The War of 1812 breaks out between the United States and Britain because of trade and border disputes, as well as disagreements about freedom of the seas. The Treaty of Ghent ends the war in 1814.

1823 President James Monroe issues the Monroe Doctrine, warning that the Americas are not open for colonization.

Salem witch trials

Drafting the Declaration of Independence

James Monroe

1836 Texas declares independence from Mexico. In response, the Mexican army attacks and kills the 189 Texans defending the Alamo.

1838 In what is known as the Trail of Tears, European settlers force 16,000 Cherokees to leave their land in Georgia and relocate to a reservation in Oklahoma. Roughly a quarter of the Cherokees die.

1846 The Mexican-American War begins. At the end of the fighting in 1848, Mexico gives California and New Mexico (which also includes present-day Arizona, Utah, and Nevada) to the United States. In return, the U.S. agrees to pay Mexico $15 million.

1848 John Sutter strikes gold in California, kicking off the California gold rush.

1860 Tensions between the North and the South over slavery, taxes, and representation reach a boiling point, and South Carolina secedes from the United States.

1861 Mississippi, Florida, Alabama, Georgia, Louisiana, and Texas secede from the Union, and the Confederate government is formed. The first shots of the American Civil War are fired at Fort Sumter at Charleston Harbor in South Carolina. Virginia, Arkansas, Tennessee, and North Carolina also secede from the Union.

1862 The Homestead Act promises 160 acres of land to anyone who remains on the land for five years. This law encourages settlers to move west.

1863 President Abraham Lincoln issues the Emancipation Proclamation, which frees all slaves in the Confederate states. The Battle of Gettysburg is fought. It is the bloodiest battle of the Civil War.

1865 General Robert E. Lee of the Confederacy surrenders to Union general Ulysses S. Grant at Appomattox Court House in Virginia, ending the Civil War.
• President Lincoln is assassinated at Ford's Theater by John Wilkes Booth, and Andrew Johnson becomes President.
• The 13th Amendment, which puts an end to slavery, is ratified.

1867 The United States buys Alaska from Russia for $7.2 million.

1869 The transcontinental railroad is completed when the Central Pacific and Union Pacific railroads are joined at Promontory, Utah.

1890 The Battle of Wounded Knee is the last major defeat for Native American tribes.

1898 The Spanish-American War is fought. At the end of the war, Cuba is independent, and Puerto Rico, Guam, and the Philippines become territories of the United States.

1903 Wilbur and Orville Wright complete their first airplane flight at Kitty Hawk, North Carolina.

1908 Henry Ford, founder of the Ford Motor Company, builds the Model T and sells it for $950, making automobiles much more affordable than ever before.

1917 The United States enters World War I.

1920 With the passage of the 19th Amendment, women get the right to vote.

1929 The U.S. stock market crashes, and the Great Depression begins.

Battle of the Alamo

Abraham Lincoln

Wright brothers' first flight

1941 In a surprise attack, Japan bombs the U.S. fleet at Pearl Harbor in Hawaii. The United States declares war on Japan. Germany and Italy declare war on the U.S.

1945 Germany surrenders on May 7, ending the war in Europe. In August, the United States drops two atomic bombs on the Japanese cities Hiroshima and Nagasaki. Japan surrenders, ending World War II.

1946 The first bank-issued credit card is developed by John Biggins for the Flatbush National Bank of Brooklyn in New York City.

1950 North Korean Communist forces invade South Korea. American forces enter the Korean War to defend South Korea. Despite three years of bitter fighting, little land changes hands.

1954 In *Brown v. Board of Education of Topeka, Kansas,* the U.S. Supreme Court declares that segregated schools are unconstitutional.

1955 Rosa Parks is arrested for refusing to give up her bus seat to a white person, leading to a boycott of the entire bus system in Montgomery, Alabama.

1962 The United States discovers that the Soviet Union had installed missiles capable of reaching the U.S. on the island of Cuba. Known as the Cuban Missile Crisis, this event brings the U.S. and the U.S.S.R. to the brink of nuclear war. After two weeks of extremely tense negotiations, the crisis comes peacefully to an end.

1963 Martin Luther King Jr. delivers his famous "I Have a Dream" speech to a crowd of more than 250,000 people in Washington, D.C.
• President John F. Kennedy is assassinated.

1965 Civil rights advocate and black militant leader Malcolm X is killed.
• A race riot in the Watts section of Los Angeles, California, is one of the worst in history.
• President Lyndon B. Johnson authorizes air raids over North Vietnam.

1968 James Earl Ray shoots and kills Martin Luther King Jr. in Memphis, Tennessee. Riots break out across the country.

1973 The Vietnam War ends when peace accords are signed. Two years later, North Vietnam takes over Saigon (or Ho Chi Minh City), the capital of South Vietnam.

1974 Due to his involvement in the Watergate scandal, President Richard Nixon resigns. Gerald Ford becomes President.

1979 Islamic militants storm the U.S. embassy in Tehran, Iran, and 52 Americans are held hostage for 444 days.

1986 The *Challenger* space shuttle explodes, killing seven crew members, including teacher Christa McAuliffe.

1991 After Iraq invades Kuwait, the United States begins bombing raids. The first Persian Gulf War ends quickly as Iraqi forces are driven from Kuwait.

1999 President Bill Clinton is acquitted of impeachment charges.

Pearl Harbor attack

Martin Luther King Jr. at a civil rights march

Troops in Afghanistan

2000 In the extremely close election between Democrat Al Gore and Republican George W. Bush, allegations of voter fraud lead to an election recount. The U.S. Supreme Court determines the outcome, and Bush is declared the winner.

2001 On September 11, two passenger planes are hijacked and flown into the World Trade Center in New York City, causing the buildings to collapse. Another plane is flown into the Pentagon, near Washington, D.C. A fourth hijacked plane is crashed into a field in Pennsylvania by the passengers onboard before it can reach its target. The United States and Britain respond by attacking the Taliban government in Afghanistan. The U.S. government declares the War on Terror.

2003 The space shuttle *Columbia* breaks apart during reentry into Earth's atmosphere, killing all seven crew members.
• Along with its allies—Britain and other countries—the United States goes to war in Iraq. Saddam Hussein's government falls quickly, but resistance and fighting continue.

2005 Hurricane Katrina hits the Gulf Coast, destroying parts of Mississippi and Louisiana, and areas along the coast of the southeastern United States. About 80% of New Orleans, Louisiana, is flooded.

2009 Barack Obama is inaugurated on January 20, becoming America's first African-American President. He quickly signs a $787 billion economic stimulus bill to combat the severe economic downturn that began in 2008.

2010 After fierce debate in Congress and across the country, President Obama signs a bill to overhaul the country's health care system. The new law aims to extend health insurance to the 32 million Americans that did not have it before.

TIME FOR KIDS GAME

King's Dream

On August 28, 1963, Martin Luther King Jr. spoke before a crowd of 250,000 people in Washington, D.C. King's "I Have a Dream" speech became famous. Parts of what he said are below. Read each paragraph carefully. Find the words in bold in the puzzle. Words can go up, down, sideways, or diagonally.

"I say to you today, my **friends,** so even though we face the difficulties of **today** and **tomorrow,** I still have a **dream.** It is a dream deeply rooted in the **American** dream."

"I have a dream that my four little **children** will one day live in a **nation** where they will not be judged by the **color** of their skin. . ."

"From every mountainside, let **freedom** ring."

Answer on page 245.

F	G	A	H	X	C	O	L	O	R
R	D	Q	M	B	E	Z	C	N	L
E	N	T	M	E	J	X	E	F	W
E	A	O	P	J	R	A	R	R	R
D	T	D	M	U	D	I	X	F	P
O	I	A	P	L	F	H	C	I	M
M	O	Y	I	C	F	B	I	A	T
R	N	H	N	D	R	E	A	M	N
B	C	F	R	I	E	N	D	S	M
T	O	M	O	R	R	O	W	I	Y

FROM TIME FOR KIDS MAGAZINE

Make Room for the Robots

By Suzanne Zimbler

ASIMO with Yo-Yo Ma

When world-famous cellist Yo-Yo Ma announced that he would be playing with the Detroit Symphony Orchestra, every seat in the house was sold. On the evening of his performance, though, it wasn't just Yo-Yo Ma that amazed the audience.

As the lights dimmed, the conductor stepped onto the stage and lifted both arms to direct the musicians. They played a song called "The Impossible Dream." It was just like any other performance, except that ASIMO, the conductor, was only 8 years old and 4 feet (1.2 m) tall. It was also a robot.

The Honda scientists who built ASIMO equipped it with many abilities. It can run, climb stairs, kick a ball, and recognize faces. It can even help musicians make beautiful music. "The goal of the robot is to be a helper," says Honda's Alicia Jones.

ASIMO is just one of many robots being developed to complete tasks that humans usually perform. Some of the machines even have a humanoid, or human-like, appearance. Robots help out in homes and offices. They prepare food, clean floors, and even serve tea.

ROBOT NATION

Japan has more robots than any other country. Four out of every 10 worker robots are there. The Japanese government is spending millions of dollars to build even more robots. Why the rush for more electronic helpers? More than one-fifth of Japan's population is 65 or older, so there are not enough young people in the workforce.

Many of Japan's robots are designed to interact with people. An egg-shaped robot called PaPeRo (*pah*-pee-ro) assists teachers by singing and reading to kids. One Japanese hospital has three shiny robots that help out in the waiting room. They greet patients, give directions, and print out maps. "We feel this is a good division of labor," hospital spokesperson Naoya Narita says. "Robots won't ever be doctors, but they can be guides and receptionists."

HARDWORKING MACHINES

Robots have been creeping into daily life for years. Since the 1960s, they have been doing jobs that are too boring or too dangerous for humans. Some stand for long hours in factories, packaging food or putting together cars. Others milk cows on dairy farms all day long. These machines, called industrial robots, are often bolted to the floor. Unlike ASIMO, they do not have a humanoid appearance.

Now that robots are moving into our homes, many are starting to look more like humans. Trevor Blackwell's company, Anybots, makes robots. He built a dish-washing humanoid robot called Monty. To reach the sink, Monty needed to be between 5 and 6 feet (1.5 and 1.8 m) tall. The robot needed a human-like hand to pick up coffee cups. "Once you make a robot for human environments," says Blackwell, "you end up getting closer and closer to a human shape."

ASIMO serving coffee

cool new INVENTIONS

A special electric eye that could help blind people get back some of their sight. Puppies designed exactly the way you want them. Inventors are always finding ways to improve our world and our lives. Read on to discover some of the coolest inventions that have been developed recently. Which ones would you like to have? Which ones could help improve our world? Which ones just bring a smile to your face?

BRIGHT EYES

Scientists at the Massachusetts Institute of Technology (MIT) are developing an electric eye that could help the blind to see. A microchip is placed onto the eyeball. Eyeglasses equipped with a camera send images to the chip and then to the brain. Vision won't be perfect, but a person will be able to make out faces and shapes in a room.

BEETLE CONTROL

Researchers have created a way to control the flight of beetles by remote control. Cyborg beetles are live bugs that have been implanted with tiny radio antennas and electrical wires. Scientists deliver jolts to the devices, allowing them to pilot the little bugs in different directions.

A POWERFUL TELESCOPE

The Herschel Space Observatory allows scientists to see deeper into space than ever before. The high-powered telescope sends back images of places in space that have been invisible. For the next three years, Herschel will watch stars and planets being born. And we'll learn more about how the universe came to be.

Inventions

141

Can you eat the car?

Can race cars be easier on the environment? The WorldFirst F3 project is a Formula 3 race car developed in England. It has carrot fibers in its steering wheel, potato starch in its side mirrors, and cashew shells in its brake pads. It runs on a mix of chocolate and vegetable oil. Tasty!

New ways to ride

You'll never have to pedal again, thanks to this electronic ride. Honda's U3-X personal mobility device is powered by a rechargeable battery. To steer, simply lean left or right. The U3-X hits a top speed of 3.7 miles (5.9 km) per hour.

STEAM-POWERED CAR

Charles Burnett III recently broke a century-old record: the fastest land speed for a steam-powered car. Burnett was clocked at 151 miles (243 km) per hour on a track in California. The 25-foot-long (8 m) British steam car has 12 boilers. Its nickname is "the fastest kettle in the world."

BLAST OFF!

NASA is retiring its current space shuttle fleet in 2010. And the agency is already testing its next line of rockets, including the 327-foot (100-m) Ares 1 rocket. It is equipped with improved computers and better engines, giving it more reliability and power. Ares 1 could be taking astronauts out of Earth's orbit by 2015.

THE ROBO-PENGUIN

Penguins are speedy swimmers and expert divers. The birds inspired scientists at Festo's Bionic Learning Network to develop the AquaPenguin. It "flies" underwater, just like the real birds. It is highly flexible, and can move in cramped spaces and swim backward. One day, it may be used to build things.

THE SCHOOL OF ONE

A sixth-grade math class in New York City has tried a new program called School of One. Students used a special lesson plan called a daily playlist that mixes virtual tutoring, in-class instruction, and educational video games, all tailored to each pupil's needs.

TALL FARMS

Farmers are running out of land on which to raise food for a growing population. So Valcent, a Texas company, has created VertiCrop, a vertical farming system. Plants grow in rotating rows, one on top of another. The rotation gives plants just the right amount of light and nutrients. And by stacking the plants, farmers use less water.

PUPPY LOVE

In 1997, Lou Hawthorne began studying animal cloning. A clone is a genetically identical copy of a living thing, created in a lab. In 2007, his company BioArts did it. Hawthorne delivered puppies to five people who paid an average of $144,000 each for copies of their dogs. BioArts has since left the pet-cloning business.

SPIDERWEB SILK

Spiders spin webs with a material that's stronger than steel and far more flexible. Textiles expert Simon Peers and designer Nicholas Godley have unveiled an 11-foot-long (3-m) spider-silk cloth. Creating it took four years, half a million dollars, and more than 1 million golden orb spiders.

MYSTERY PERSON

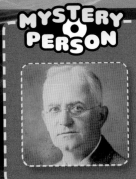

Clue 1: I was born in Waterville, New York, in 1854. In 1889, I invented roll film and a handheld box camera. It was the very first Kodak camera.

Clue 2: In 1900, I introduced a camera for kids, called the Brownie. It sold for $1.

Clue 3: My inventions helped make photography easier. Taking pictures became a popular hobby.

Who am I? _____   Answer on page 245.

Inventions

WORD WHIZ

Spelling Bee Winner: Kavya Shivashankar
Winning Word: LAODICEAN

A record 293 students participated in the 82nd annual Scripps National Spelling Bee, held May 26 to 28, 2009. In her fourth year as a spelling bee competitor, 13-year-old Kavya Shivashankar finally took the top prize. In 2006, Kavya placed 10th in the spelling bee. The following year, she moved up to eighth place, and in 2008, finished fourth. She plans to be a neurosurgeon when she grows up. Kavya beat out 11 other finalists and clinched the title by correctly spelling *Laodicean*.

WHAT DOES LAODICEAN MEAN? Indifferent to, or not interested in, religion or politics

The Newest Words in the Dictionary

To keep up with advances in technology and new cultural trends, dictionaries add new words every year. Here are a few of the words added to the Merriam-Webster dictionary at the end of 2009.

carbon footprint: the negative impact that a person or business has on the environment. More specifically, the term refers to the amount of carbon emitted by a person or action during a particular period of time.

frenemy: someone who pretends to be a friend but who is actually an enemy

goji (*goh*-jee): the dark red berry of the thorny Asian shrub *Lycium barbarum*. This cherrylike berry is often dried and used to make fruit drinks.

locavore (*loh*-kuh-vor): someone who eats foods that have been locally grown, whenever it is possible

reggaeton (ray-gay-tone): a style of music that combines hip hop with Caribbean and Latin American rhythms. Reggaeton was originally popular in Puerto Rico.

shawarma (sheh-*war*-muh): a sandwich made of sliced lamb, chicken, or vegetables, wrapped in pita bread. It is usually served with tahini, a paste made from sesame seeds.

staycation: a vacation spent at home or close to home

vlog: a blog that features videos

webisode: an episode of a show that can be viewed on a website

רח׳/מעלות נחלת שבעה
Hebrew

معلوت نحلات شيعة
Arabic

MA'ALOT NAHALAT SHIVA' ST
Latin

Alphabets

An alphabet is a set of letters or symbols used to write down language. There are many alphabets in use today, including the Latin (or Roman) alphabet, which is used for modern English, as well as for many western European languages such as French, Italian, Spanish, Swedish, and Portuguese. Some of the other alphabets used around the world are the Greek, Arabic, Cyrillic, and Hebrew alphabets.

- The Greek alphabet, which currently uses 24 letters, was developed around 1000 B.C.

- The Arabic alphabet is used to write many languages, including Persian (spoken in Iran), Urdu (spoken in Pakistan), and Hausa (spoken in Niger, northern Nigeria, and other African countries).

Menu written in the Greek and Latin alphabets

MYSTERY PERSON

Clue 1: In 1821, I invented a written version of the Cherokee language.

Clue 2: I didn't know how to read or write. Still, I created an alphabet of 86 symbols representing each syllable of my language.

Clue 3: Today, Cherokees all around the country can read and write their language because of my invention.

Who am I? _____

Answer on page 245.

- More than 50 languages, including Russian, are written using the Cyrillic alphabet.

- The Hebrew alphabet is written and read from right to left.

TRY IT OUT!

Say It in Hawaiian

There are only 12 letters in the Hawaiian alphabet. They are a, e, i, o, u, h, k, l, m, n, p, and w. The main language of the islands used to be Hawaiian. Today, most Hawaiians speak English, but they still use many words from the native language.

ALOHA!

Say these Hawaiian words and phrases.

ENGLISH	HAWAIIAN	HOW YOU SAY IT
hello	aloha	ah-*loh*-hah
family	'ohana	oh-*hah*-nah
teacher	kumu	*koo*-moo
child	keiki	*kay*-kee
man	kane	*kah*-nay
woman	wahine	vah-*hee*-nay
house	hale	*hah*-lay
thank you	mahalo	mah-*hah*-loh

Language

WHAT IS MATHEMATICS?

Mathematics is the study of figures and numbers. It deals with shapes, sizes, amounts, and patterns. There are many branches of mathematics, including arithmetic (addition, subtraction, multiplication, and division), algebra, geometry, and statistics.

GEOMETRIC TERMS

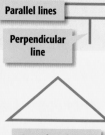

Right angle

90°

Obtuse angle

Acute angle

135°

45°

0°

An **angle** is formed every time two lines meet, or intersect. A **right angle** is an angle that measures 90°. An **acute angle** measures less than 90°, and an **obtuse angle** measures more than 90°.

Parallel lines

Perpendicular line

Parallel lines are lines that will never meet, or intersect. **Perpendicular lines** form a right angle where they meet.

A **triangle** has three sides. In an **equilateral triangle,** all sides are the same length. An **isosceles triangle** has at least two sides of the same length. In a **scalene triangle,** each side is a different length. A **right triangle** is a triangle with a right angle. On a right triangle, the side opposite the right angle is called the **hypotenuse.**

Isosceles triangle

A **quadrilateral** is a geometric figure with four sides. A **rectangle** is a quadrilateral with four right angles. A **square** is a rectangle with four equal sides. A **trapezoid** is a quadrilateral with one set of parallel sides. A **parallelogram** is a four-sided figure with two pairs of parallel sides. A **rhombus** is a parallelogram with sides of equal length.

Trapezoid

How Many Sides?

Shapes get their names based on the number of sides they have. A polygon is a closed figure with three or more sides.

NUMBER OF SIDES	NAME	SHAPE
3	triangle, trigon	
4	quadrilateral, tetragon	
5	pentagon	
6	hexagon	

NUMBER OF SIDES	NAME	SHAPE
7	heptagon	
8	octagon	
9	nonagon, enneagon	
10	decagon	

COMMON FORMULAS

To find the AREA of a TRIANGLE:
Multiply the base of the triangle by the height of the triangle. Divide by 2.

area = (base x height) ÷ 2

Example: area = (6 x 8) ÷ 2, or 24 square units

To find the AREA of a RECTANGLE:
Multiply the base of the rectangle by its height.

area = base x height

Example: area = 6 x 3, or 18 square units

To find the AREA of a SQUARE:
Multiply the length of one side of the square by itself.

area = side x side

Example: area = 4 x 4, or 16 square units

The **radius** of a circle is the length between the center of the circle and any point on the perimeter of the circle.

To find the AREA of a CIRCLE:
Multiply the radius by itself. Then multiply the product by 3.14 (which is also known as π, or **pi**):

area = radius x radius x 3.14
(or area = πr^2)

Example: area = 5 x 5 x 3.14, or 78.5 square units

The **diameter** of a circle is the length of a straight line beginning on the perimeter of the circle, passing through the center and ending on the perimeter of the circle. The diameter is twice as long as the radius. The **circumference** of a circle is the distance around the entire circle.

To find the CIRCUMFERENCE of a CIRCLE:
Multiply the diameter by 3.14.

circumference = diameter x 3.14
(or circumference = diameter x π)

Example: circumference = 10 x 3.14, or 31.4

Easy As Pi?

The number 3.14, used in some common mathematical formulas (above), is π rounded to two decimal places. Pronounced like *pie*, π is a Greek letter. The actual value of π continues for trillions of digits. Here are the first 50 digits after the decimal point:

3.14159265358979323846264338327950288419716939937510

Math

Writing Numbers Like the Romans Did

The ancient Romans came up with a numbering system that uses letters to represent numbers. The basic Roman numerals are I for 1, V for 5, X for 10, L for 50, C for 100, D for 500, and M for 1,000. Numbers are made by stringing these letters together.

- If a smaller number comes after a larger number, the numbers are added together. For example: VI = 6, XII = 12, and CLXI = 161.

- If a larger number comes after a smaller number, the smaller number is subtracted from the larger number. For example, IV = 4, XIX = 19, CCXXIV = 224.

Here are some more Roman numerals for you to learn in MMXI (2011).

I	1	XVI	16
II	2	XVII	17
III	3	XVIII	18
IV	4	XIX	19
V	5	XX	20
VI	6	XXX	30
VII	7	XL	40
VIII	8	L	50
IX	9	LX	60
X	10	LXX	70
XI	11	LXXX	80
XII	12	XC	90
XIII	13	C	100
XIV	14	D	500
XV	15	M	1,000

Evens and Odds

Even numbers end in 0, 2, 4, 6, or 8. Odd numbers end in 1, 3, 5, 7, or 9.

Based on whether numbers are even or odd, you can predict whether their sums and remainders will be even or odd. Here is how.

ADDITION

even + even = even
odd + odd = even
even + odd = odd

SUBTRACTION

even − even = even
odd − odd = even
even − odd = odd
odd − even = odd

guess what?

You've probably heard the words *millions*, *billions*, and *trillions* before. There are words for even bigger numbers. For example, a **quadrillion** is 1,000,000,000,000,000. A googol is a 1 followed by 100 zeroes and a **googolplex** is a 1 followed by a googol of zeroes.

WHAT IS PRIME?

A **prime number** is a number greater than 1 that can be divided (without a remainder) only by itself and the number 1.

For example, 11 is a prime number. It can be divided by 1 and 11. Dividing it by any other number would leave a remainder:

$$11 \div 2 = 5.5 \text{ and } 11 \div 3 = 3.67$$

Here are the first 10 prime numbers:

2	3	5	7	11	13	17	19	23	29

guess what? *The only even number that is a prime number is 2. Why is that? Because all other even numbers can be divided by 2.*

Holiday Giving

The holidays are a time for giving, but you want to make sure to stay within your budget. Imagine that you want to buy gifts for four people. You have $50 to spend at a winter sale. Write the names of the items you choose and the price of each one on the lines below. Then add everything up. Be sure to spend $50 or less.

1. _____ $ _____

2. _____ $ _____

3. _____ $ _____

4. _____ $ _____

Answers on page 245.

Movies and TV

FROM TIME FOR KIDS MAGAZINE

Live from the Teen Choice Awards

TFK REPORTER CLAIRE EPTING MET UP WITH SOME WINNING PERSONALITIES AT THE 2009 TEEN CHOICE AWARDS

By Claire Epting

Robert Pattinson and Kristen Stewart of the Twilight Saga

What do Miley Cyrus, Miranda Cosgrove, and Zac Efron have in common? They all attended the 11th annual Teen Choice Awards, hosted by the Jonas Brothers, which took place on August 9, 2009. Teenagers from 13 to 19 years old voted online for their favorite stars in categories such as Choice Comedy or Choice Animated Show. There were even some unusual categories, such as Choice TV Villain.

Who were some of the winners? The movie *Twilight* won nine awards. The Jonas Brothers won five awards, and TV's *Hannah Montana* took home three awards. During the show, there were musical performances by the Jonas Brothers, Miley Cyrus, and the Black Eyed Peas.

Before the awards ceremony began, stars made their way down the green carpet (as opposed to the typical red carpet). The carpet is where reporters can interview the celebrities before the big show. Afterwards, reporters and photographers head into a special room to watch the show on a monitor and interview some of the winners.

THE STARS SPEAK

Jennette McCurdy (who plays Sam on the TV show *iCarly*) shared her favorite past *iCarly* episode: "I liked the one where I got to play a twin. I got to play two different characters so I loved that."

Nathan Kress, who plays Freddie on *iCarly*, said that he got to fence on his favorite episode. "Neither Jerry [Trainor] nor I had ever learned how to fence, so they got a trainer to teach us the moves," Nathan said. And Miranda Cosgrove, who plays Carly in *iCarly*, says that her favorite episode had not aired yet, but was filled with all of the bloopers from the show.

Have you ever wondered what music is on the iPods of today's teen stars? Miranda Cosgrove's most played song was "I Gotta Feeling" by the Black Eyed Peas. Emily Osment, of *Hannah Montana*, shared that her most played song was "Wand" by the Flaming Lips.

The 2009 Teen Choice Awards were a huge success. Many voters participated to make it great. It was amazing to be there, and it was neat to get some information on what is happening next for the talented teen entertainers.

Zac Efron

Emily Osment

MOVIES

ACTOR, MUSIC/DANCE: Zac Efron, *High School Musical 3: Senior Year*
ACTOR, ACTION ADVENTURE: Hugh Jackman, *X-Men Origins: Wolverine*
ACTOR, COMEDY: Zac Efron, *17 Again*
ACTOR, DRAMA: Robert Pattinson, *Twilight*
ACTRESS, MUSIC/DANCE: Miley Cyrus, *Hannah Montana: The Movie*
ACTRESS, ACTION ADVENTURE: Jordana Brewster, *Fast & Furious*
ACTRESS, COMEDY: Anne Hathaway, *Bride Wars*
ACTRESS, DRAMA: Kristen Stewart, *Twilight*
HISSY FIT: Miley Cyrus, *Hannah Montana: The Movie*
ACTION ADVENTURE: *X-Men Origins: Wolverine*
BROMANTIC COMEDY: *Marley & Me*
COMEDY: *Night at the Museum: Battle of the Smithsonian*
DRAMA: *Twilight*
FRESH FACE FEMALE: Ashley Greene, *Twilight*
FRESH FACE MALE: Taylor Lautner, *Twilight*
HORROR/THRILLER: *Friday the 13th*
LIPLOCK: Kristen Stewart and Robert Pattinson, *Twilight*
MUSIC/DANCE: *High School Musical 3: Senior Year*
ROCKSTAR MOMENT: Zac Efron, *17 Again*
ROMANCE: *Twilight*
RUMBLE: Robert Pattinson vs. Cam Gigandet, *Twilight*
VILLAIN: Cam Gigandet, *Twilight*

TELEVISION

ACTOR, ACTION ADVENTURE: Tom Welling, *Smallville*
ACTOR, COMEDY: Jonas Brothers, *Jonas*
ACTOR, DRAMA: Chace Crawford, *Gossip Girl*
ACTRESS, ACTION ADVENTURE: Hayden Panettiere, *Heroes*
ACTRESS, COMEDY: Miley Cyrus, *Hannah Montana*
ACTRESS, DRAMA: Leighton Meester, *Gossip Girl*
ANIMATED SHOW: *SpongeBob SquarePants*
BREAKOUT STAR, FEMALE: Demi Lovato, *Sonny with a Chance*
BREAKOUT STAR, MALE: Frankie Jonas, *Jonas*
FAB-U-LOUS: Miss Jay, *America's Next Top Model*
PARENTAL UNIT: Billy Ray Cyrus, *Hannah Montana*
PERSONALITY: Ryan Seacrest , *American Idol, E! News*
REALITY/VARIETY STAR, FEMALE: Lauren Conrad, *The Hills*
REALITY/VARIETY STAR, MALE: Adam Lambert, *American Idol*
ACTION ADVENTURE: *Heroes*
BREAKOUT SHOW: *Jonas*
COMEDY: *Hannah Montana*
DRAMA: *Gossip Girl*
REALITY: *The Hills*
REALITY COMPETITION: *American Idol*
SIDEKICK: Emily Osment, *Hannah Montana*
VILLAIN: Ed Westwick, *Gossip Girl*

AUGUST 10, 2009

Michelle Trachtenberg and Zac Efron in *17 Again*

Jonas Brothers

Movies and TV

151

82nd Annual Academy Awards

MARCH 7, 2010

Sandra Bullock

And the Oscar Goes To . . .

On March 7, 2010, the top names in Hollywood gathered for the Academy Awards. Here are some of the night's big winners.

The special effects team behind Avatar

BEST PICTURE: *The Hurt Locker*
BEST ANIMATED FEATURE: *Up*
BEST DIRECTOR: Kathryn Bigelow, *The Hurt Locker*
BEST FEATURE DOCUMENTARY: *The Cove*
BEST ACTOR: Jeff Bridges, *Crazy Heart*
BEST ACTRESS: Sandra Bullock, *The Blind Side*
BEST ORIGINAL SONG: "The Weary Kind," (Theme from *Crazy Heart*)
BEST ORIGINAL SCORE: *Up*
BEST ORIGINAL SCREENPLAY: *The Hurt Locker*
BEST VISUAL EFFECTS: *Avatar*
BEST CINEMATOGRAPHY: *Avatar*
BEST COSTUME DESIGN: *The Young Victoria*
BEST MAKEUP: *Star Trek*

Star Trek

guess what?

Kathryn Bigelow made history in 2010, becoming the first woman to win the Oscar for Best Director.

TOP 10 Best-Selling Movies of 2009

RANK	TITLE	MONEY MADE	OPENING DATE
1.	*Transformers: Revenge of the Fallen*	$402,111,870	6/24/2009
2.	*Harry Potter and the Half-Blood Prince*	$301,948,049	7/15/2009
3.	*Up*	$293,004,164	5/29/2009
4.	*The Hangover*	$277,283,642	6/5/2009
5.	*Star Trek*	$257,730,019	5/8/2009
6.	*The Twilight Saga: New Moon*	$255,363,052	11/20/2009
7.	*Monsters vs. Aliens*	$198,351,526	3/27/2009
8.	*Ice Age: Dawn of the Dinosaurs*	$196,573,705	7/1/2009
9.	*X-Men Origins: Wolverine*	$179,883,157	5/1/2009
10.	*Night at the Museum: Battle of the Smithsonian*	$177,243,721	5/22/2009

Source: The Nielsen Company/*The Hollywood Reporter*
Note: Data from January 1–December 6, 2009, in the United States and Canada only.

People's Choice Awards

Glee

MOVIES

MOVIE ACTOR: Johnny Depp
MOVIE ACTRESS: Sandra Bullock
ACTION STAR: Hugh Jackman
COMEDY STAR: Jim Carrey
BREAKOUT MOVIE ACTRESS: Miley Cyrus
BREAKOUT MOVIE ACTOR: Taylor Lautner
ON-SCREEN TEAM: Robert Pattinson, Kristen Stewart, and Taylor Lautner, *The Twilight Saga*
FAMILY MOVIE: *Up*
MOVIE FRANCHISE: The Twilight Saga
COMEDY MOVIE: *The Proposal*
FAVORITE MOVIE: *Twilight*

TELEVISION

TV DRAMA: *House*
TV COMEDY: *The Big Bang Theory*
TV DRAMA ACTOR: Hugh Laurie
TV DRAMA ACTRESS: Katherine Heigl
TV COMEDY ACTOR: Steve Carell
TV COMEDY ACTRESS: Alyson Hannigan
TV OBSESSION: *True Blood*
TV TALK SHOW: *The Ellen DeGeneres Show*
TV SCI-FI/FANTASY: *Supernatural*
TV COMPETITION SHOW: *American Idol*
ANIMAL SHOW: *Dog Whisperer*
NEW TV DRAMA: *The Vampire Diaries*
NEW TV COMEDY: *Glee*

Alyson Hannigan

guess what?

2010 was a busy year for Sandra Bullock. She won an Oscar, a Golden Globe, and a People's Choice Award for her great performance in *The Blind Side*. But, she also took home a Razzie Award for Worst Actress for her work in the film *All About Steve*.

Hugh Jackman

TOP 10 Highest-Grossing Movies in the U.S.

RANK	MOVIE TITLE	YEAR RELEASED	U.S. BOX OFFICE TOTAL
1.	*Avatar*	2009	$740,408,054
2.	*Titanic*	1997	$600,779,824
3.	*The Dark Knight*	2008	$533,316,061
4.	*Star Wars*	1977	$460,935,665
5.	*Shrek 2*	2004	$436,471,036
6.	*E.T.: The Extra-Terrestrial*	1982	$434,949,459
7.	*Star Wars: Episode 1: The Phantom Menace*	1999	$431,065,444
8.	*Pirates of the Caribbean: Dead Man's Chest*	2006	$423,032,628
9.	*Spider-Man*	2002	$403,706,375
10.	*Transformers: Revenge of the Fallen*	2009	$402,076,689

Movies and TV

Nickelodeon Kids' Choice Awards

SATURDAY, MARCH 27, 2010

MOVIES

Favorite Movie: *Alvin and the Chipmunks: The Squeakquel*

Favorite Movie Actor: Taylor Lautner in *The Twilight Saga: New Moon*

Favorite Movie Actress: Miley Cyrus in *Hannah Montana: The Movie*

Favorite Animated Movie: *Up*

Cutest Movie Couple: Jacob and Bella (Taylor Lautner and Kristen Stewart) from *The Twilight Saga: New Moon*

TELEVISION

Favorite Reality Show: *American Idol*

Favorite TV Show: *iCarly*

Favorite TV Actress: Selena Gomez

Favorite TV Actor: Dylan Sprouse

Favorite Cartoon: *SpongeBob SquarePants*

Selena Gomez

iCarly star Miranda Cosgrove accepts the award for Favorite TV Show

MOVIE MUSICALS

High School Musical 3: Senior Year

With glitzy numbers like the ones in *Dreamgirls* and catchy tunes like the songs from *High School Musical*, movie musicals are hugely popular right now. But they aren't a new phenomenon. *The Jazz Singer* was released in 1927, and *Meet Me in St. Louis* in 1944. Gene Kelly danced across the screen in *Singin' in the Rain* in 1952, and actress Julie Andrews delighted audiences as Maria in the film version of *The Sound of Music* in 1965.

Singin' in the Rain

A Film Festival for Kids

TFK REPORTS ON THE CHICAGO INTERNATIONAL CHILDREN'S FILM FESTIVAL

By TFK Kid Reporter Meghan Pfau

For 26 years, the Chicago International Children's Film Festival (CICFF) has featured interesting and thoughtful children's movies. More than 200 films were screened as part of the 2009 festival. It is the largest annual film festival in North America and the only Academy Award–qualifying children's film festival in the world. Winners in the short film category go on to compete in the Oscars! The films come from more than 40 countries. More than 25,000 people attend.

Animators work with kids at a CICFF workshop.

Audience members

FOR KIDS, BY KIDS

The festival involves young people in many ways. "We don't just show kids movies. We ask kids to think about what they are watching," CICFF Director Nicole Drieske told TFK. "Five minutes before the lights go down, we have a talk with everybody. We talk about what's going on in our minds when we are watching a movie," she explained. "Movies teach us so much. If we're not paying attention to what we are watching, we aren't learning as much as we could." Viewers vote, giving their opinions at the end of each movie. The CICFF staff wants kids to feel like they are an important part of the festival.

Kids can also attend workshops led by filmmakers, media professionals, and celebrities. And young talent takes part in the CICFF. Eleven-year-old Shiropa Purna wrote and directed *Our Boat Is Our Address*, which was featured in the festival. "My dad is a director, and he taught me many things," Shiropa said.

A children's jury meets in August to watch more than 100 movies that will appear in the festival. They rate the films based on plot, character, setting, acting, sound, and cinematography. The jury awards more than a dozen prizes. The awards are announced at the festival's Closing Night Award Ceremony.

For more information, go to cicff.org.

MYSTERY PERSON

Clue 1: I am a British actress and singer. I made my film debut in 1964 as a magical nanny named Mary Poppins.

Clue 2: More than 40 years ago, I starred as Maria in *The Sound of Music*, one of the most popular movie musicals ever.

Clue 3: I am also an author. My books include *Mandy* and *The Last of the Really Great Whangdoodles*.

Who am I? _____

Answer on page 245.

Music

A Chat with Justin Bieber

TFK TALKS TO THE RISING POP STAR

By TFK Kid Reporter Sarah Horbacewicz

Justin Bieber joins Usher onstage at Madison Square Garden in December 2009.

When Justin Bieber was 12, he entered a singing competition in his hometown of Stratford, Ontario, Canada, and won second place. He wanted to share the news with family members, so he posted clips from the contest on YouTube. Over time, Justin added more videos of himself singing, and his relatives weren't the only ones to take notice. More than 55 million fans also logged on to watch Justin perform the songs of his favorite artists, including Usher, Ne-Yo, and Stevie Wonder.

At 15, Justin already had two hit singles of his own, and his first album, *One World*, was a huge success. Justin talked to TFK Kid Reporter Sarah Horbacewicz about how music has changed his life.

TFK: At 15, you released your first album. Can you tell me how this happened?

JUSTIN BIEBER: It started on YouTube. I put videos up just for friends and family, and it got really big on the Internet. Scooter Braun, who is now my manager, saw the videos. He flew me down to Atlanta, where I got to meet Usher.

TFK: How would you describe your style of music?

JUSTIN: I would describe my style of music as R&B pop music.

TFK: Do you think your success has changed your life in any way?

JUSTIN: Yeah, I've gotten to travel the world, and I don't think I would ever have been able to do that. That was a lot of fun, and so is being able to meet all these great and really nice people, like you.

TFK: What do you like to do when you're not singing or performing?

JUSTIN: When I'm not singing or performing, I like to just hang out with my friends, go golfing, go to the movies—just regular stuff.

TFK: How do you balance school and your music career?

JUSTIN: School is always really important, more important than my music. I have a tutor, and she travels with me.

TFK: Whom do you look up to?

JUSTIN: I look up to Michael Jackson as an artist. I look up to Usher. I look up to a lot of different people.

TFK: Do you have any new celebrity friends, and do you still hang out with your old friends?

JUSTIN: I still hang out with my old friends, but I'm also friends with Taylor Swift.

TFK: Did music come naturally to you, or did you push yourself to become who you are today?

JUSTIN: I really didn't try to do any of this, so I guess it came naturally.

TFK: How much do you practice?

JUSTIN: I probably should practice more, but I practice every day, pretty much.

THE AMERICAN MUSIC AWARDS

november 22, 2009

ARTIST OF THE YEAR: Taylor Swift

FAVORITE MALE ARTIST, POP OR ROCK: Michael Jackson

FAVORITE FEMALE ARTIST, POP OR ROCK: Taylor Swift

FAVORITE BAND, DUO OR GROUP, POP OR ROCK: The Black Eyed Peas

FAVORITE ALBUM, POP OR ROCK: *Number Ones,* Michael Jackson

FAVORITE MALE ARTIST, COUNTRY: Keith Urban

FAVORITE FEMALE ARTIST, COUNTRY: Taylor Swift

FAVORITE BAND, DUO OR GROUP, COUNTRY: Rascal Flatts

FAVORITE ALBUM, COUNTRY: *Fearless,* Taylor Swift

FAVORITE MALE ARTIST, SOUL/RHYTHM & BLUES: Michael Jackson

FAVORITE FEMALE ARTIST, SOUL/RHYTHM & BLUES: Beyoncé

FAVORITE BAND, DUO OR GROUP, SOUL/RHYTHM & BLUES: The Black Eyed Peas

FAVORITE ALBUM, SOUL/RHYTHM & BLUES: *Number Ones*, Michael Jackson

FAVORITE MALE ARTIST, RAP/HIP-HOP: Jay-Z

FAVORITE ALBUM, RAP/HIP-HOP: *Blueprint 3,* Jay-Z

FAVORITE ARTIST, ALTERNATIVE ROCK: Green Day

FAVORITE ARTIST, LATIN: Aventura

FAVORITE ALBUM: *Twilight* soundtrack

T-MOBILE BREAKTHROUGH ARTIST AWARD: Gloriana

guess what? Michael Jackson's album, *Thriller*, is the best-selling album of all time.

Alicia Keys and Jay-Z

The Black Eyed Peas

Keith Urban

2010 Nickelodeon Kids' Choice Awards

March 27, 2010

Favorite Male Singer: **Jay-Z**

Favorite Female Singer: **Taylor Swift**

Favorite Music Group: **The Black Eyed Peas**

Favorite Song: **"You Belong with Me," Taylor Swift**

Music

TEEN CHOICE AWARDS

AUGUST 10, 2009

ALBUM, FEMALE ARTIST: *Fearless*, Taylor Swift

ALBUM, GROUP: *Lines, Vines and Trying Times*, Jonas Brothers

ALBUM, MALE ARTIST: *We Sing, We Dance, We Steal Things*, Jason Mraz

FEMALE ARTIST: Taylor Swift

MALE ARTIST: Jason Mraz

BREAKOUT ARTIST: David Archuleta

HOOK UP: "Just Dance," Lady Gaga featuring Colby O'Donis

SINGLE: "The Climb," Miley Cyrus

LOVE SONG: "Crush," David Archuleta

R&B ARTIST: Beyoncé

R&B TRACK: "Single Ladies (Put a Ring on It)," Beyoncé

RAP ARTIST: Kanye West

RAP/HIP-HOP TRACK: "Boom Boom Pow," The Black Eyed Peas

ROCK GROUP: Paramore

ROCK TRACK: "Decode," Paramore

SOUNDTRACK: *Twilight*

SUMMER SONG: "Before the Storm," Jonas Brothers featuring Miley Cyrus

TOUR: David Archuleta/Demi Lovato

Jason Mraz

Jason Mraz grew up in Virginia and became interested in musical theater as a young man. After high school, he spent a year studying musical theater in New York City but then began concentrating on playing the guitar and writing his own songs. *We Sing, We Dance, We Steal Things* is Mraz's third album. Of the 12 songs featured on the CD, "I'm Yours" is probably the best known. It climbed to the Number 6 spot on the Billboard Hot 100, which is a weekly list of the most popular songs in the country. The song spent 76 weeks on the charts—that's almost a year and a half!

guess what?

Jason Mraz is a vegan. That means he doesn't eat any meat or dairy products—only food derived from plants.

Miley Cyrus

Paramore

158

MTV VIDEO MUSIC AWARDS

SEPTEMBER 13, 2009

Beyoncé

VIDEO OF THE YEAR: "Single Ladies (Put a Ring on It)," Beyoncé

BEST MALE VIDEO: "Live Your Life," T.I.

BEST FEMALE VIDEO: "You Belong with Me," Taylor Swift

BEST ROCK VIDEO: "21 Guns," Green Day

BEST HIP-HOP VIDEO: "We Made You," Eminem

BEST POP VIDEO: "Womanizer," Britney Spears

BEST ART DIRECTION: "Paparazzi," Lady Gaga

BEST CHOREOGRAPHY: "Single Ladies (Put a Ring on It)," Beyoncé

BEST NEW ARTIST: Lady Gaga

BEST DIRECTION: "21 Guns," Green Day

BEST EDITING: "Single Ladies (Put a Ring on It)," Beyoncé

BREAKTHROUGH VIDEO: "Lessons Learned," Matt and Kim

Green Day

Taylor Swift

Singer-songwriter Taylor Swift was born in Wyomissing, Pennsylvania, on December 13, 1989. A music lover from an early age, she performed at local fairs, sporting events, and karaoke contests. Swift was only 14 years old when SONY/ATV Publishing hired her to write songs–the youngest person ever to be a staff songwriter at the company. She scored her first country hit with the song "Tim McGraw" in 2006. Later, her *Romeo and Juliet*–themed song "Love Story" was a hit on both country and pop charts. Swift chalks up her success to writing music that her fans can relate to. She has said, "If you listen to my albums, it's like reading my diary."

Music

GRAMMY AWARDS

JANUARY 31, 2010

Kings of Leon

RECORD OF THE YEAR: *Use Somebody,* Kings of Leon

ALBUM OF THE YEAR: *Fearless,* Taylor Swift

SONG OF THE YEAR: "Single Ladies (Put a Ring on It)," Beyoncé

BEST FEMALE POP VOCAL PERFORMANCE: "Halo," Beyoncé

Taylor Swift

BEST MALE POP VOCAL PERFORMANCE: "Make It Mine," Jason Mraz

BEST POP PERFORMANCE BY A DUO OR GROUP: "I Gotta Feeling," The Black Eyed Peas

BEST POP COLLABORATION: "Lucky," Jason Mraz and Colbie Caillat

BEST POP VOCAL ALBUM: *The E.N.D.*, The Black Eyed Peas

BEST SOLO ROCK VOCAL PERFORMANCE: "Working on a Dream," Bruce Springsteen

BEST ROCK SONG: "Use Somebody," Kings of Leon

BEST ROCK ALBUM: *21st Century Breakdown*, Green Day

BEST DANCE RECORDING: "Poker Face," Lady Gaga

BEST ELECTRONIC/DANCE ALBUM: *The Fame*, Lady Gaga

Lady Gaga

BEST R&B SONG: "Single Ladies (Put a Ring on It)," Beyoncé

BEST CONTEMPORARY R&B ALBUM: *I Am . . . Sasha Fierce*, Beyoncé

BEST RAP SOLO PERFORMANCE: "D.O.A. (Death of Auto-Tune)," Jay-Z

BEST RAP SONG: "Run This Town," Jay-Z, Rihanna, and Kanye West

BEST FEMALE COUNTRY VOCAL PERFORMANCE: "White Horse," Taylor Swift

BEST MALE COUNTRY VOCAL PERFORMANCE: "Sweet Thing," Keith Urban

BEST COUNTRY SONG: "White Horse," Taylor Swift

BEST COUNTRY ALBUM: *Fearless,* Taylor Swift

BEST LATIN POP ALBUM: *Sin Frenos,* La Quinta Estación

BEST MUSICAL ALBUM FOR CHILDREN: *Family Time*, Ziggy Marley

Zac Brown

BEST MUSICAL SHOW ALBUM: *West Side Story*

BEST NEW ARTIST: Zac Brown Band

Got Rhythm?

By Vickie An and Josephine Bila

Do you enjoy singing along to the radio? Can you picture yourself onstage being cheered on by thousands of adoring fans? Here are a few games that will transform you into a virtual musician or DJ.

RHYTHM HEAVEN

If you ever find yourself tapping your foot to a beat or snapping your fingers in time with a catchy tune, then *Rhythm Heaven* may be the game for you. To play, simply tap, hold, flick, or slide your stylus to the beat of the music on the Nintendo DS touch screen.

With more than 50 imaginative mini-games, *Rhythm Heaven* provides hours of game play and lots of variety. Each stage presents new challenges that range from singing along with the glee club to playing table tennis. Players must successfully complete the rhythm tests in order to move on to the next round, collect medals, and unlock special content.

BAND HERO

Pop music may be fun to listen to, but now it's fun to play—with your own band members! The makers of *Guitar Hero* have now added *Band Hero* to the musical mix. Put Mom on the drums and Dad on the bass, while you play guitar or sing to all your favorite tunes. The game's featured artists include Taylor Swift, Fall Out Boy, and the Jackson 5. Go ahead and rock your way to superstardom!

LEGO ROCK BAND

Are you ready to rock? This new family-friendly game merges the multiplayer music experience of *Rock Band* with the creativity and humor of the Lego video games. Players will be able to customize their own avatars, instruments, bandmates, and entourages. Strum and sing along to current pop hits from groups like the All-American Rejects or classic chart-toppers like Queen and David Bowie.

As you successfully complete songs and rock challenges, you'll collect Lego studs that will unlock additional content and special vehicles that will take your band on tour. You'll perform in all kinds of venues, from local clubs to huge stadiums and even outer space! Isn't it time you built your inner rock star?

MYSTERY PERSON

Clue 1: I was born and raised in the early 1900s in New Orleans, Louisiana. The city is known as the birthplace of jazz.

Clue 2: I was an amazing trumpeter and one of the most influential jazz artists in history. My hits include "What a Wonderful World."

Clue 3: I also appeared in several films. The last one was *Hello, Dolly* in 1969. I died in 1971.

Who am I? _____

Answer on page 245.

Music

Remembering Lincoln

By Brenda Iasevoli

More than 200 years after his birth, Abraham Lincoln still captures our imagination. He is the bearded man in the stovepipe hat, and the face on the penny and the five-dollar bill. But who is the man behind the image? Why does he still matter?

"Abraham Lincoln lived a great American story," Harold Holzer, a leading expert on Lincoln, told TFK. "He showed that any young person in this country, regardless of where he starts or how poor he is, can rise to the highest opportunities."

BORN IN A LOG CABIN

Lincoln was born in Kentucky on February 12, 1809. His parents were poor farmers. Young Abe's mother and father were uneducated. Lincoln attended school for no more than a year. But he read every chance he got. He did not go to law school. Instead, he studied on his own and earned a law license.

In 1858, Lincoln ran for the U.S. Senate. He spoke against slavery. Lincoln did not win the Senate seat, but his words impressed voters. Two years later, he was elected the 16th President of the United States. He promised to keep slavery out of new states in the West. "If slavery is not wrong," he said, "nothing is wrong."

NORTH VS. SOUTH

People in the South depended on slaves to work on farms. Southerners saw Lincoln's election as a threat to their way of life. Within months of the election, seven states broke away from the Union. They formed the Confederate States of America. Later, four more states joined the Confederacy.

Lincoln was determined to keep the United States together. In his first speech as President, he said, "We are not enemies, but friends." He said that he did not intend to outlaw existing slavery. But on April 12, 1861, the long and bloody Civil War between the North and South began.

Almost two years later, Lincoln signed the Emancipation Proclamation. "If ever my name goes into history, it will be for this act, and my whole soul is in it," Lincoln said. "Free, free, free," an ex-slave told a Washington newspaper after the Proclamation. "Oh how good it is to be free, and to know that what I earn is mine and that no man can ever say he owns my body or my soul."

A NOBLE IDEA LIVES ON

In his inaugural address, President Obama told Americans, "The time has come. . . to carry forward that precious gift, that noble idea, passed on from generation to generation: the God-given promise that all are equal, all are free, and all deserve a chance to pursue their full measure of happiness." Lincoln would have agreed.

Abraham and Tad Lincoln

Lincoln's Life

Abraham Lincoln was a farm boy who grew up to become President. He led the United States during the Civil War.

1809 On February 12, Abraham Lincoln is born in a one-room log cabin in Kentucky.

1816 The Lincoln family moves to a farm in southern Indiana.

1837 Lincoln moves to Springfield, Illinois, and begins practicing law.

1842 He marries Mary Todd. They eventually have four children: Robert, Eddie, Willie, and Tad.

1847 Lincoln is elected to the U.S. House of Representatives.

1858 While running for the U.S. Senate against Stephen A. Douglas, Lincoln debates Douglas seven times, opposing slavery. Lincoln loses the race, but gains national attention.

1860 Lincoln is elected the 16th President. Within months, seven Southern states secede, or break away, from the Union. They form the Confederacy, and are later joined by four more states.

1861 On April 12, Confederates open fire on Fort Sumter, in Charleston, South Carolina. The Civil War begins.

1863 On January 1, Lincoln signs the Emancipation Proclamation. It frees the slaves in seceding states. From July 1 to 3, Union and Confederate soldiers battle in Gettysburg, Pennsylvania. On November 19, Lincoln goes to the battlefield and gives his most famous speech, the Gettysburg Address.

1864 Lincoln is reelected President.

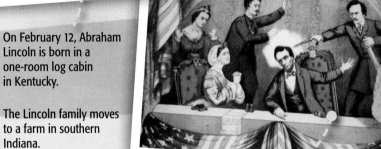

1865 The Civil War ends on April 9. Five days later, Lincoln is shot and killed by John Wilkes Booth while watching a play at Ford's Theater in Washington, D.C. On December 6, the 13th Amendment is passed. It permanently outlaws slavery.

TOP 5 Oldest Presidents

Abraham Lincoln was 51 years old when he won the presidential election. At age 42, Theodore Roosevelt was the youngest person to serve as President. Here are the nation's oldest leaders.

1. **Ronald Reagan,** 69 years old
2. **William Henry Harrison,** 68 years old
3. **James Buchanan,** 65 years old
4. **Zachary Taylor,** 64 years old
5. **George H. W. Bush,** 64 years old

1

George Washington **SERVED 1789–1797**

Born: February 22, 1732, in Virginia   Died: December 14, 1799
Political Party: None (first term), Federalist (second term)
Vice President: John Adams   First Lady: Martha Dandridge Custis

guess what? *George Washington was inaugurated in New York in 1789 and in Philadelphia in 1793. He is the only President to be inaugurated in two cities.*

2

John Adams **SERVED 1797–1801**

Born: October 30, 1735, in Massachusetts   Died: July 4, 1826
Political Party: Federalist
Vice President: Thomas Jefferson   First Lady: Abigail Smith

guess what? *On July 4, 1826, John Adams's last words were, "Thomas Jefferson survives." Adams was not aware that Jefferson had died shortly before him on the very same day.*

3

Thomas Jefferson **SERVED 1801–1809**

Born: April 13, 1743, in Virginia   Died: July 4, 1826
Political Party: Democratic-Republican
Vice Presidents: Aaron Burr, George Clinton
First Lady: Martha Wayles Skelton

guess what? *Although Thomas Jefferson was a talented writer, he was not a gifted public speaker. He conducted most of his business, including discussions with members of Congress and his Cabinet, in writing. Jefferson's two inaugural addresses were his only public speeches.*

4

James Madison **SERVED 1809–1817**

Born: March 16, 1751, in Virginia   Died: June 28, 1836
Political Party: Democratic-Republican
Vice Presidents: George Clinton, Elbridge Gerry
First Lady: Dorothy "Dolley" Payne Todd

guess what? *James Madison was the primary author of the U.S. Constitution. He signed the historic document in 1787. He and George Washington are the only two signers of the Constitution to go on to become President.*

5

James Monroe **SERVED 1817–1825**

Born: April 28, 1758, in Virginia   Died: July 4, 1831
Political Party: Democratic-Republican
Vice President: Daniel D. Tompkins   First Lady: Elizabeth "Eliza" Kortright

guess what? *James Monroe ran for his second term with very little opposition. He received all but one of the electoral votes. At the time, there were 235 electors. Today there are 538.*

6

John Quincy Adams **SERVED 1825–1829**

Born: July 11, 1767, in Massachusetts   Died: February 23, 1848
Political Party: Democratic-Republican
Vice President: John C. Calhoun   First Lady: Louisa Catherine Johnson

guess what? *John Quincy Adams is the only person to serve in the House of Representatives after being President.*

Andrew Jackson  SERVED 1829–1837 ⑦

Born: March 15, 1767, in South Carolina **Died:** June 8, 1845
Political Party: Democratic
Vice Presidents: John C. Calhoun, Martin Van Buren
First Lady: Rachel Donelson Robards

 Andrew Jackson was the first President to face an assassination attempt. The would-be assassin's gun misfired and the President overpowered him.

Martin Van Buren SERVED 1837–1841 ⑧

Born: December 5, 1782, in New York **Died:** July 24, 1862
Political Party: Democratic
Vice President: Richard M. Johnson **First Lady:** Hannah Hoes

 Martin Van Buren's ancestors were from the Netherlands. Both he and his wife, Hannah, grew up speaking Dutch at home.

William Henry Harrison
 SERVED 1841 ⑨

Born: February 9, 1773, in Virginia **Died:** April 4, 1841
Political Party: Whig
Vice President: John Tyler **First Lady:** Anna Tuthill Symmes

 William Henry Harrison was the first presidential candidate to use a campaign slogan. His slogan, "Tippecanoe and Tyler Too," referred to the Battle of Tippecanoe, a conflict fought between U.S. forces and Native American warriors in the Indiana Territory in 1811.

John Tyler SERVED 1841–1845 ⑩

Born: March 29, 1790, in Virginia **Died:** January 18, 1862
Political Party: Whig
Vice President: None **First Ladies:** Letitia Christian (d. 1842), Julia Gardiner

 John Tyler named his Virginia estate Sherwood Forest, likening himself to the heroic outlaw Robin Hood.

James K. Polk SERVED 1845–1849 ⑪

Born: November 2, 1795, in North Carolina **Died:** June 15, 1849
Political Party: Democratic
Vice President: George M. Dallas **First Lady:** Sarah Childress

 During James Polk's term in office, First Lady Sarah Childress Polk did not allow dancing in the White House.

Zachary Taylor SERVED 1849–1850 ⑫

Born: November 24, 1784, in Virginia **Died:** July 9, 1850
Political Party: Whig
Vice President: Millard Fillmore **First Lady:** Margaret Mackall Smith

 Zachary Taylor found out that he had been nominated for the presidency a few days late because when his notification letter arrived, he was asked to pay for the postage and refused.

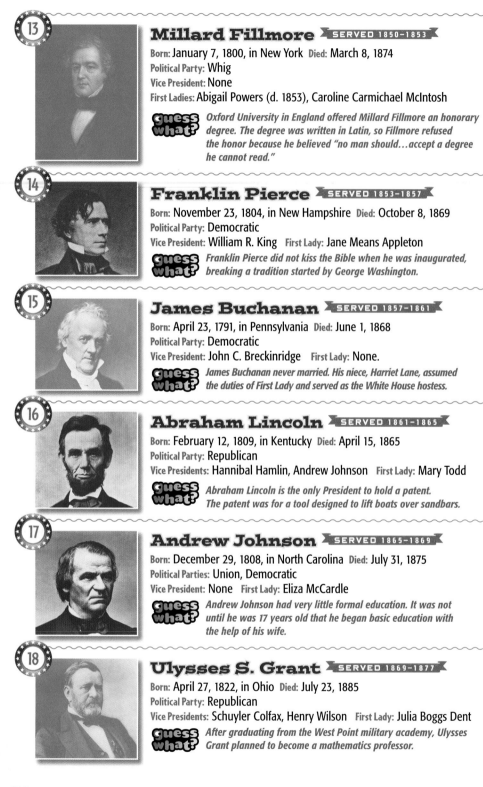

Millard Fillmore — SERVED 1850–1853

13

Born: January 7, 1800, in New York **Died:** March 8, 1874
Political Party: Whig
Vice President: None
First Ladies: Abigail Powers (d. 1853), Caroline Carmichael McIntosh

guess what? *Oxford University in England offered Millard Fillmore an honorary degree. The degree was written in Latin, so Fillmore refused the honor because he believed "no man should…accept a degree he cannot read."*

Franklin Pierce — SERVED 1853–1857

14

Born: November 23, 1804, in New Hampshire **Died:** October 8, 1869
Political Party: Democratic
Vice President: William R. King **First Lady:** Jane Means Appleton

guess what? *Franklin Pierce did not kiss the Bible when he was inaugurated, breaking a tradition started by George Washington.*

James Buchanan — SERVED 1857–1861

15

Born: April 23, 1791, in Pennsylvania **Died:** June 1, 1868
Political Party: Democratic
Vice President: John C. Breckinridge **First Lady:** None.

guess what? *James Buchanan never married. His niece, Harriet Lane, assumed the duties of First Lady and served as the White House hostess.*

Abraham Lincoln — SERVED 1861–1865

16

Born: February 12, 1809, in Kentucky **Died:** April 15, 1865
Political Party: Republican
Vice Presidents: Hannibal Hamlin, Andrew Johnson **First Lady:** Mary Todd

guess what? *Abraham Lincoln is the only President to hold a patent. The patent was for a tool designed to lift boats over sandbars.*

Andrew Johnson — SERVED 1865–1869

17

Born: December 29, 1808, in North Carolina **Died:** July 31, 1875
Political Parties: Union, Democratic
Vice President: None **First Lady:** Eliza McCardle

guess what? *Andrew Johnson had very little formal education. It was not until he was 17 years old that he began basic education with the help of his wife.*

Ulysses S. Grant — SERVED 1869–1877

18

Born: April 27, 1822, in Ohio **Died:** July 23, 1885
Political Party: Republican
Vice Presidents: Schuyler Colfax, Henry Wilson **First Lady:** Julia Boggs Dent

guess what? *After graduating from the West Point military academy, Ulysses Grant planned to become a mathematics professor.*

Rutherford B. Hayes

 SERVED 1877–1881

Born: October 4, 1822, in Ohio **Died:** January 17, 1893
Political Party: Republican
Vice President: William A. Wheeler **First Lady:** Lucy Ware Webb

Rutherford B. Hayes hosted the first Easter egg roll at the White House in 1878.

 19

James A. Garfield

Born: November 19, 1831, in Ohio **Died:** September 19, 1881
Political Party: Republican
Vice President: Chester A. Arthur **First Lady:** Lucretia Rudolph

James Garfield's mother, Eliza Ballou Garfield, was the first mother of a President to witness her son's inauguration.

 20

Chester A. Arthur

SERVED 1881–1885

Born: October 5, 1829, in Vermont **Died:** November 18, 1886
Political Party: Republican
Vice President: None **First Lady:** Ellen Lewis Herndon

Chester Arthur suffered from Bright's disease, a kidney disease that was fatal at the time. Although he struggled with the illness during his presidency, he kept his disease secret from the public.

21

Grover Cleveland SERVED 1885–1889 22

Born: March 18, 1837, in New Jersey **Died:** June 24, 1908
Political Party: Democratic
Vice President: Thomas A. Hendricks **First Lady:** Frances Folsom

The Baby Ruth candy bar was named after Grover Cleveland's daughter Ruth.

Benjamin Harrison

SERVED 1889–1893

Born: August 20, 1833, in Ohio **Died:** March 13, 1901
Political Party: Republican
Vice President: Levi P. Morton
First Ladies: Caroline Lavina Scott (d. 1892), Mary Scott Lord Dimmick

Benjamin Harrison was nicknamed Little Ben because of his small stature—he was only 5 feet, 6 inches tall (168 cm).

23

Grover Cleveland SERVED 1893–1897 24

Born: March 18, 1837, in New Jersey **Died:** June 24, 1908
Political Party: Democratic
Vice President: Adlai E. Stevenson **First Lady:** Frances Folsom

When Grover Cleveland claimed he was going on a fishing trip during the summer of 1893, he was actually getting a cancerous growth removed from his mouth. The public did not discover this until 1917, nearly 10 years after his death.

Presidents

William McKinley SERVED 1897–1901

Born: January 29, 1843, in Ohio **Died:** September 14, 1901
Political Party: Republican
Vice Presidents: Garret A. Hobart, Theodore Roosevelt **First Lady:** Ida Saxton

guess what? *William McKinley often wore a red carnation in the lapel of his jacket. The state of Ohio, where McKinley was born and raised, selected the red carnation as its official state flower in honor of President McKinley.*

Theodore Roosevelt SERVED 1901–1909

Born: October 27, 1858, in New York **Died:** January 6, 1919
Political Party: Republican
Vice President: Charles W. Fairbanks **First Lady:** Edith Kermit Carow

guess what? *Teddy Roosevelt was the first American to win a Nobel Peace Prize. He was given the award in 1906 for his work negotiating the end of the Russo-Japanese War.*

William H. Taft SERVED 1909–1913

Born: September 15, 1857, in Ohio **Died:** March 8, 1930
Political Party: Republican
Vice President: James S. Sherman **First Lady:** Helen Herron

guess what? *At more than 300 pounds (136 kg), William Taft was the heaviest President. A larger bathtub had to be installed in the White House to accommodate his size.*

Woodrow Wilson SERVED 1913–1921

Born: December 28, 1856, in Virginia **Died:** February 3, 1924
Political Party: Democratic
Vice President: Thomas R. Marshall
First Ladies: Ellen Louise Axson (d. 1914), Edith Bolling Galt

guess what? *To save money on lawn care during World War I, Woodrow Wilson brought in sheep to graze on the White House grounds. The sheep were also used as part of a fundraiser—their wool was sold to raise money for the Red Cross.*

Warren G. Harding SERVED 1921–1923

Born: November 2, 1865, in Ohio **Died:** August 2, 1923
Political Party: Republican
Vice President: Calvin Coolidge **First Lady:** Florence Kling

guess what? *Warren Harding was the first President to visit both Alaska and Canada.*

Calvin Coolidge SERVED 1923–1929

Born: July 4, 1872, in Vermont **Died:** January 5, 1933
Political Party: Republican
Vice President: Charles G. Dawes **First Lady:** Grace Anna Goodhue

guess what? *In 1923, Calvin Coolidge became the first President to have his State of the Union address broadcast on the radio.*

Herbert C. Hoover
 SERVED 1929–1933 **31**

Born: August 10, 1874, in Iowa **Died:** October 20, 1964
Political Party: Republican
Vice President: Charles Curtis **First Lady:** Lou Henry

Herbert Hoover and his wife, Lou, lived in China during the Boxer Rebellion. During the conflict, he risked his life to save a group of Chinese children in the city of Tientsin.

Franklin D. Roosevelt
 SERVED 1933–1945 **32**

Born: January 30, 1882, in New York **Died:** April 12, 1945
Political Party: Democratic
Vice Presidents: John Garner, Henry Wallace, Harry S Truman
First Lady: Anna Eleanor Roosevelt

When Franklin D. Roosevelt selected Frances Perkins to be the secretary of labor in 1933, it was the first time a woman was appointed to the U.S. Cabinet.

Harry S Truman
 SERVED 1945–1953 **33**

Born: May 8, 1884, in Missouri **Died:** December 26, 1972
Political Party: Democratic
Vice President: Alben W. Barkley
First Lady: Elizabeth "Bess" Virginia Wallace

As a young person, Harry Truman woke up on many mornings at 5 a.m. to practice the piano for two hours.

Dwight D. Eisenhower
SERVED 1953–1961 **34**

Born: October 14, 1890, in Texas **Died:** March 28, 1969
Political Party: Republican
Vice President: Richard M. Nixon **First Lady:** Mamie Geneva Doud

Dwight Eisenhower spent 38 years as a member of the U.S. Army. During that time, he lived in 27 different homes.

John F. Kennedy
SERVED 1961–1963 **35**

Born: May 29, 1917, in Massachusetts **Died:** November 22, 1963
Political Party: Democratic
Vice President: Lyndon B. Johnson **First Lady:** Jacqueline Lee Bouvier

John F. Kennedy was the first President to hold a televised press conference.

Lyndon B. Johnson
 **SERVED 1963–1969** **36**

Born: August 27, 1908, in Texas **Died:** January 22, 1973
Political Party: Democratic
Vice President: Hubert H. Humphrey
First Lady: Claudia Alta "Lady Bird" Taylor

 Lyndon Johnson worked as a janitor to support himself while attending Southwest Texas State Teachers College at San Marcos, Texas.

Presidents

37

Richard M. Nixon SERVED 1969–1974

Born: January 9, 1913, in California Died: April 22, 1994
Political Party: Republican
Vice Presidents: Spiro T. Agnew, Gerald R. Ford
First Lady: Thelma Catherine "Pat" Ryan

guess what? *Richard Nixon loved to bowl.*

38

Gerald R. Ford SERVED 1974–1977

Born: July 14, 1913, in Nebraska Died: December 26, 2006
Political Party: Republican
Vice President: Nelson A. Rockefeller
First Lady: Elizabeth "Betty" Anne Bloomer Warren

guess what? *Gerald Ford was a dedicated supporter of America's space program. In 1958, he was part of the House Select Committee on Astronautics and Space Exploration, which helped to establish NASA (National Aeronautics and Space Administration).*

39

Jimmy Carter SERVED 1977–1981

Born: October 1, 1924, in Georgia
Political Party: Democratic
Vice President: Walter F. Mondale First Lady: Rosalynn Smith

guess what? *Jimmy Carter grew up on a peanut farm in a tiny town outside of Plains, Georgia. The town's population was only about 600 people.*

40

Ronald Reagan SERVED 1981–1989

Born: February 6, 1911, in Illinois Died: June 5, 2004
Political Party: Republican
Vice President: George H.W. Bush First Lady: Nancy Davis

guess what? *Before becoming President, Ronald Reagan had a career as an actor. Once, while filming a movie, another actor fired a pistol too close to Reagan's head. The incident left him hard of hearing in his right ear.*

41

George H.W. Bush SERVED 1989–1993

Born: June 12, 1924, in Massachusetts
Political Party: Republican
Vice President: J. Danforth Quayle First Lady: Barbara Pierce

guess what? *George H.W. Bush was the first Vice President since Martin Van Buren to win a presidential election. He was also the first former Vice President since Martin Van Buren to lose when running for reelection.*

42

Bill Clinton SERVED 1993–2001

Born: August 19, 1946, in Arkansas
Political Party: Democratic
Vice President: Albert Gore Jr. First Lady: Hillary Rodham

guess what? *The U.S. Secret Service gave Bill Clinton the code name Eagle. Hillary Clinton was known as Evergreen, and the Clinton's only daughter, Chelsea, was called Energy.*

George W. Bush
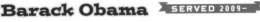

Born: July 6, 1946, in Connecticut
Political Party: Republican
Vice President: Richard B. Cheney   **First Lady:** Laura Welch

George W. Bush was the first son of a President to become President since 1825, when John Quincy Adams became President. (His father was John Adams, the nation's second President.)

Barack Obama

Born: August 4, 1961, in Hawaii
Political Party: Democratic
Vice President: Joe Biden   **First Lady:** Michelle Robinson

On his Inauguration Day, Barack Obama invited the Jonas Brothers to the White House as a surprise for his daughters, Malia and Sasha.

Presidential Succession

This list shows the order of people who would take over if a sitting President died, resigned, or was removed from office.

1. Vice President
2. Speaker of the House
3. President Pro Tempore of the Senate
4. Secretary of State
5. Secretary of the Treasury
6. Secretary of Defense
7. Attorney General
8. Secretary of the Interior
9. Secretary of Agriculture
10. Secretary of Commerce
11. Secretary of Labor
12. Secretary of Health and Human Services
13. Secretary of Housing and Urban Development
14. Secretary of Transportation
15. Secretary of Energy
16. Secretary of Education
17. Secretary of Veterans Affairs
18. Secretary of Homeland Security

MYSTERY PERSON

Clue 1: I served as the ninth President of the United States. I was born in Virginia in 1773.

Clue 2: My 1840 campaign slogan was "Tippecanoe and Tyler too."

Clue 3: My presidential term was the shortest in U.S. history. It lasted only a month. I fell sick after my inauguration. I was the first President to die in office.

Who am I? _____

Answer on page 245.

Migration Marvel

A NEW STUDY PROVES THAT THE ARCTIC TERN MAKES THE LONGEST YEARLY MIGRATION IN THE WORLD

By Brenda Iasevoli

Arctic tern in Iceland

An international team of scientists has officially crowned the Arctic tern the king of long-distance migration. Every year, the tiny bird flies nearly 45,000 miles (72,420 km) on its trip from the northern tip of Greenland to the shores of Antarctica and back again. That's equal to 60 trips around the Earth in the bird's lifetime.

"This is a mind-boggling achievement for a bird of just over 100 grams [about 3.5 ounces]," says Carsten Egevang of the Greenland Institute of Natural Resources. He was one of the main scientists on the tern study.

TRACKING TERNS

Scientists have known for years that the bitty bird, which weighs as much as a stick of butter, makes a lengthy migration. But scientists could never before prove that it was the longest in the world. The instruments used to follow large animals, such as geese, penguins, and seals, were too big for the terns to carry.

The development of tiny tracking devices has allowed scientists from Greenland, Denmark, the United States, Great Britain, and Iceland to map the Arctic tern's massive pole-to-pole migration. Scientists attached devices called geolocators to the legs of 50 birds in Greenland and 20 in Iceland. The geolocators are about the size of a small paperclip.

WHAT A TRIP!

What did the scientists learn? The terns make a month-long stop in the middle of the North Atlantic Ocean to feed on small fish and shrimp-like animals called krill. As they continue their journey south, half of the birds fly down the coast of Africa. The others fly across the Atlantic Ocean and down the coast of South America. The two groups meet in Antarctica.

The scientists were surprised to find that the birds did not take the shortest route back to their breeding grounds in Greenland. Instead, they flew in an S-shaped pattern over the Atlantic, adding 1,000 miles (1,609 km) to their journey. Ian Stenhouse, a scientist on the study, says that the birds follow wind systems to help them on their return trip. "They get a lift from the wind," Stenhouse told TFK, "and this allows them to make the return journey in about half the time they spent going south."

But the biggest discovery of all was how far these birds actually travel each year. Scientists had estimated the round-trip to be about 20,000 miles (32,187 km). The new tracking instruments showed that the Arctic tern travels twice that distance.

Migration routes of the Arctic tern

MONERA This kingdom consists of one-celled bacteria that don't have a nucleus. Some are able to move, and others aren't. Some can make their own food to live on, but others need to feed on things outside themselves.

Bacteria

Paramecia

FUNGI These organisms have more than one cell, and their cells have nuclei. Fungi generally can't move. They must rely on outside sources for their food. This kingdom includes molds, mushrooms, and yeast.

Mold

The Five Kingdoms

PROTISTA The one-celled organisms of this kingdom share the same characteristics as those in the monera kingdom except that they have a nucleus. Examples of protista are amoebas, paramecia, and some one-celled algae.

Every form of life belongs to one of five kingdoms.

ANIMALS The animal kingdom consists of multicellular organisms that move and rely on outside sources for food. In general, they are the most complex creatures on Earth, with most having the ability to communicate and form social groups. Examples of animals are sponges, jellyfish, insects, amphibians, fish, and mammals, including humans. (For more on the animal kingdom, see page 17.)

Trees

PLANTS The plant kingdom consists of multicellular organisms that have nuclei and remain in one place. In a process called photosynthesis, plants use sunlight and a chemical called chlorophyll to produce their own food. Some plants produce flowers and fruit; others don't. Examples of the plant kingdom are multicellular algae, ferns, mosses, trees, shrubs, wildflowers, fruits, and vegetables.

Bees

Branches of Science

Science is the field of knowledge that systematically studies and organizes information, and draws conclusions based on measurable results. Traditionally, scientists have classified their fields into three branches: physical sciences, earth sciences, and life sciences. Social sciences, technology, and mathematics may also be included. Each branch has many fields of study; some are described here.

A chemistry teacher displays a model of molecules.

PHYSICAL SCIENCES These sciences study the properties of energy and matter, as well as their relationship to one another. **Physics** seeks to explain how the universe behaves through the workings of matter, energy, force, and time. **Chemistry** is the study of chemical elements and how they interact on an atomic level. **Astronomy** is the study of space, its galaxies, and all heavenly objects.

EARTH SCIENCES These sciences focus on the Earth and study its composition and structure. **Geology** is the study of Earth's rock formations. **Geography** concerns the study and mapping of Earth's terrain. **Oceanography** focuses on Earth's oceans and their currents and habitats. **Meteorology** is the study of weather. **Paleontology** focuses on the remains of ancient plants and animals.

guess what?

Oceanographers study the oceans, which cover more than 70% of Earth's surface. The average depth of the ocean is 2.5 miles (4 km). Scientists estimate that 90% of ocean life exists in the deepest parts of the ocean, known as the abyss.

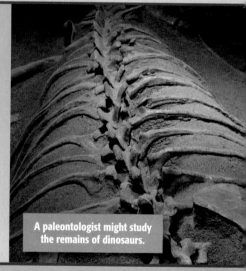

A paleontologist might study the remains of dinosaurs.

LIFE SCIENCES These sciences explore the nature of living things. **Biology** covers how living things evolve, reproduce, thrive, and relate to one another. It is further divided into many branches, including **botany**, which focuses on plants; **zoology,** which deals with animals; and **microbiology,** which zeroes in on microscopic organisms.

going green

There are several new types of scientific study dedicated to learning about the environment and devising ways to solve environmental problems. For example, environmental chemists may investigate air, water, and soil pollution, and an atmospheric scientist may study greenhouse gases or pollutants found in the air.

Botanist

SOCIAL SCIENCES These sciences investigate how humans behave and live together. **Psychology** explores individual human behavior, and **sociology** analyzes group behavior among humans. **Anthropology** studies human physical traits, as well as cultures and languages. **Economics** is the study of how money, goods, and businesses affect society. **Law** focuses on the rules of society, and **political science** examines governmental processes and institutions.

Psychologist

guess what?

Archaeology is a branch of anthropology that deals with the life and culture of ancient peoples. Louis and Mary Leakey were a husband-and-wife team of archaeologists and anthropologists who uncovered fossils in 1959 in Tanzania, Africa, that were about 1.75 million years old. In 1960, Mary Leakey found the bones of *Homo habilis*, an ancestor of humans that lived roughly 2 million years ago. These scientists proved that humans were much older than previously thought.

Computer scientist

TECHNOLOGY This branch is concerned with the practical application of scientific knowledge. **Engineering** is concerned with the design and construction of objects, machines, and systems. **Biotechnology** is the application of biological processes to create medicines and vaccines, and to alter food and crops. **Computer science** focuses on meeting industrial needs by creating computers and developing new software.

MATHEMATICS This science differs from other branches because it deals with concepts rather than physical evidence. Its focus is on measuring numeric relationships, analyzing data, and predicting outcomes. **Arithmetic** uses only numbers to solve problems, while **algebra** uses both numbers and unknown variables in the form of letters. **Geometry** is the study of two- and three-dimensional shapes. **Calculus** involves the computation of problems that contain constantly changing measurements. Nearly all scientists use mathematics in their research.

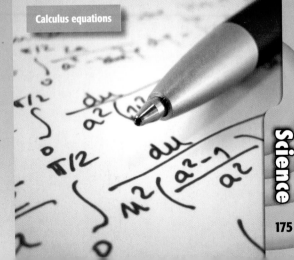
Calculus equations

Science

PERIODIC TABLE OF ELEMENTS

Elements are the building blocks of all matter. They are substances so tiny they cannot be divided into any other substances. Some common elements are carbon, oxygen, nitrogen, and sodium. There are currently 118 elements on the periodic table.

The smallest unit of each element is an atom. Atoms are made up of three kinds of particles: protons, electrons, and neutrons. Each element has a unique number of protons. The elements on the periodic table are organized by their atomic number, which is the number of protons in the nucleus of the element. The periodic table also lists the atomic mass of an element, which refers to the number of protons and neutrons found in an element.

FAMILIES

- Nonmetals
- Alkali metals
- Alkaline Earth metals
- Transition elements
- Other metals
- Metalloids
- Halogens
- Noble gases
- Lanthanides
- Actinides

Period	Group 1	2	3	4	5	6	7	8	9	10
1	1 H 1.008									
2	3 Li 6.941	4 Be 9.012								
3	11 Na 22.99	12 Mg 24.31								
4	19 K 39.10	20 Ca 40.08	21 Sc 44.96	22 Ti 47.88	23 V 50.94	24 Cr 52	25 Mn 54.94	26 Fe 55.85	27 Co 58.93	28 Ni 58.69
5	37 Rb 85.47	38 Sr 87.62	39 Y 88.91	40 Zr 91.22	41 Nb 92.91	42 Mo 95.96	43 Tc (98)	44 Ru 101.1	45 Rh 102.9	46 Pd 106.4
6	55 Cs 132.9	56 Ba 137.3	57 La 138.9	72 Hf 178.5	73 Ta 180.9	74 W 183.9	75 Re 186.2	76 Os 190.2	77 Ir 192.2	78 Pt 195.1
7	87 Fr (223)	88 Ra (226)	89 Ac (227)	104 Rf (267)	105 Db (268)	106 Sg (271)	107 Bh (272)	108 Hs (270)	109 Mt (276)	110 Ds (281)

58 Ce 140.1	59 Pr 140.9	60 Nd 144.2	61 Pm (147)	62 Sm 150.4	63 Eu 152	64 Gd 157.3
90 Th 232	91 Pa (231)	92 U (238)	93 Np (237)	94 Pu (244)	95 Am (243)	96 Cm (247)

				18
				2 **He** 4.003

13	**14**	**15**	**16**	**17**	
5 **B** 10.81	6 **C** 12.01	7 **N** 14.01	8 **O** 16	9 **F** 19	10 **Ne** 20.18
13 **Al** 26.98	14 **Si** 28.09	15 **P** 30.97	16 **S** 32.07	17 **Cl** 35.45	18 **Ar** 39.95

11	**12**						
29 **Cu** 63.55	30 **Zn** 65.39	31 **Ga** 69.72	32 **Ge** 72.64	33 **As** 74.92	34 **Se** 78.96	35 **Br** 79.9	36 **Kr** 83.8
47 **Ag** 107.9	48 **Cd** 112.4	49 **In** 114.8	50 **Sn** 118.7	51 **Sb** 121.8	52 **Te** 127.6	53 **I** 126.9	54 **Xe** 131.3
79 **Au** 197	80 **Hg** 200.5	81 **Tl** 204.4	82 **Pb** 207.2	83 **Bi** 209	84 **Po** (209)	85 **At** (210)	86 **Rn** (222)
111 **Rg** (272)	112 **Cn** (277)	113 **Uut** (284)	114 **Uuq** (289)	115 **Uup** (288)	116 **Uuh** (293)	117 **Uus** 0	118 **Uuo** (294)

65 **Tb** 158.9	66 **Dy** 162.5	67 **Ho** 164.9	68 **Er** 167.3	69 **Tm** 168.9	70 **Yb** 173	71 **Lu** 175
97 **Bk** (247)	98 **Cf** (251)	99 **Es** (252)	100 **Fm** (257)	101 **Md** (258)	102 **No** (259)	103 **Lr** (262)

Science

POLICE LINE

REAL–LIFE CSI: Sleuthing with Science

THE SCENE: A dead man lies faceup on the lawn by the front door to a small country hotel. When the crime scene investigation (CSI) team arrives, they find that the man has been shot. Muddy footprints lead toward an empty garage, where tire marks lead down the driveway. The man has no identification on him, his clothes are torn, and his hands are bloody, as if a struggle took place. What can the team do with these clues and others to solve the crime?

To find out About the crime

- A medical examiner can remove the bullet and send it to a ballistics lab, where an expert will examine it. Groove marks on the bullet will match the inside of the barrel of the gun that fired it.

- Investigators can make casts and molds of the footprints to determine the estimated height and weight of each possible suspect.

- The tire tracks can be photographed and compared with those made by a suspect's vehicle.

- The chemical composition of any unrecognizable material can be determined by various techniques, such as gas chromatography, mass spectrometry, and laser ablation spectrometry. These processes burn a tiny part of the evidence, turning it into a gas, which is then analyzed for the elements it contains.

guess what?

The markings in the iris, or colored part of the human eye, are different for every human being. Today, there are machines that can scan these physical traits and record that data for future reference. Biometrics, the measurement of unique life characteristics, is becoming a valuable tool in the high-tech security field.

To find out About the Victim

- The medical examiner can do an autopsy on the body to determine the time of death. He or she would look for any substances in the stomach that might indicate what the victim recently ate or drank. An autopsy might also reveal whether a victim has been poisoned.

- The victim's sweat, tears, saliva, and blood can be analyzed to reveal his DNA, which can be used to determine his identity.

- If the victim has been dead for a while, there may be flies or other insects on or in the body. Based on the insects found at the scene, a forensic entomologist (a scientist who specializes in insects) might be able to determine how long the body has been lying at the site.

- Information about the victim's teeth can be matched with dental records to help in identification.

To find out About the Murderer

- If the medical examiner finds any foreign blood or hair at the scene, or skin under the victim's fingernails, the DNA of these samples can help to identify the person they came from.

- Investigators can dust objects that the murderer might have touched, such as the garage door handle, in order to find fingerprints.

- If a suspect is caught soon after the shooting, special tape can be applied to his or her fingers. When examined under an electron microscope, the tape will reveal whether any gunpowder residue is present. If there is, it may prove that a suspect had recently fired a gun.

What Is an Entomologist?

Entomology is the scientific study of insects, and entomologists are the scientists who work in this branch of zoology. Some entomologists study the life cycle, characteristics, and behavior of different kinds of insects. Others work to control insect populations or keep insects from transmitting diseases to humans or livestock. Insects make up the largest class in the animal kingdom. There are nearly 10,000,000,000,000,000,000 (10 quintillion) insects in the world, and new ones are still being identified. They include 5-inch-long (13 cm) beetles, locusts that can fly at a speed of 21 miles (33 km) per hour, and poisonous ants.

Insects in the Garden TFK GAME

Count all the insects. Color in one box in the graph for each insect you count. Answer on page 245.

INSECT COUNT										
Ladybugs										
Dragonflies										
Butterflies										
Honeybees										
	1	2	3	4	5	6	7	8	9	10

Science

Saturn's Super-Sized Ring

NASA SCIENTISTS DISCOVER A HUGE NEW RING AROUND SATURN

By Suzanne Zimbler

When you think of Saturn, you probably picture a planet surrounded by colorful rings. For years, Saturn was known to have seven main rings. But in October 2009, NASA scientists announced that they had spotted an eighth.

This never-before-seen ring is not only Saturn's biggest, but it is also the largest in our solar system. "This is one super-sized ring," said Anne Verbiscer, one of the astronomers who worked on the study. According to scientists, the ring is so huge that it would take 1 billion Earths to fill it.

Here is an artist's depiction of Saturn inside the newly discovered ring. Notice how small the planet is compared to the giant ring.

The enormous ring around Saturn is made up of ice and dust particles. "The particles are so far apart," says Verbiscer, "that if you were to stand in the ring, you wouldn't even know it."

SEEING RINGS

Four hundred years ago, Galileo got the first glimpse of Saturn's rings using his telescope. NASA scientists also used a telescope to spot the new ring. The Spitzer telescope, launched in 2003, orbits the sun while taking pictures of faraway objects in space.

The new ring is almost invisible to the human eye. But the Spitzer telescope can detect the glow of extremely cold objects, such as the giant ring, which is -316°F (-158°C).

MADE OF MOONDUST

The colossal hoop circles Saturn from a distance of 8 million miles. It is 50 times farther away from Saturn than the planet's other rings. It also has a completely different tilt.

The giant ring is made up of a thin layer of dust. Scientists think the dust comes from Saturn's moon

There are many craters on the surface of Saturn's moon, Iapetus.

Phoebe. Why? Phoebe orbits within the ring. Its dents and marks make it clear that Phoebe has been hit many times by space rocks and clumps of ice. Each time Phoebe is hit, dust flies into space and goes into orbit, adding particles to the giant ring.

MOON-MADE MYSTERY

The discovery of the new ring may also provide scientists with an answer to a mystery. Another of Saturn's moons, Iapetus, has a bright side and a very dark side. Scientists have long wondered why. With the discovery of the new ring, they now believe that dust from the giant ring is moving toward Saturn and slamming into Iapetus.

"Astronomers have long suspected that there is a connection between Phoebe and the dark material on Iapetus," said scientist Douglas Hamilton. "This new ring provides convincing evidence of that relationship."

a Galactic Glossary

The term **CELESTIAL BODY** refers to an object found in space, such as a star or a planet.

A **MOON** is a natural satellite made of rock or ice that orbits a planet or other solar body. Mercury and Venus have no moons. Mars has two. Neptune has 13. Uranus has 27, and Jupiter has 62! Some moons orbit dwarf planets that are large enough to have a field of gravity to hold them in an orbit. Earth has just one moon, which is about 240,000 miles (386,000 km) away.

Four of Jupiter's moons: Io, Europa, Ganymede, and Callisto

A **LIGHT-YEAR** is the distance light travels in one year, about 5.88 trillion miles (9.5 trillion km). Other than the sun, the closest stars to Earth are Alpha and Proxima Centauri. They are 4.2 and 4.4 light-years away. That's far!

A **COMET** is made up mostly of ice, dust, and gases, and moves in an **elliptical orbit** around the sun. An elliptical orbit is oval-shaped, rather than circular. Some comets may take less than 200 years to move around the sun; others can take thousands of years. Because the paths of comets may take them deep into space before they come back toward the sun, they are only seen for short periods of time. Halley's Comet, for example, is only seen on Earth every 76 years. Some scientists say that comets look like big, dirty snowballs.

Solar eclipse

An **ECLIPSE** happens when one celestial body falls into the shadow of another. The most common types of eclipses are **solar** (when the moon passes between Earth and the sun) and **lunar** (when the full moon passes through some portion of Earth's shadow). Sometimes stars eclipse one another, too. A lunar eclipse can be seen from the entire half of the Earth facing it, while a solar eclipse can only be seen by people along a narrow path on the surface of Earth.

METEOROIDS are rocks found in space. They are usually fragments of comets or asteroids. When a meteoroid enters Earth's atmosphere, it usually burns up. If it does not, it is known as a **meteor** or a **falling star**. Meteors that hit the ground are called **meteorites**. The largest meteorite ever recorded was found in Namibia. It weighed 66 tons (60 m tons).

Meteorite

Barringer Meteorite Crater in Arizona

From the Universe to You

The UNIVERSE consists of billions of stars. Some of these stars have planets orbiting them. Scientists aren't sure if every star has other bodies orbiting it, and many stars are simply too far away to observe with today's tools. A GALAXY is a large collection of stars, dust, and gas held together by gravity. A typical galaxy consists of billions of stars. It is estimated that there are 50 billion galaxies in the universe!

UNIVERSE
▼
GALAXIES
▼
THE MILKY WAY
▼
OUR SOLAR SYSTEM
▼
EARTH
▼
YOU

THE SOLAR SYSTEM

Our solar system is the space neighborhood that includes one star (the sun) and its eight large planets, a few dwarf planets, about 170 moons, and a lot of space junk (such as bits of rock and ice).

Our sun and its planets exist in an area of space called the Milky Way galaxy. The Milky Way is huge. If it were possible to travel at the speed of light (186,282 miles per second/299,792 km per second), it would take 100,000 years to go from one end of the Milky Way to the other. There are other galaxies out there, far beyond the edges of the Milky Way. Together, all the galaxies make up the universe.

Planets move around the sun. Early astronomers were able to see the six planets closest to the sun simply by looking up, but Uranus, Neptune, and Pluto (which is now considered a dwarf planet) can be seen only by telescope. Mercury, Venus, Earth, and Mars are called the terrestrial planets because they have solid, rocky bodies. The outer four planets do not have surfaces because they are made up of gases.

guess what?

Stars and planets look almost exactly alike in the night sky, but there are a couple of ways to tell them apart. Because stars are so much farther away from us than planets are, they appear to twinkle. A planet's light remains steady.

PLANETS

MERCURY

How big is it? **With a diameter of 3,025 miles (4,868.3 km), it is less than half the size of Earth.**

Where is it? **About 36 million miles (57.9 million km) from the sun**

How's the weather? **The average surface temperature is 354°F (179°C).**

Moons: **0** Rings: **0**

MARS

How big is it? **With a diameter of 4,222 miles (6,795 km), it is roughly half as big as Earth.**

Where is it? **About 141.71 million miles (227.9 million km) from the sun**

How's the weather? **The average surface temperature is −82°F (−63°C).**

Moons: **2** Rings: **0**

URANUS

How big is it? **With a diameter of 31,693 miles (51,005 km), it is about four times the size of Earth.**

Where is it? **About 1.78 billion miles (2.87 billion km) from the sun**

How's the weather? **The average surface temperature is −353°F (−214°C).**

Moons: **27** Rings: **13**

VENUS

How big is it? **With a diameter of 7,504 miles (12,077 km), it is a little smaller than Earth.**

Where is it? **About 67.24 million miles (108.2 million km) from the sun**

How's the weather? **The average surface temperature is 847°F (463°C).**

Moons: **0** Rings: **0**

EARTH

How big is it? **Earth has a diameter of 7,926.2 miles (12,756 km).**

Where is it? **About 92.9 million miles (149.6 million km) from the sun**

How's the weather? **The average surface temperature is 59°F (15°C).**

Moons: **1** Rings: **0**

JUPITER

How big is it? **At 88,650 miles (142,668 km), its diameter is 11 times bigger than Earth's.**

Where is it? **About 483.9 million miles (778.3 million km) from the sun**

How's the weather? **The average surface temperature is −238°F (−150°C).**

Moons: **62** Rings: **3**

SATURN

How big is it? **With a diameter of 74,732 miles (120,270 km), it is 9 1/2 times the size of Earth.**

Where is it? **About 885.9 million miles (1.43 billion km) from the sun**

How's the weather? **The average surface temperature is −285°F (−176°C).**

Moons: **62** Rings: **Thousands**

NEPTUNE

How big is it? **With a diameter of 30,707 miles (49,418 km), it is four times bigger than Earth.**

Where is it? **About 2.8 billion miles (4.5 billion km) from the sun**

How's the weather? **The average surface temperature is −373°F (−225°C).**

Moons: **13** Rings: **9, made up of thousands of "ringlets"**

SPACE FIRSTS

People have been studying space since ancient times. Until the 1950s, however, all of this exploration took place on the ground. Here are some of the many milestones in space exploration that have occurred since then.

1969 moon landing

SpaceShipOne

Sally Ride

1957 Russian scientists launch *Sputnik*, the first manmade satellite, into space.

1958 NASA (National Aeronautics and Space Administration) is founded. It launches *Explorer 1*, the first U.S. satellite, into the atmosphere.

1961 Cosmonaut (the Russian equivalent of an astronaut) Yuri Gagarin becomes the first person to see Earth from space. Later that year, aboard the *Freedom 7*, Alan Shepard is the first American in space.

1962 Astronaut John Glenn is the first American to orbit Earth in a spaceship.

1969 American Neil Armstrong walks on the surface of the moon.

1971 The Russians launch Salyut I, the first space station.

1976 NASA's *Viking I* lands on Mars.

1978 NASA's *Pioneer 1* and *Pioneer 2* reach Venus's atmosphere.

This 1979 photo montage of Jupiter and its moons was taken by *Voyager*.

1979–81 NASA's *Voyager* craft passes Jupiter and Saturn, taking the first close-up pictures of these planets.

1981 The first space shuttle, *Columbia*, is launched by NASA.

1983 America's first woman astronaut, Sally Ride, travels into space.

1990 The Hubble Space Telescope is launched.

1998 Construction begins on the International Space Station (ISS).

2001 The *NEAR Shoemaker* spacecraft touches down on an asteroid.

2002 NASA's Mars *Odyssey* space probe maps the surface of Mars.

2003 China launches *Shenzhou 5*, its first manned space mission.

2004 *SpaceShipOne*, the first privately launched spacecraft, lifts off from Mojave, California.

2008 India launches its first unmanned moon mission.

New Views of Space

The Hubble Space Telescope soars through space, 350 miles (563 km) above Earth. It has a crystal-clear view of the universe and has sent pictures of deep space back to Earth since 1990. Some of these images are close-ups of the planets and of stars being born.

Astronauts from the space shuttle spent 13 days repairing the space telescope in May 2009. After the repairs were complete, NASA released amazing new photos from the "eye in the sky."

HUBBLE'S NEW START

Hubble's new parts are more sensitive to light. They make the telescope's pictures brighter and clearer than ever before. "This is truly Hubble's new beginning," says NASA's Edward Weiler. The new batch of photos taken by Hubble shows galaxies, planets, and nebulas. One photo shows gassy areas that look like butterfly wings. The glow is hot gas and dust. Hubble could not capture such an amazing level of detail before its recent round of repairs.

Over the next few years, the space telescope will take pictures of our solar system and more distant worlds. Scientists hope that Hubble will create a picture-perfect portrait of our universe.

photo of a dying star in July 2009. What looks like colorful butterfly wings is actually a mass of incredibly hot gas. The gas is more than 36,000°F (19,982°C), and is moving through space faster than 600,000 miles (965,606 km) per hour.

Using the newly installed Wide Field Camera 3, Hubble captured this image of the approximately 100,000 stars in the center of the giant star cluster, Omega Centauri. Omega Centauri is one of the biggest star clusters orbiting the Milky Way galaxy and can even be seen without a telescope.

guess what? The Hubble Space Telescope circles Earth every 97 minutes, traveling at about 5 miles (8 km) per second.

Stephan's Quintet is a group of five galaxies located within the Pegasus constellation, about 300 million light-years away. The different colors indicate the different ages of the stars in the photo. A young star appears blue; an aging star looks red.

This photo of Jupiter is the clearest one ever taken of the giant planet. The dark spot on the bottom of the planet is debris from a comet or asteroid that entered Jupiter's atmosphere and broke apart.

Space

An astronaut captured this photo of the entire International Space Station in 2005, while aboard the space shuttle *Discovery*. The body of water in the background is the Caspian Sea.

Food on the International Space Station is often served in bags. The bags can be attached to walls, trays, or shelves using Velcro. This space meal includes beefsteak, creamed spinach, crackers, cheese spread, shortbread cookies, and candy-coated peanuts.

Laboratory in the Sky

Launched in 1998, the International Space Station (ISS) got its first permanent crew by 2000. This high-tech space lab is a collaboration between NASA and the space programs of Russia, Japan, Canada, Brazil, and 11 nations that are part of the European Space Agency (ESA). While in orbit, astronauts from around the world perform scientific research and work to build and maintain the station. Many of their experiments focus on humans' ability to live and work in space over long periods of time. The station has a greenhouse aboard, which can be used to determine if people living on Mars could grow plants for food and oxygen. The ISS crew also studies the physiological effects of weightless living and exposure to radiation in space.

guess what? *Because the International Space Station orbits close to Earth, it can be seen with the naked eye.*

Everyday Routines in Space

In space, astronauts need to do many of the same things they do every day at home—such as eating meals, brushing their teeth, and going to the bathroom. Without gravity, everything floats. So how do they do it?

Astronauts eat some foods, like fruits, the same way they would on Earth. Other dishes are dehydrated and need added water to make a meal. Storing food can be tricky because there are no refrigerators in space. After brushing their teeth, astronauts either swallow the toothpaste or spit it into a washcloth. As for going to the bathroom, the cabin contains a toilet that collects solid wastes and releases

Astronauts even play games aboard the ISS.

liquids into space, where they vaporize. The trick is to close the lid before any waste floats into the cabin due to the lack of gravity.

guess what? *Astronauts have condiments—like ketchup and hot sauce—in space. Unlike at home, salt and pepper are available only in liquid form. If an astronaut tried to shake out the tiny salt grains or pepper flakes, they would drift all over the cabin!*

Aboard the International Space Station, astronauts do not always have access to fresh fruit and vegetables. These deliveries make them very happy!

SPACE SUITS

An astronaut's space suit is like a traveling home, containing all the things needed to sustain and protect life. Space suits provide oxygen to breathe and pressurization to keep the astronaut's blood from boiling in space. Temperatures in space vary greatly, from 248°F to −148°F (120°C to −100°C). An astronaut's body heat is trapped inside a suit, so to maintain a normal body temperature, the suit contains an undergarment that carries cold liquid close to the skin.

The main part of the HELMET is made of clear plastic. The clear bubble is covered by a visor coated with a thin layer of gold. The gold protects the astronaut's eyes by filtering out the harmful rays from the sun.

Astronauts cannot see the displays and control module while wearing a space suit. In order to see the settings, an astronaut will wear a small MIRROR on his or her wrist. The settings on the module are written backward so they appear normally when viewed in a mirror.

SAFETY TETHERS keep astronauts from drifting off into space.

The PRIMARY LIFE SUPPORT SUBSYSTEM (PLSS) looks like a backpack. It contains an oxygen tank, water-cooling equipment, a radio, a fan, and a back-up battery.

The DISPLAYS AND CONTROL MODULE, attached to the front of the suit, contains the electronic display and control panel for the entire space suit.

The LOWER TORSO ASSEMBLY includes pants, boots, and the lower half of the waist closure. The closure is metal and connects the lower torso assembly to the hard upper torso. The red stripe on the pants helps to identify the astronaut inside the suit. (Another astronaut's suit may feature a white stripe, or it may have a red-and-white pattern instead.)

guess what?

Most dust is harmless, but dust in space can be incredibly dangerous. Space suits are built to protect astronauts from the dust that can travel faster than a speeding bullet!

MYSTERY PERSON

Clue 1: I was born in Worcester, Massachusetts, in 1882.

Clue 2: When I was 17, my biggest wish was to one day fly humans to Mars. In 1926, I launched the first liquid-fuel rocket.

Clue 3: My inventions helped later space exploration get off the ground. I am sometimes called the father of space flight.

Who am I? _____

Answer on page 245.

Space

Sports

FROM TIME FOR KIDS MAGAZINE

Q and A with Tony Hawk

By Jeff Dooley

Many consider Tony Hawk to be the greatest skateboarder of all time. In 2009, he released a skateboarding video game, *Tony Hawk: Ride*, which features a brand-new skateboard-like platform (instead of a controller) that allows players to move just like the pros, performing spins, kick flips, and grabs on their way to a perfect run. Read on to find out more!

TFK: What excites you about *Tony Hawk: Ride*?

TONY HAWK: How the board maneuvers and how it responds. The board senses every kind of motion on it. It senses your hands and your feet coming in, so you can push the board with your feet and bring your hand in for grabs. When I first came up with the idea, I didn't know we could make it this advanced and responsive, so you can feel like you are really on a skateboard. Once they put in the infrared sensors, it was like, "Oh, this is it."

TFK: Do you think people who don't skate will be able to pick up the video game pretty quickly?

HAWK: Oh, yeah—we've seen plenty do that already. It's funny, because my wife got on it and instantly did this trick that I had been trying to do, and I was like, "How'd you do that one?"

TFK: When you were starting out as a young skater, did you ever question whether or not you wanted to keep doing it?

HAWK: No. When I first went to the skate park, and I saw what was really possible—these guys were flying out of empty swimming pools—I was like, "I want to do that. I want to fly." So then I started going to skate parks on a regular basis. Every time I went skating, I would learn something. Even if it was just a subtle technique, I was getting better at it. And I never felt like I was getting better at basketball or baseball.

TFK: Who are some of the skaters you enjoy watching now?

HAWK: I really like watching Bob Burnquist because he's well rounded and really innovative. I also like Chaz Ortiz. I don't know if you've heard of a kid named Alex Perelson, but he's the new vert skater. He won the 2009 Maloof Cup last summer when he pulled his first 900 in the finals.

TFK: What advice do you have for young skaters who are just starting out?

HAWK: Take it slow. This stuff takes years to learn. It takes repeated attempts. It takes perseverance. A lot of people think they're just going to go in, learn a kick flip, get some coverage, get sponsored, and make money, but it takes a long time to develop all those skills. And you've got to work at it. It's fun, but it's a job.

TFK: You are someone who achieved a great deal of success at a very young age. What advice do you have for kids who hope to make a similar impact?

HAWK: The best advice I can give kids is, "Do what you love doing," even if it doesn't seem like it's the coolest thing at the time. If you enjoy it, you have to follow it, because ultimately you're going to be happy going to work every day. Just believe in yourself and do something because you love it.

Tony Hawk and his son Riley in 2009

X Games

The X Games, held every winter and summer, showcase the best in extreme sports. Athletes from all over the world participate, showing off their skills with a skateboard, snowboard, bike, rally car, snowmobile, or pair of skis. Some events are based on pure speed, while others reward competitors for style and tricks.

2010 WINTER X GAMES WINNERS

SKIING: **Tyler Walker** (Mono Skier X), **Bobby Brown** (Big Air), **Chris Del Bosco** (Men's Skier X), **Ophelie David** (Women's Skier X), **Bobby Brown** (Men's Slopestyle), **Kaya Turski** (Women's Slopestyle), **Kevin Rolland** (Men's SuperPipe), **Jen Hudak** (Women's SuperPipe), **Peter Olenick** (SuperPipe High Air)

SNOWBOARDING: **Halldor Helgason** (Big Air), **Nate Holland** (Men's Snowboarder X), **Lindsey Jacobellis** (Women's Snowboarder X), **Eero Ettala** (Men's Slopestyle), **Jenny Jones** (Women's Slopestyle), **Shaun White** (Men's SuperPipe), **Gretchen Bleiler** (Women's SuperPipe)

SNOWMOBILING: **Levi LaVallee** (Knock Out), **Justin Hoyer** (Freestyle), **Tucker Hibbert** (Snocross), **Heath Frisby** (Best Trick), **Mike Schultz** (Snocross Adaptive)

2009 SUMMER X GAMES WINNERS

SKATEBOARDING: **Jake Brown** (Big Air), **Danny Way** (Big Air Rail Jam), **Marisa Dal Santo** (Women's Street), **Paul Rodriguez** (Men's Street), **Lyn-Z Adams Hawkins** (Women's Vert), **Pierre-Luc Gagnon** (Men's Vert), **Sam Bosworth** (Vert Jam), **Rune Glifberg** (SuperPark)

MOTO X: **Kyle Loza** (Best Trick), **TIE: Ricky Carmichael** and **Ronnie Renner** (Step Up), **Josh Hansen** (Men's Racing), **Ashley Fiolek** (Women's Racing), **Ivan Lazzarini** (SuperMoto), **Blake Williams** (Freestyle)

BMX: **Garrett Reynolds** (Street), **Kevin Robinson** (Big Air), **Scotty Cranmer** (Park), **Jamie Bestwick** (Vert)

RALLY CAR RACING: **Kenny Brack**

Gretchen Bleiler

Blake Williams

RECORD BREAKER

On December 31, 2009, in front of a crowd of 20,000 people, extreme-sports legend Travis Pastrana broke the world record for longest rally car jump. The previous record was 171 feet (52 m). Pastrana jumped his trademark Red Bull rally car a whopping 269 feet (82 m). The winner of four straight Rally America championships, Pastrana is also the first person ever to do a double backflip on a motorcycle.

Sports

189

FOOTBALL

Super Bowl XLIV

Super Bowl MVP Drew Brees

The Indianapolis Colts and the New Orleans Saints went head to head in Super Bowl XLIV on February 7, 2010, in Miami, Florida. It had been a storybook season for the Saints, who made it to the Super Bowl for the first time in their 43-year history. But their success went beyond football. The Saints come from New Orleans, a city still struggling to rebuild and thrive after being devastated by Hurricane Katrina in 2005. For the players and the city, a win for the Saints would be an amazing boost.

The Colts, led by regular-season MVP quarterback Peyton Manning, came into the Super Bowl as the favorite, and right from the start, they showed why. They took the early lead after a field goal and a 19-yard touchdown pass from Manning to wide receiver Pierre Garçon. They were leading 10–6 at half time and looked like they were in control of the game.

But Saints coach Sean Payton had different ideas. He called some of the gutsiest plays in Super Bowl history, helping the Saints take the lead at the start of the second half. The Saints were up 24–17 with three minutes and 12 seconds left in the fourth quarter. The Colts were trying to tie the game, but Saints defender Tracy Porter intercepted a pass by Manning. Porter then returned the ball 74 yards for a touchdown to seal the championship

for the Saints. Final score: Saints 31, Colts 17.

Quarterback Drew Brees was named MVP after completing 32 passes (out of 39 attempts) and throwing for 288 yards and two touchdowns. His 32 completions tied a Super Bowl record. But the victory was about more than just him. "We play for so much more than ourselves," he explained. "We played for our city." He asked, "Four years ago, who would've thought that we'd be here? . . . But the organization and the city decided to rebuild together. And that's what we did."

Regular-season MVP Peyton Manning

guess what? The Roman numerals XLIV stand for the number 44. Super Bowl XLIV is the 44th in NFL history. For more on Roman numerals, see page 148.

2009–2010 NFL AWARD WINNERS

MOST VALUABLE PLAYER Peyton Manning, quarterback, Indianapolis Colts

OFFENSIVE PLAYER OF THE YEAR Chris Johnson, running back, Tennessee Titans

DEFENSIVE PLAYER OF THE YEAR Charles Woodson, cornerback, Green Bay Packers

OFFENSIVE ROOKIE OF THE YEAR Percy Harvin, wide receiver, Minnesota Vikings

DEFENSIVE ROOKIE OF THE YEAR Brian Cushing, linebacker, Houston Texans

COACH OF THE YEAR Marvin Lewis, Cincinnati Bengals

COMEBACK PLAYER OF THE YEAR Tom Brady, quarterback, New England Patriots

Chris Johnson

Texas vs. Alabama

Crimson Tide Comes Out on Top

The final game of the BCS (Bowl Championship Series) marks the end of the college football season every year. Last year's game, held in Pasadena, California, on January 7, 2010, pitted the Texas Longhorns against the Alabama Crimson Tide. After remaining undefeated throughout the regular season, the Crimson Tide beat the Longhorns 37–21 in the BCS Championship Game.

Mark Ingram

2010 BCS BOWL GAMES AND SCORES

ROSE BOWL (Pasadena, California)
Ohio State 26, Oregon 17

SUGAR BOWL (New Orleans, Louisiana)
Florida 51, Cincinnati 24

ORANGE BOWL (Miami, Florida)
Iowa 24, Georgia Tech 14

FIESTA BOWL (Glendale, Arizona)
Boise State 17, Texas Christian 10

GATOR BOWL (Jacksonville, Florida)
Florida State 33, West Virginia 21

Heisman Trophy

Every year, the Heisman award, named after legendary coach John Heisman, is given to the most outstanding player in college football, "whose performance best exhibits the pursuit of excellence with integrity." The winner of this important award is chosen by a panel of sportswriters from around the country.

Days before playing in the BCS Championship Game, Alabama sophomore running back Mark Ingram took home the Heisman Trophy. In the closest vote in the Heisman Committee's 75-year history, Ingram became the first-ever Heisman winner from Alabama. He also became the second player ever to win the Heisman and the BCS title in the same year (Matt Leinart of University of Southern California did it in 2004). It was the third straight year that the Heisman was won by a sophomore.

RECORD BREAKER

With the win over Texas in the BCS Championship Game, Alabama coach Nick Saban became the only coach to win two BCS championships at two different schools. He was the coach at Louisiana State University (LSU) when he earned his first BCS championship victory in 2003.

BASEBALL

Zack Greinke

2009 MLB LEAGUE LEADERS

BATTING
HOME RUNS
American League: (TIE) Carlos Pena, first baseman, Tampa Bay Rays, and Mark Teixeira, first baseman, New York Yankees, 39
National League: Albert Pujols, first baseman, St. Louis Cardinals, 47
BATTING AVERAGE
American League: Joe Mauer, catcher, Minnesota Twins, .365
National League: Hanley Ramirez, shortstop, Florida Marlins, .342

PITCHING
EARNED RUN AVERAGE
American League: Zack Greinke, Kansas City Royals, 2.16
National League: Chris Carpenter, St. Louis Cardinals, 2.24
STRIKEOUTS
American League: Justin Verlander, Detroit Tigers, 269
National League: Tim Lincecum, San Francisco Giants, 261

2009 MLB AWARD WINNERS

MOST VALUABLE PLAYER
American League: Joe Mauer, catcher, Minnesota Twins
National League: Albert Pujols, first baseman, St. Louis Cardinals

CY YOUNG AWARD (BEST PITCHER)
American League: Zack Greinke, Kansas City Royals
National League: Tim Lincecum, San Francisco Giants

ROOKIE OF THE YEAR
American League: Andrew Bailey, relief pitcher, Oakland Athletics
National League: Chris Coghlan, outfielder, Florida Marlins

MANAGER OF THE YEAR
American League: Mike Scioscia, Los Angeles Angels of Anaheim
National League: Jim Tracy, Colorado Rockies

Joe Mauer

Derek Jeter

guess what?

On June 4, 2009, San Francisco Giants pitcher Randy Johnson won his 300th career game, becoming the 24th player (and only the sixth lefty) ever to do so.

RECORD BREAKER

On August 16, 2009, Yankees captain Derek Jeter set the record for most hits as a shortstop with 2,674, passing Luis Aparicio. Less than a month later, Jeter passed Lou Gehrig for most hits ever as a New York Yankee, with 2,722. Gehrig's record had stood for more than seven decades.

2009 World Series

The 2008 champion Philadelphia Phillies returned to the World Series in 2009. This time, they went up against the New York Yankees, who were playing in their 40th World Series. To get there, the Yankees had beaten the Minnesota Twins and Los Angeles Angels of Anaheim in the American League playoffs. They had finished the regular season with the best record in the league (103–59) and were favored to win the series.

Though the Phillies won Game 1 in New York, the Yankees came out on top in the next three games. They only needed one more victory to win the championship. The Phillies rallied in Game 5, but when the series returned to New York for Game 6, the powerful Yankee bats were too much. The Yankees won 7–3, clinching their 27th World Series title, by far the most of any team. Outfielder Hideki Matsui was named MVP of the series after driving in six runs in Game 6. Matsui tied the record for most RBI (runs batted in) in one World Series game.

guess what? *Hideki Matsui became the first-ever Japanese-born player to be named World Series MVP.*

Chula Vista's Nick Conlin slides home.

Little League World Series

On August 30, 2009, the Park View Little League team of Chula Vista, California, beat the Kuei-Shan Little League team of Taoyuan, Chinese Taipei, 6–3. Representing the Western Region of the United States, Chula Vista was down 3–0 in the final game before rallying for the win. They are the fifth U.S. team in a row to win the Little League World Series.

guess what? *The Park View team of Chula Vista is the sixth team from California to take home the top prize at the Little League World Series.*

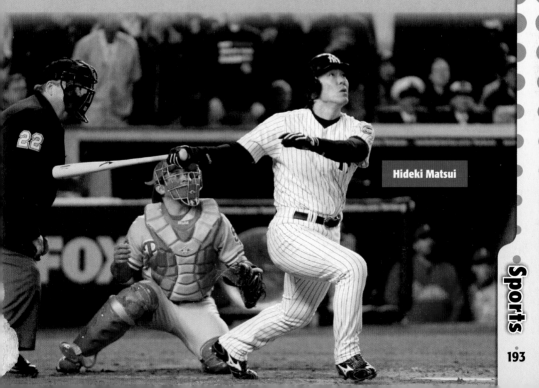
Hideki Matsui

BASKETBALL

NBA Regular Season

2008–2009 NBA LEADERS

SCORING

NAME	TEAM	GAMES PLAYED	POINTS PER GAME
1. Dwyane Wade	Miami Heat	79	30.2
2. LeBron James	Cleveland Cavaliers	81	28.4
3. Kobe Bryant	Los Angeles Lakers	82	26.8

ASSISTS

NAME	TEAM	GAMES PLAYED	ASSISTS PER GAME
1. Chris Paul	New Orleans Hornets	78	11
2. Deron Williams	Utah Jazz	68	10.7
3. Steve Nash	Phoenix Suns	74	9.7

REBOUNDS

NAME	TEAM	GAMES PLAYED	REBOUNDS PER GAME
1. Dwight Howard	Orlando Magic	79	13.8
2. Troy Murphy	Indiana Pacers	73	11.8
3. David Lee	New York Knicks	81	11.7

Dwyane Wade

NBA Finals

In 2009, the Los Angeles Lakers returned to the NBA finals for the second year in a row. They lost to the Boston Celtics in 2008, but won their 15th NBA championship by beating the Orlando Magic four games to one. The Magic, playing in only their second-ever NBA finals, have still never won a title. Though the Lakers won four out of five games, the series featured some very close contests. Two games went into overtime, and another was decided by only four points. In the end, the Lakers' experience helped them win over a much younger Magic team. The series ended with Game 5, when the Lakers won 99–86. It marked the fourth championship for superstar Kobe Bryant, who carried the team throughout the playoffs. Bryant led the Lakers in scoring, assists, free-throw shooting, and minutes played.

Kobe Bryant

guess what?

In 2009, Los Angeles Lakers coach Phil Jackson set his own personal record when the Lakers won the 2009 title. That victory was his 10th NBA championship, enabling him to surpass legendary Boston Celtics coach Red Auerbach for most wins. Jackson's first six wins were in the '90s as coach of the Chicago Bulls. He won his most recent titles as coach of the Lakers.

going green

In April 2009, the NBA partnered with the Natural Resources Defense Council (NRDC) for the first-ever NBA Green Week. To raise money and awareness for protecting the environment, all 30 NBA teams hosted community service events, including tree plantings, recycling drives, and park cleanup days.

WNBA Regular Season

WNBA finals

2009 WNBA Championship

The Phoenix Mercury defeated the Indiana Fever, three games to two, to capture their second WNBA title. Diana Taurasi was named Finals MVP.

GAME 1: Mercury 120, Fever 116 (OT)

GAME 2: Fever 93, Mercury 84

GAME 3: Fever 86, Mercury 85

GAME 4: Mercury 90, Fever 77

GAME 5: Mercury 94, Fever 86

2009 WNBA SEASON LEADERS

SCORING

NAME	TEAM	GAMES PLAYED	POINTS PER GAME
1. Diana Taurasi	Phoenix Mercury	31	20.4
2. Becky Hammon	San Antonio Silver Stars	31	19.5
3. Lauren Jackson	Seattle Storm	26	19.2

ASSISTS

NAME	TEAM	GAMES PLAYED	ASSISTS PER GAME
1. Sue Bird	Seattle Storm	31	5.8
2. Ticha Penicheiro	Sacramento Monarchs	30	5.2
3. Becky Hammon	San Antonio Silver Stars	31	5.0
3. Cappie Poindexter	Phoenix Mercury	34	5.0

REBOUNDS

NAME	TEAM	GAMES PLAYED	REBOUNDS PER GAME
1. Candace Parker	Los Angeles Sparks	25	9.8
2. Erika de Souza	Atlanta Dream	34	9.1
3. Candice Dupree	Chicago Sky	34	7.9
3. Crystal Langhorne	Washington Mystics	34	7.9

Diana Taurasi

College Basketball

2009 NCAA MEN'S DIVISION I CHAMPIONSHIP

TEAM	1ST HALF POINTS	2ND HALF POINTS	FINAL SCORE
North Carolina Tar Heels	55	34	89
Michigan State Spartans	34	38	72

2009 NCAA WOMEN'S DIVISION I CHAMPIONSHIP

TEAM	1ST HALF POINTS	2ND HALF POINTS	FINAL SCORE
Connecticut Huskies	39	37	76
Louisville Cardinals	25	29	54

Sports

HOCKEY

2009 Stanley Cup

In a rematch of the 2008 Stanley Cup final, the Pittsburgh Penguins and the Detroit Red Wings battled again for hockey's highest honor. But this time, it was the Penguins who took home the big silver trophy. The series was not decided until Game 7. Maxime Talbot of the Penguins scored two goals in the second period, and the Penguins won the game, 2–1, to clinch the title. It was only the third time a player had ever scored both of his team's goals in Game 7 of a Stanley Cup final. Penguins' center Evgeni Malkin was named postseason MVP, leading all players with 36 points.

Guess what? *Just two days after the Penguins claimed the Stanley Cup, the Lakers won Game 5 against the Magic to win the NBA championship. Both the Lakers and the Penguins had been runners-up the year before, losing in the 2008 finals.*

2009 NHL AWARD WINNERS

Like most professional sports leagues, the NHL hands out end-of-season awards to its best players and coaches. Here are some of the awards given out in 2009.

AWARD	AWARDED TO...	2009 WINNER (TEAM)
Hart Memorial Trophy	Most valuable player	Alex Ovechkin (Capitals)
Vezina Trophy	Best goalie	Tim Thomas (Bruins)
James Norris Memorial Trophy	Outstanding defenseman	Zdeno Chara (Bruins)
Calder Memorial Trophy	Outstanding rookie	Steve Mason (Blue Jackets)
Lady Byng Memorial Trophy	Player who displays sportsmanship and gentlemanly conduct	Pavel Datsyuk (Red Wings)
Frank J. Selke Trophy	Outstanding defensive forward	Pavel Datsyuk (Red Wings)
Jack Adams Award	Outstanding coach	Claude Julien (Bruins)
Lester B. Pearson Award	Most outstanding player as voted by fellow NHL members	Alex Ovechkin (Capitals)

Alex Ovechkin

Stanley Cup finals

BROUGHT TO YOU BY THE EDITORS OF **Sports Illustrated KIDS**

2010 World Cup

Soccer is the world's most popular sport. And the World Cup is the world's biggest soccer tournament. It is played every four years. In 2010, it is being held for the 19th time from June 11 to July 11 in South Africa. It is the first time the World Cup is taking place in Africa. The tournament begins with eight groups of four teams. Each team plays the other three teams in its group. The top two teams in each group move on to the next round. Here are the opening-round groupings for the 2010 World Cup.

GROUP A: South Africa, Mexico, Uruguay, France

GROUP B: Nigeria, Greece, South Korea, Argentina

GROUP C: England, United States, Algeria, Slovenia

GROUP D: Germany, Australia, Serbia, Ghana

GROUP E: Cameroon, Denmark, Japan, Netherlands

GROUP F: Italy, Paraguay, New Zealand, Slovakia

GROUP G: Brazil, North Korea, Côte d'Ivoire, Portugal

GROUP H: Spain, Switzerland, Honduras, Chile

U.S. vs. Spain at the Confederations Cup

U.S. vs. Brazil

In the 2006 World Cup final, Italy defeated France 5–3.

2009 Confederations Cup

The U.S. men's soccer team pulled off perhaps the biggest victory in its history in 2009, when it beat Spain 2–0 in the semifinals of the FIFA Confederations Cup. Not only was it the first time that the United States had ever advanced to a FIFA tournament final, but they did it against the top team in the world. Prior to taking on the U.S. team, Spain had won 15 straight matches and hadn't lost in 35 games (a tie for the all-time record). The U.S. team ended Spain's streak, pulling off one of the biggest upsets in international soccer history.

The United States then advanced to the final match against Brazil, taking a 2–0 lead in the first half. But Brazil fought back, tying up the game and eventually winning 3–2.

guess what? The World Cup has never been won by a team from somewhere other than Europe or South America. In fact, a non-European or non–South American team has never even made it to the World Cup finals. In 1930, the United States made it as far as the semifinals. South Korea advanced to the semifinals in 2002 to take on Germany.

Sports

2009 Daytona 500

2009 CHASE FOR THE SPRINT CUP RACE RESULTS

The Sprint Cup Series consists of 36 races, starting with the prestigious Daytona 500, and is considered the top racing series of the National Association for Stock Car Auto Racing (NASCAR). The first 26 races make up the regular season as drivers rack up points for their finishes. After that, the 12 drivers with the most points compete in the Chase, the final 10 races of the series. The driver with the most points after those 10 races is awarded the Sprint Cup, NASCAR's greatest prize. In 2009, the Chase ended in the Ford 400 on November 22. Here's how the Chase went down.

RACE	TRACK	WINNER
SYLVANIA 300	New Hampshire Motor Speedway	Mark Martin
AAA 400	Dover International Speedway	Jimmie Johnson
PRICE CHOPPER 400 PRESENTED BY KRAFT FOODS	Kansas Speedway	Tony Stewart
PEPSI 500	Auto Club Speedway	Jimmie Johnson
NASCAR BANKING 500 ONLY FROM BANK OF AMERICA	Lowe's Motor Speedway	Jimmie Johnson
TUMS FAST RELIEF 500	Martinsville Speedway	Denny Hamlin
AMP ENERGY 500	Talladega Superspeedway	Jamie McMurray
DICKIES 500	Texas Motor Speedway	Kurt Busch
CHECKER O'REILLY AUTO PARTS 500 PRESENTED BY PENNZOIL	Phoenix International Raceway	Jimmie Johnson
FORD 400	Homestead-Miami Speedway	Denny Hamlin

2009 CHASE FOR THE SPRINT CUP FINAL STANDINGS

	DRIVER	TOTAL POINTS
1.	Jimmie Johnson	6,652
2.	Mark Martin	6,511
3.	Jeff Gordon	6,473

Indianapolis 500

The Indianapolis 500, or Indy 500, is one of the largest single-day sporting events in the world. Held at the Indianapolis Motor Speedway, the race covers a full 500 miles (804.7 km) and is viewed live by more than 250,000 people. The 93rd Indy 500 took place on May 24, 2009, and was won by Helio Castroneves. It was Castroneves's third Indy 500 victory.

In 2008, Jimmie Johnson tied the record for most consecutive championships. A year later, he broke it. When Johnson finished first in the Chase for the Sprint Cup final standings for the fourth year in a row, he topped the record first set by Cale Yarborough, who won the title in 1976, 1977, and 1978. As Johnson finished in fifth place in the final race of the year (Ford 400), knowing that he had secured enough points for a first-place win, he shouted, "How 'bout some history!"

TENNIS

2009 TENNIS CHAMPIONS

Serena Williams

AUSTRALIAN OPEN
MEN'S SINGLES: Rafael Nadal
MEN'S DOUBLES: Bob Bryan, Mike Bryan
WOMEN'S SINGLES: Serena Williams
WOMEN'S DOUBLES: Serena Williams, Venus Williams

FRENCH OPEN
MEN'S SINGLES: Roger Federer
MEN'S DOUBLES: Lukas Dlouhy, Leander Paes
WOMEN'S SINGLES: Svetlana Kuznetsova
WOMEN'S DOUBLES: Anabel Medina Garrigues, Virginia Ruano Pascual

WIMBLEDON
MEN'S SINGLES: Roger Federer
MEN'S DOUBLES: Daniel Nestor, Nenad Zimonjic
WOMEN'S SINGLES: Serena Williams
WOMEN'S DOUBLES: Serena Williams, Venus Williams

Juan Martín del Potro

U.S. OPEN
MEN'S SINGLES: Juan Martín del Potro
MEN'S DOUBLES: Lukas Dlouhy, Leander Paes
WOMEN'S SINGLES: Kim Clijsters
WOMEN'S DOUBLES: Serena Williams, Venus Williams

DAVIS CUP (MEN'S INTERNATIONAL TEAM TENNIS)
Spain beat the Czech Republic five matches to none.

FED CUP (WOMEN'S INTERNATIONAL TEAM TENNIS)
Italy defeated the United States four matches to none.

TOP 5 Winners of Major Men's Tournaments

The four major tennis tournaments (the Australian Open, French Open, Wimbledon, and the U.S. Open) are known as Grand Slam events. Roger Federer has won the most!

PLAYER	NUMBER OF GRAND SLAM EVENTS WON
1. Roger Federer	16
2. Pete Sampras	14
3. Roy Emerson	12
4. Rod Laver	11
5. Björn Borg	11

GOLF

2009 MAJOR EVENT WINNERS

MEN
MASTERS: Angel Cabrera
U.S. OPEN: Lucas Glover
BRITISH OPEN: Stewart Cink
PGA CHAMPIONSHIP: Y.E. Yang
U.S. AMATEUR CHAMPIONSHIP: Byeong-Hun An

WOMEN
KRAFT NABISCO CHAMPIONSHIP: Brittany Lincicome
LPGA CHAMPIONSHIP: Anna Nordqvist
U.S. WOMEN'S OPEN: Eun-Hee Ji
WOMEN'S BRITISH OPEN: Catriona Matthew
U.S. AMATEUR CHAMPIONSHIP: Jennifer Song

Y.E. Yang

guess what?
There are three types of golf clubs: woods, irons, and putters. Each type of club is used for a different purpose. Woods are used for driving the ball long distances, usually off of the tee. Putters are used for the shortest shots, when golfers need to roll the ball along the green and into the hole. Irons are used for everything in between.

GYMNASTICS

WORLD CHAMPIONSHIPS

The 2009 World Artistic Gymnastics Championships were held for the 41st time in London, England, from October 13 to 18, 2009. Here are the gold-medal winners.

EVENT	GOLD MEDAL	COUNTRY
Men's Individual All-Around	Kohei Uchimura	Japan
Men's Floor	Marian Dragulescu	Romania
Men's Pommel Horse	Zhang Hongtao	China
Men's Rings	Yan Mingyong	China
Men's Vault	Marian Dragulescu	Romania
Men's Parallel Bars	Wang Guanyin	China
Men's High Bar	Zou Kai	China
Women's Individual All-Around	Bridget Sloan	USA
Women's Vault	Kayla Williams	USA
Women's Uneven Bars	He Kexin	China
Women's Balance Beam	Deng Linlin	China
Women's Floor	Elizabeth Tweddle	Great Britain

Bridget Sloan

College Gymnastics

In 2009, the NCAA Women's Gymnastics Championship was won by the University of Georgia Bulldogs. It was their fifth consecutive NCAA title and 10th overall. On the men's side, Stanford University took the top title. It was the first time since 2001 that the title went to a school other than the University of Oklahoma or Penn State.

SURFING

2009 World Surfing Champions

There are three champions recognized every year by the Association of Surfing Professionals (ASP). The titles for best male, female, and longboard surfer are awarded based on points that surfers receive in competitions on the ASP World Tour. In 2009, all three winners came from Australia. Mick Fanning was crowned men's champion for the second time. Stephanie Gilmore took home the women's championship for the third time in a row, and Harley Ingleby was named longboard champ for the first time.

Mick Fanning

guess what? 2009 marked the second time that all three world surfing champions came from Australia. In 1991, Aussies Damien Hardman, Wendy Botha, and Martin McMillan took home the titles. Of the 90 World Surfing Championships awarded, 40 of them have gone to Australians.

CYCLING

2009 Tour de France

Alberto Contador won his second Tour de France title in 2009, beating out Andy Schleck and legend Lance Armstrong to claim the victory. He became only the second Spanish rider to win the race twice. He last won the Tour de France in 2007.

Alberto Contador

2009 TOUR DE FRANCE TOP FINISHES

The Tour de France is an exhausting bike race over a 2,142-mile (3,570-km) course through England, Belgium, Spain, and France. Here are the first five riders to complete the race in 2009.

RANK	NAME	COUNTRY	RACE TIME
1.	Alberto Contador	Spain	85 hours, 48 minutes, 35 seconds
2.	Andy Schleck	Luxembourg	85 hours, 52 minutes, 46 seconds
3.	Lance Armstrong	USA	85 hours, 53 minutes, 59 seconds
4.	Bradley Wiggins	Great Britain	85 hours, 54 minutes, 36 seconds
5.	Frank Schleck	Luxembourg	85 hours, 54 minutes, 39 seconds

guess what?

Traditionally, the rider in the lead during the Tour de France wears a bright yellow shirt. Called the *maillot jaune* (*my*-oh zhon) in French, the yellow jersey is worn both as an honor and as a way of easily identifying the rider in first place. The tradition began in the 1919 Tour de France.

Michael Phelps

SWIMMING

2009 FINA WORLD SWIMMING CHAMPIONSHIPS

The 2009 FINA World Swimming Championships were held in Rome, Italy, from July 17 to August 2, 2009. They featured events in all five aquatic categories: diving, swimming, open water swimming, synchronized swimming, and water polo. Here are some results.

DISCIPLINE	EVENT	GOLD MEDAL
Swimming	Men's 4x100 Meter Medley Relay	USA
Swimming	Women's 4x100 Meter Medley Relay	China
Open Water Swimming	Men's 25-kilometer Open Water	Valerio Cleri (Italy)
Open Water Swimming	Women's 25-kilometer Open Water	Angela Maurer (Germany)
Diving	Men's 10-meter Platform	Tom Daley (Great Britain)
Diving	Women's 10-meter Platform	Paola Espinosa (Mexico)
Synchronized Swimming	Team Technical Routine	Russia
Synchronized Swimming	Team Free Routine	Russia
Water Polo	Men's Tournament	Serbia
Water Polo	Women's Tournament	USA

RECORD BREAKER

After winning an impressive eight medals in the 2008 Summer Olympics, swimmer Michael Phelps continued to break records in 2009. In the 100-meter butterfly event at the FINA World Championships, Phelps broke his own world record of 50.22 seconds, finishing the race in 49.82 seconds.

Paola Espinosa

Sports

WINTER OLYMPICS 2010

Bilodeau

The 2010 Winter Olympics were held in Vancouver, British Columbia, Canada, from February 12 to 28, 2010. Officially known as the XXI Olympic Winter Games, the Olympics included 86 different events and featured more than 2,600 athletes from 82 countries.

Canada Ends Drought

Canada has hosted the Olympics three times. Montreal was the site of the 1976 Summer Olympics, and the 1988 Winter Olympics were held in Calgary. But, believe it or not, the Canadians didn't win any gold medals during either of those Olympics. That all changed on the third day of the 2010 Olympics when Alexandre Bilodeau took home the gold in freestyle mogul skiing. In all, Canada won 14 gold medals, the most of any nation. Canada also set a new Olympic record for the most gold medals won by a country at a single Winter Games.

Oh Yes for Ohno!

Apolo Ohno became the most decorated American Winter Olympian in 2010, winning three medals in speed skating for the United States. Ohno took the

guess what? In 2010, the United States men's bobsled team won their first gold medal in the four-man event since 1948.

silver medal in the 1,500-meter individual race and the bronze in both the 1,000-meter individual race and the 5,000-meter relay. Ohno didn't win any gold medals in 2010, but he now has a lifetime total of eight medals—the most Winter Olympics medals ever won by an American. Speed skater Bonnie Blair held the previous record with six.

Apolo Ohno

Figure Skating

U.S. MEN WIN BIG

Kim Yu-Na

American Evan Lysacek won the gold medal in the men's figure-skating competition, putting the United States on top of the podium for the first time in this event since 1988, when Brian Boitano won the gold. Lysacek upset the defending gold medalist Evgeni Plushenko of Russia to win the event, which surprised many viewers.

KIM YU-NA BREAKS A WOMEN'S FIGURE-SKATING RECORD

South Korean Kim Yu-Na did more than just win the gold medal in women's figure skating. She made history while doing it. The favorite coming into the Olympics, Kim did not disappoint even the highest expectations. She shattered the previous Olympic record by posting a score of 228.56. She even beat her own personal best by 18 points! Japanese skater Mao Asada won the silver, and Canadian Joannie Rochette took the bronze.

Shaun White Does It Again

Shaun White

American snowboarder Shaun White won the gold medal in the half-pipe event for the second straight Olympics. He had recently taken top honors in the same event in the 2010 X Games. Snowboarders generally take two passes at the half-pipe, and the judges only count the higher of the two scores. White's first run down the half-pipe scored such high marks that he didn't even need to do a second run to secure the win. But he did it anyway, and landed one of the toughest tricks in snowboarding history. It is called the Double McTwist 1260. Not only did White create it, but he is the only person in the world who has ever landed it.

guess what? *Because of his bright red hair and the incredible height he reaches in his jumps, Shaun White has earned the nickname The Flying Tomato.*

Hockey Showdown

The United States and Canada faced off in the final game of the men's Olympic hockey tournament. The U.S. team went into the game undefeated, having beaten Canada 5–3 in an earlier part of the tournament. Canada was up 2–1 late in the game. But with 24 seconds left, American Zach Parise tied the game to send it to overtime. Seven minutes and 40 seconds into overtime, Canadian star Sidney Crosby scored to capture the gold medal for the host nation. More than 27 million people tuned in to watch the exciting game.

U.S. vs. Canada

guess what? U.S. cross-country skier Kris Freeman was diagnosed with Type 1 diabetes in 2002, but he did not let his illness stand in the way of his competing in the 2010 games. While he didn't win any medals, Freeman serves as an inspiration to anyone who wants to fulfill Olympic-sized dreams.

RECORD BREAKER

The U.S. alpine skiing team had its best-ever Olympic Games, winning more medals than any nation. Led by Lindsey Vonn, who injured her shin just days before the Games started, the Americans took home 8 medals (out of 30 possible).

Lindsey Vonn

FINAL MEDAL COUNT BY COUNTRY

COUNTRY	GOLD MEDALS	SILVER MEDALS	BRONZE MEDALS	TOTAL MEDALS
1. United States	9	15	13	37
2. Germany	10	13	7	30
3. Canada	14	7	5	26
4. Norway	9	8	6	23
5. Austria	4	6	6	16

UPCOMING OLYMPIC GAMES

2012 (SUMMER) - **London, England**

2014 (WINTER) - **Sochi, Russia**

2016 (SUMMER) - **Rio de Janeiro, Brazil**

Sports

HORSE RACING

Mine That Bird

2009 Triple Crown

The three biggest horse races in the United States are the Kentucky Derby at Churchill Downs in Louisville, Kentucky; the Preakness Stakes at Pimlico Race Course in Baltimore, Maryland; and the Belmont Stakes at Belmont Park in Elmont, New York. These three races take place within a five-week period from early May to early June, and make up the Triple Crown of Thoroughbred Racing, or Triple Crown, for short.

The 2009 Triple Crown racing season was an exciting one. Long shot Mine That Bird rallied from last place to win the Kentucky Derby at 50–1 odds. It was one of the biggest upsets in Kentucky Derby history, second only to Donerail's 91–1 shocker in 1913. In another surprise, Mine That Bird jockey Calvin Borel decided to ride a different horse in the Preakness Stakes. He chose to ride the undefeated filly Rachel Alexandra. It was the first time ever that the Derby-winning jockey and the Derby-winning horse competed separately in the Preakness. At the Preakness, Rachel Alexandra just barely beat Mine That Bird for the win. For the final leg of the Triple Crown, the Belmont Stakes, Rachel Alexandra's owners decided not to race her, so Borel switched back to Mine That Bird. It would have been the first time ever that a jockey won all three Triple Crown races on two different horses. But that did not happen. Mine That Bird finished third in the Belmont, losing to Summer Bird, his own half brother.

DOGSLEDDING

Iditarod

The Iditarod is an annual dogsledding race covering more than 1,150 miles (1,917 km) across the mountain ranges, frozen rivers, and forests of Alaska. It's been called The Last Great Race on Earth. In 2009, two-time defending champion Lance Mackey took first place with a time of 9 days, 21 hours, 38 minutes, and 46 seconds.

Lance Mackey and his team

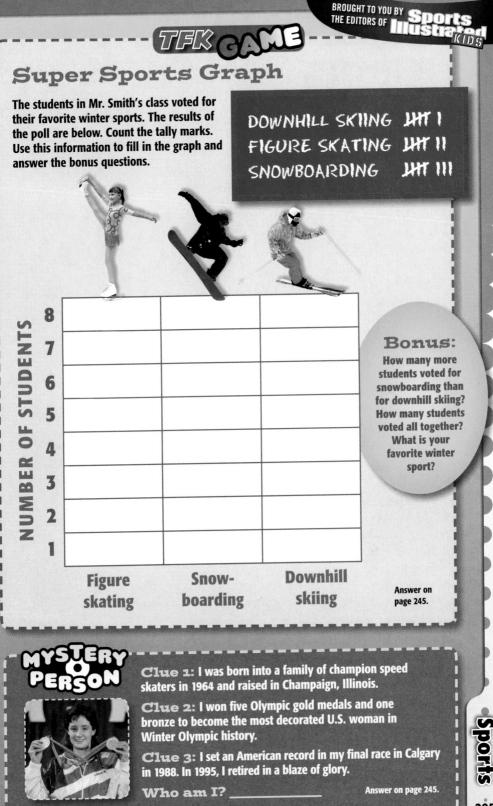

TFK GAME

Super Sports Graph

The students in Mr. Smith's class voted for their favorite winter sports. The results of the poll are below. Count the tally marks. Use this information to fill in the graph and answer the bonus questions.

DOWNHILL SKIING ~~LHT~~ I
FIGURE SKATING ~~LHT~~ II
SNOWBOARDING ~~LHT~~ III

NUMBER OF STUDENTS

8
7
6
5
4
3
2
1

Figure skating   Snow-boarding   Downhill skiing

Bonus:
How many more students voted for snowboarding than for downhill skiing? How many students voted all together? What is your favorite winter sport?

Answer on page 245.

MYSTERY PERSON

Clue 1: I was born into a family of champion speed skaters in 1964 and raised in Champaign, Illinois.

Clue 2: I won five Olympic gold medals and one bronze to become the most decorated U.S. woman in Winter Olympic history.

Clue 3: I set an American record in my final race in Calgary in 1988. In 1995, I retired in a blaze of glory.

Who am I? _____   Answer on page 245.

Sports

United States

ALABAMA

CAPITAL: Montgomery

LARGEST CITY: Birmingham

POSTAL CODE: AL

LAND AREA: 50,750 square miles (131,443 sq km)

POPULATION (2009): 4,708,708

ENTERED UNION (RANK): December 14, 1819 (22)

MOTTO: *Audemus jura nostra defendere.* (We dare maintain our rights.)

TREE: Southern longleaf pine

FLOWER: Camellia

BIRD: Yellowhammer (also known as the northern flicker or yellow-shafted flicker)

NICKNAMES: Yellowhammer State, Cotton State, Heart of Dixie

FAMOUS ALABAMIAN: Secretary of State Condoleezza Rice

guess what? *Russell Cave National Monument, found in northeastern Alabama, is home to many artifacts left by people who lived there more than 9,000 years ago. Archaeologists have found tools, weapons, and even bones in the cave passages.*

Birmingham

Montgomery

Yellowhammer

ALASKA

CAPITAL: Juneau

LARGEST CITY: Anchorage

POSTAL CODE: AK

LAND AREA: 570,374 square miles (1,477,267 sq km)

POPULATION (2009): 698,473

ENTERED UNION (RANK): January 3, 1959 (49)

MOTTO: North to the future

TREE: Sitka spruce

FLOWER: Forget-me-not

BIRD: Willow ptarmigan

NICKNAMES: The Last Frontier, Land of the Midnight Sun

FAMOUS ALASKAN: Curt Schilling, baseball player

guess what? *In 1927, Alaska's state flag was designed by Benny Benson, who was only 13 years old at the time.*

Anchorage

Juneau

Willow ptarmigan

ARIZONA

CAPITAL: Phoenix

LARGEST CITY: Phoenix

POSTAL CODE: AZ

LAND AREA: 113,642 square miles (296,400 sq km)

POPULATION (2009): 6,595,778

ENTERED UNION (RANK): February 14, 1912 (48)

MOTTO: *Ditat deus.* (God enriches.)

TREE: Palo verde

FLOWER: Saguaro cactus blossom

BIRD: Cactus wren

NICKNAME: Grand Canyon State

FAMOUS ARIZONAN: Geronimo, Native American leader

guess what? *Arizona is home to the saguaro cactus, which can grow as tall as a five-story building and live as long as 200 years.*

Phoenix

Geronimo

ARKANSAS

ARKANSAS

CAPITAL: Little Rock

LARGEST CITY: Little Rock

POSTAL CODE: AR

LAND AREA: 52,075 square miles (134,874 sq km)

POPULATION (2009): 2,889,450

ENTERED UNION (RANK): June 15, 1836 (25)

MOTTO: *Regnat populus.* (The people rule.)

TREE: Pine

FLOWER: Apple blossom

BIRD: Mockingbird

NICKNAME: Natural State

FAMOUS ARKANSAN: Bill Clinton, 42nd U.S. President

guess what? *Stuttgart, Arkansas, is home to the World Championship Duck Calling Contest.*

Little Rock

Apple blossom

CALIFORNIA

CAPITAL: Sacramento

LARGEST CITY: Los Angeles

POSTAL CODE: CA

LAND AREA: 155,973 square miles (403,970 sq km)

POPULATION (2009): 36,961,664

ENTERED UNION (RANK): September 9, 1850 (31)

MOTTO: *Eureka!* (I have found it!)

TREE: California redwood

FLOWER: Golden poppy

BIRD: California valley quail

NICKNAME: Golden State

FAMOUS CALIFORNIAN: Julia Child, chef and author

Guess what? Nearly all of the artichokes grown in the United States are farmed in California.

Artichokes

COLORADO

CAPITAL: Denver

LARGEST CITY: Denver

POSTAL CODE: CO

LAND AREA: 103,730 square miles (268,660 sq km)

POPULATION (2009): 5,024,748

ENTERED UNION (RANK): August 1, 1876 (38)

MOTTO: *Nil sine numine* (Nothing without the Deity)

TREE: Colorado blue spruce

FLOWER: Rocky Mountain columbine

BIRD: Lark bunting

NICKNAME: Centennial State

FAMOUS COLORADAN: Jack Dempsey, boxer

Guess what? Katherine Lee Bates composed the song "America the Beautiful" after seeing the view from Pikes Peak, near Colorado Springs.

Pikes Peak

CONNECTICUT

CAPITAL: Hartford

LARGEST CITY: Bridgeport

POSTAL CODE: CT

LAND AREA: 5,018 square miles (12,997 sq km)

POPULATION (2009): 3,518,288

ENTERED UNION (RANK): January 9, 1788 (5)

MOTTO: *Qui transtulit sustinet.* (He who transplanted still sustains.)

TREE: White oak

FLOWER: Mountain laurel

BIRD: American robin

NICKNAMES: Constitution State, Nutmeg State

FAMOUS NUTMEGGER: Harriet Beecher Stowe, abolitionist and novelist who wrote *Uncle Tom's Cabin*

 The praying mantis is the state insect of Connecticut.

Praying mantis

Hartford
Bridgeport

DELAWARE

CAPITAL: Dover

LARGEST CITY: Wilmington

POSTAL CODE: DE

LAND AREA: 1,955 square miles (5,063 sq km)

POPULATION (2009): 885,122

ENTERED UNION (RANK): December 7, 1787 (1)

MOTTO: Liberty and independence

TREE: American holly

FLOWER: Peach blossom

BIRD: Blue hen chicken

NICKNAMES: Diamond State, First State, Small Wonder

FAMOUS DELAWAREAN: Henry Heimlich, surgeon and inventor of the Heimlich maneuver

guess what? *Thomas Jefferson once described Delaware as a diamond: "small, but of great value." For this reason, Delaware is sometimes referred to as the Diamond State.*

Wilmington
Dover

Peach blossom

FLORIDA

CAPITAL: Tallahassee

LARGEST CITY: Jacksonville

POSTAL CODE: FL

LAND AREA: 53,927 square miles (139,670 sq km)

POPULATION (2009): 18,537,969

ENTERED UNION (RANK): March 3, 1845 (27)

MOTTO: In God we trust.

TREE: Sabal palm

FLOWER: Orange blossom

BIRD: Mockingbird

NICKNAME: Sunshine State

FAMOUS FLORIDIAN: Aaron Carter, singer

guess what? *The process for making artificial ice was developed in sunny Florida. Dr. John Gorrie of Apalachicola patented the technique in 1851.*

Tallahassee

Jacksonville

Mockingbird

GEORGIA

CAPITAL: Atlanta

LARGEST CITY: Atlanta

POSTAL CODE: GA

LAND AREA: 57,919 square miles (150,010 sq km)

POPULATION (2009): 9,829,211

ENTERED UNION (RANK): January 2, 1788 (4)

MOTTO: Wisdom, justice, and moderation

TREE: Live oak

FLOWER: Cherokee rose

BIRD: Brown thrasher

NICKNAMES: Peach State, Empire State of the South

FAMOUS GEORGIAN: Margaret Mitchell, author of *Gone with the Wind*

guess what? *Georgia produces one of the sweetest varieties of onions, the Vidalia. It grows only in the fields surrounding the towns of Vidalia and Glennville, Georgia.*

Atlanta

Atlanta skyline

HAWAII

CAPITAL: Honolulu
(on the island of Oahu)

LARGEST CITY: Honolulu

POSTAL CODE: HI

LAND AREA: 6,423 square miles
(16,636 sq km)

POPULATION (2009): 1,295,178

ENTERED UNION (RANK):
August 21, 1959 (50)

MOTTO: *Ua mau ke ea o ka aina i ka pono.* (The life of the land is perpetuated in righteousness.)

TREE: Kuku'i (candlenut)

FLOWER: Yellow hibiscus

BIRD: Nene (Hawaiian goose)

NICKNAME: Aloha State

FAMOUS HAWAIIAN: Barack Obama, 44th U.S. President

 Hawaii is the only U.S. state that grows coffee.

PACIFIC OCEAN

Honolulu

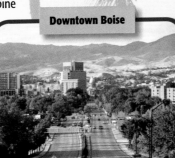

President Obama

IDAHO

CAPITAL: Boise

LARGEST CITY: Boise

POSTAL CODE: ID

LAND AREA: 82,751 square miles
(214,325 sq km)

POPULATION (2009): 1,545,801

ENTERED UNION (RANK):
July 3, 1890 (43)

MOTTO: *Esto perpetua.*
(Let it be perpetual.)

TREE: Western white pine

FLOWER: Syringa

BIRD: Mountain bluebird

NICKNAME: Gem State

FAMOUS IDAHOAN: Gutzon Borglum, Mount Rushmore sculptor

guess what? *In 1805, the explorers Lewis and Clark became the first non-native Americans to visit Idaho.*

Downtown Boise

Boise

ILLINOIS

ILLINOIS

CAPITAL: Springfield

LARGEST CITY: Chicago

POSTAL CODE: IL

LAND AREA: 55,593 square miles (143,986 sq km)

POPULATION (2009): 12,910,409

ENTERED UNION (RANK): December 3, 1818 (21)

MOTTO: State sovereignty, national union

TREE: White oak

FLOWER: Purple violet

BIRD: Cardinal

NICKNAMES: Prairie State, Land of Lincoln

FAMOUS ILLINOISAN: Ernest Hemingway, writer

guess what? *Every year on St. Patrick's Day, the city of Chicago dyes the Chicago River green, in honor of the city's Irish roots.*

The Chicago River on St. Patrick's Day

Chicago

Springfield

INDIANA

CAPITAL: Indianapolis

LARGEST CITY: Indianapolis

POSTAL CODE: IN

LAND AREA: 35,870 square miles (92,903 sq km)

POPULATION (2009): 6,423,113

ENTERED UNION (RANK): December 11, 1816 (19)

MOTTO: The crossroads of America

TREE: Tulip tree, or yellow poplar

FLOWER: Peony

BIRD: Cardinal

NICKNAMES: Hoosier State, Crossroads of America

FAMOUS INDIANAN OR HOOSIER: Michael Jackson, pop star

guess what? *The town of Santa Claus, Indiana, receives more than half a million letters and requests every year around Christmastime. It was originally called Santa Fe, but when town leaders registered for a post office in 1856, they found out there already was a Santa Fe, Indiana. The town residents voted to keep Santa in the town's name, swapping Claus for Fe.*

Indianapolis

A leaf from a tulip tree

IOWA

CAPITAL: Des Moines

LARGEST CITY: Des Moines

POSTAL CODE: IA

LAND AREA: 55,875 square miles (144,716 sq km)

POPULATION (2009): 3,007,856

ENTERED UNION (RANK): December 28, 1846 (29)

MOTTO: Our liberties we prize, and our rights we will maintain.

TREE: Oak

FLOWER: Wild prairie rose

BIRD: Eastern goldfinch (also known as the American goldfinch)

NICKNAME: Hawkeye State

FAMOUS IOWAN: William "Buffalo Bill" Cody, scout and entertainer

guess what? *Iowa is the only U.S. state bordered to the east and west by water. The Mississippi River is Iowa's eastern border, and the Missouri River is to the west.*

Des Moines

An oak tree in Iowa

KANSAS

CAPITAL: Topeka

LARGEST CITY: Wichita

POSTAL CODE: KS

LAND AREA: 81,823 square miles (211,922 sq km)

POPULATION (2009): 2,818,747

ENTERED UNION (RANK): January 29, 1861 (34)

MOTTO: *Ad astra per aspera* (To the stars through difficulties)

TREE: Cottonwood

FLOWER: Sunflower

BIRD: Western meadowlark

NICKNAMES: Sunflower State, Jayhawk State, Wheat State

FAMOUS KANSAN: Amelia Earhart, first woman to fly solo across the Atlantic Ocean

guess what? *In 1990, wheat farmers in Kansas produced enough wheat to make 33 billion loaves of bread. If distributed among the world's population, that would have been enough bread for each person on Earth to have five loaves.*

KANSAS

Topeka

Wichita

Amelia Earhart

United States

213

KENTUCKY

CAPITAL: Frankfort

LARGEST CITY: Louisville

POSTAL CODE: KY

LAND AREA: 39,732 square miles (102,906 sq km)

POPULATION (2009): 4,314,113

ENTERED UNION (RANK): June 1, 1792 (15)

MOTTO: United we stand, divided we fall.

TREE: Tulip poplar

FLOWER: Goldenrod

BIRD: Kentucky cardinal

NICKNAME: Bluegrass State

FAMOUS KENTUCKIAN: Muhammad Ali, boxer

 Part of the oath of office for a Kentucky governor involves swearing that he or she has never participated in a duel.

Louisville · Frankfort

Goldenrod

LOUISIANA

CAPITAL: Baton Rouge

LARGEST CITY: New Orleans

POSTAL CODE: LA

LAND AREA: 43,566 square miles (112,836 sq km)

POPULATION (2009): 4,492,076

ENTERED UNION (RANK): April 30, 1812 (18)

MOTTO: Union, justice, and confidence

TREE: Bald cypress

FLOWER: Magnolia

BIRD: Eastern brown pelican

NICKNAME: Pelican State

FAMOUS LOUISIANAN: Peyton Manning, football player

guess what? *Louisiana is the only state in the union that doesn't subdivide into counties. Instead, it splits into smaller political units known as parishes.*

New Orleans

Baton Rouge

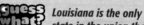

Statue of jazz legend Louis Armstrong in New Orleans

MAINE

CAPITAL: Augusta

LARGEST CITY: Portland

POSTAL CODE: ME

LAND AREA: 30,865 square miles (79,940 sq km)

POPULATION (2009): 1,318,301

ENTERED UNION (RANK): March 15, 1820 (23)

MOTTO: *Dirigo.* (I lead.)

TREE: White pine

FLOWER: White pine cone and tassel

BIRD: Black-capped chickadee

NICKNAME: Pine Tree State

FAMOUS MAINER: Stephen King, best-selling author

guess what? Ninety percent of the lobsters caught in the United States are found off the coast of Maine.

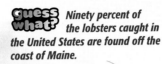

Maine lobster

Augusta ⊛

Portland ●

MARYLAND

CAPITAL: Annapolis

LARGEST CITY: Baltimore

POSTAL CODE: MD

LAND AREA: 9,775 square miles (25,317 sq km)

POPULATION (2009): 5,699,478

ENTERED UNION (RANK): April 28, 1788 (7)

MOTTO: *Fatti maschii, parole femine* (Manly deeds, womanly words)

TREE: White oak

FLOWER: Black-eyed Susan

BIRD: Baltimore oriole

NICKNAMES: Free State, Old Line State

FAMOUS MARYLANDER: Mary Downing Hahn, children's book author

guess what? The state sport in Maryland is jousting. Once enjoyed by medieval knights, jousting involves two contestants mounted on horses, who charge each other and attempt to dismount each other with a lance.

Baltimore

Annapolis ⊛

Black-eyed Susan

MASSACHUSETTS

CAPITAL: Boston
LARGEST CITY: Boston
POSTAL CODE: MA
LAND AREA: 7,838 square miles (20,300 sq km)
POPULATION (2009): 6,593,587
ENTERED UNION (RANK): February 6, 1788 (6)
MOTTO: *Ense petit placidam sub libertate quietem.* (By the sword we seek peace, but peace only under liberty.)
TREE: American elm
FLOWER: Mayflower
BIRD: Black-capped chickadee

NICKNAMES: Bay State, Old Colony State, Baked Bean State
FAMOUS BAY STATER: Dr. Seuss, children's book author

guess what? *Originally known as mintonette, the sport of volleyball was invented in Holyoke, Massachusetts, by William G. Morgan.*

Boston ✪

Black-capped chickadee

MICHIGAN

CAPITAL: Lansing
LARGEST CITY: Detroit
POSTAL CODE: MI
LAND AREA: 56,809 square miles (147,135 sq km)
POPULATION (2009): 9,969,727
ENTERED UNION (RANK): January 26, 1837 (26)
MOTTO: *Si quaeris peninsulam amoenam circumspice.* (If you seek a pleasant peninsula, look about you.)
TREE: White pine
FLOWER: Apple blossom
BIRD: American robin
NICKNAMES: Wolverine State, Great Lakes State

FAMOUS MICHIGANDER OR MICHIGANIAN: Taylor Lautner, actor

guess what? *Motown Records, famous for producing such artists as Stevie Wonder, the Supremes, Marvin Gaye, and the Jackson 5, was originally headquartered in Detroit.*

American robin

Lansing ✪

Detroit ●

MINNESOTA

CAPITAL: St. Paul

LARGEST CITY: Minneapolis

POSTAL CODE: MN

LAND AREA: 79,617 square miles (206,208 sq km)

POPULATION (2009): 5,266,214

ENTERED UNION (RANK): May 11, 1858 (32)

MOTTO: *L'Étoile du nord* (Star of the north)

TREE: Red (or Norway) pine

FLOWER: Pink and white lady's slipper

BIRD: Common loon

NICKNAMES: North Star State, Gopher State, Land of 10,000 Lakes

FAMOUS MINNESOTAN: Judy Garland, actress best known as Dorothy in *The Wizard of Oz*

 guess what? *Minneapolis is home to an extensive system of elevated, enclosed walkways. It is possible to walk 8 miles (13 km) without ever setting foot outside.*

Minneapolis

Minneapolis

St. Paul

MISSISSIPPI

CAPITAL: Jackson

LARGEST CITY: Jackson

POSTAL CODE: MS

LAND AREA: 46,914 square miles (121,507 sq km)

POPULATION (2009): 2,951,996

ENTERED UNION (RANK): December 10, 1817 (20)

MOTTO: *Virtute et armis* (By valor and arms)

TREE: Magnolia

FLOWER: Magnolia

BIRD: Mockingbird

NICKNAME: Magnolia State

FAMOUS MISSISSIPPIAN: Jim Henson, puppeteer and creator of the Muppets

guess what? *Every four years, Jackson hosts the USA International Ballet Competition, often referred to as the Olympics of Dance. The competition brings in dancers from around the world for two weeks, and awards prizes ranging from master classes to contracts with professional companies.*

Jackson

Magnolia

United States

MISSOURI

CAPITAL: Jefferson City

LARGEST CITY: Kansas City

POSTAL CODE: MO

LAND AREA: 68,898 square miles (178,446 sq km)

POPULATION (2009): 5,987,580

ENTERED UNION (RANK): August 10, 1821 (24)

MOTTO: *Salus populi suprema lex esto.* (The welfare of the people shall be the supreme law.)

TREE: Flowering dogwood

FLOWER: Hawthorn

BIRD: Bluebird

NICKNAME: Show Me State

FAMOUS MISSOURIAN: Bess Truman, First Lady

guess what? At 630 feet (192 m), the Gateway Arch in St. Louis is the tallest man-made monument in the United States. Completed in 1965, the monument stands as a symbol of the Gateway to the West, in honor of the historic Lewis and Clark expedition.

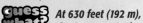
The Gateway Arch

MONTANA

CAPITAL: Helena

LARGEST CITY: Billings

POSTAL CODE: MT

LAND AREA: 145,556 square miles (376,990 sq km)

POPULATION (2009): 974,989

ENTERED UNION (RANK): November 8, 1889 (41)

MOTTO: *Oro y plata* (Gold and silver)

TREE: Ponderosa pine

FLOWER: Bitterroot

BIRD: Western meadowlark

NICKNAME: Treasure State

FAMOUS MONTANAN: Evel Knievel, motorcycle daredevil

guess what? Montana has two state gemstones: agate and sapphire. The Yogo sapphire from Montana is the only North American stone included in England's famous Crown Jewels.

State capitol in Helena

NEBRASKA

CAPITAL: Lincoln

LARGEST CITY: Omaha

POSTAL CODE: NE

LAND AREA: 76,878 square miles (199,114 sq km)

POPULATION (2009): 1,796,619

ENTERED UNION (RANK): March 1, 1867 (37)

MOTTO: Equality before the law

TREE: Eastern cottonwood

FLOWER: Goldenrod

BIRD: Western meadowlark

NICKNAMES: Cornhusker State, Beef State

FAMOUS NEBRASKAN: Malcolm X, civil rights leader

guess what? Chimney Rock, which is 325 feet (99 m) tall, was used as a trail marker for caravans crossing the country on the Oregon Trail. The sight of this rock signaled the end of the seemingly endless Nebraska plains.

Omaha

Lincoln

Chimney Rock

NEVADA

CAPITAL: Carson City

LARGEST CITY: Las Vegas

POSTAL CODE: NV

LAND AREA: 109,806 square miles (284,397 sq km)

POPULATION (2009): 2,643,085

ENTERED UNION (RANK): October 31, 1864 (36)

MOTTO: All for our country

TREE: Single-leaf piñon pine

FLOWER: Sagebrush

BIRD: Mountain bluebird

NICKNAMES: Sagebrush State, Silver State, Battle Born State

FAMOUS NEVADAN: Harry Reid, U.S. Senator

guess what? Nevada's Death Valley is the lowest point in the Western Hemisphere, and the driest area of the United States. In this desert landscape, the kangaroo rat can live its entire life without ever drinking water.

Carson City

Las Vegas

Harry Reid

NEW HAMPSHIRE

CAPITAL: Concord

LARGEST CITY: Manchester

POSTAL CODE: NH

LAND AREA: 8,969 square miles (23,230 sq km)

POPULATION (2009): 1,324,575

ENTERED UNION (RANK): June 21, 1788 (9)

MOTTO: Live free or die.

TREE: White birch (also known as the canoe or paper birch)

FLOWER: Purple lilac

BIRD: Purple finch

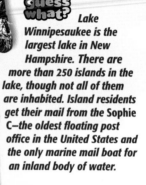

NICKNAME: Granite State

FAMOUS NEW HAMPSHIRITE: Alan Shepard, first American in space

guess what? *Lake Winnipesaukee is the largest lake in New Hampshire. There are more than 250 islands in the lake, though not all of them are inhabited. Island residents get their mail from the Sophie C—the oldest floating post office in the United States and the only marine mail boat for an inland body of water.*

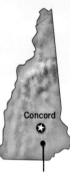

Concord

Manchester

Alan Shepard

NEW JERSEY

CAPITAL: Trenton

LARGEST CITY: Newark

POSTAL CODE: NJ

LAND AREA: 7,419 square miles (19,215 sq km)

POPULATION (2009): 8,707,739

ENTERED UNION (RANK): December 18, 1787 (3)

MOTTO: Liberty and prosperity

TREE: Red oak

FLOWER: Common meadow violet

BIRD: Eastern (or American) goldfinch

NICKNAME: Garden State

FAMOUS NEW JERSEYITE: Bruce Springsteen, singer and songwriter

guess what? *Paterson, New Jersey, is home to what is probably the world's largest collection of spoons. Housed at the Lambert Castle Museum, the collection contains 5,400 items.*

Violet

Newark

Trenton

NEW MEXICO

CAPITAL: Santa Fe

LARGEST CITY: Albuquerque

POSTAL CODE: NM

LAND AREA: 121,365 square miles (314,335 sq km)

POPULATION (2009): 2,009,671

ENTERED UNION (RANK): January 6, 1912 (47)

MOTTO: *Crescit eundo.* (It grows as it goes.)

TREE: Piñon pine

FLOWER: Yucca

BIRD: Roadrunner

NICKNAMES: Land of Enchantment, Cactus State

FAMOUS NEW MEXICAN: William Hanna, animator

guess what? Las Cruces, New Mexico, hosts the annual Whole Enchilada Fiesta. Each year, up to 70,000 people gather for the event, which ends in the creation of an enormous enchilada. The ingredients for this project include 750 pounds (340 kg) of stone-ground corn for making tortillas, 175 gallons (662 L) of vegetable oil, 75 gallons (284 L) of red chile sauce, 175 pounds (79 kg) of grated cheese, and 50 pounds (23 kg) of chopped onions.

Santa Fe

Albuquerque

Roadrunner

NEW YORK

CAPITAL: Albany

LARGEST CITY: New York

POSTAL CODE: NY

LAND AREA: 47,224 square miles (122,310 sq km)

POPULATION (2009): 19,541,453

ENTERED UNION (RANK): July 26, 1788 (11)

MOTTO: *Excelsior* (Ever upward)

TREE: Sugar maple

FLOWER: Rose

BIRD: Bluebird

NICKNAME: Empire State

FAMOUS NEW YORKER: Shirley Chisholm, first black woman elected to the U.S. Congress

guess what? In 1861, Matthew Vassar founded Vassar College in Poughkeepsie, New York. He sought to provide women with a liberal arts education equal to that of the best men's colleges of the time. Originally a women-only institution, Vassar began admitting men in 1969.

Albany

New York

Shirley Chisholm

NORTH CAROLINA

CAPITAL: Raleigh

LARGEST CITY: Charlotte

POSTAL CODE: NC

LAND AREA: 48,708 square miles (126,154 sq km)

POPULATION (2009): 9,380,884

ENTERED UNION (RANK): November 21, 1789 (12)

MOTTO: *Esse quam videri* (To be rather than to seem)

TREE: Pine

FLOWER: Flowering dogwood

BIRD: Cardinal

NICKNAME: Tar Heel State

FAMOUS NORTH CAROLINIAN: Fantasia Barrino, *American Idol* winner

guess what? North Carolina produces more sweet potatoes than any other state in the nation.

Dogwood

NORTH DAKOTA

CAPITAL: Bismarck

LARGEST CITY: Fargo

POSTAL CODE: ND

LAND AREA: 68,994 square miles (178,694 sq km)

POPULATION (2009): 646,844

ENTERED UNION (RANK): November 2, 1889 (39)

MOTTO: Liberty and union, now and forever, one and inseparable

TREE: American elm

FLOWER: Wild prairie rose

BIRD: Western meadowlark

NICKNAMES: Sioux State, Flickertail State, Peace Garden State, Rough Rider State

FAMOUS NORTH DAKOTAN: Josh Duhamel, actor

guess what? The world's largest intact triceratops skull can be viewed at the Dakota Dinosaur Museum in Dickinson, North Dakota. The skull weighs about 1,500 pounds (680 kg).

Elm trees

OHIO

CAPITAL: Columbus

LARGEST CITY: Columbus

POSTAL CODE: OH

LAND AREA: 40,953 square miles (106,068 sq km)

POPULATION (2009): 11,542,645

ENTERED UNION (RANK): March 1, 1803 (17)

MOTTO: With God, all things are possible.

TREE: Buckeye

FLOWER: Scarlet carnation

BIRD: Cardinal

NICKNAME: Buckeye State

FAMOUS OHIOAN: Thomas Edison, inventor

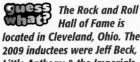 *The Rock and Roll Hall of Fame is located in Cleveland, Ohio. The 2009 inductees were Jeff Beck, Little Anthony & the Imperials, Metallica, Run-DMC, and Bobby Womack.*

Columbus

The Rock and Roll Hall of Fame

OKLAHOMA

CAPITAL: Oklahoma City

LARGEST CITY: Oklahoma City

POSTAL CODE: OK

LAND AREA: 68,679 square miles (177,879 sq km)

POPULATION (2009): 3,687,050

ENTERED UNION (RANK): November 16, 1907 (46)

MOTTO: *Labor omnia vincit.* (Labor conquers all things.)

TREE: Eastern redbud

FLOWER: Mistletoe

BIRD: Scissor-tailed flycatcher

NICKNAME: Sooner State

FAMOUS OKLAHOMAN: Mickey Mantle, baseball player

 *More than 400,000 Native Americans live in Oklahoma. That is the second-highest population of Native residents in the country.*

Longhorn cattle in Oklahoma

Oklahoma City

OREGON

CAPITAL: Salem

LARGEST CITY: Portland

POSTAL CODE: OR

LAND AREA: 96,003 square miles (248,648 sq km)

POPULATION (2009): 3,825,657

ENTERED UNION (RANK): February 14, 1859 (33)

MOTTO: *Alis volat propriis.* (She flies with her own wings.)

TREE: Douglas fir

FLOWER: Oregon grape

BIRD: Western meadowlark

NICKNAME: Beaver State

FAMOUS OREGONIAN: Matt Groening, creator of *The Simpsons*

guess what? The International Museum of Carousel Art, located in Hood River, Oregon, houses the world's largest collection of antique carousel art and carousel horses.

Portland

Salem

Douglas fir

PENNSYLVANIA

CAPITAL: Harrisburg

LARGEST CITY: Philadelphia

POSTAL CODE: PA

LAND AREA: 44,820 square miles (116,084 sq km)

POPULATION (2009): 12,604,767

ENTERED UNION (RANK): December 12, 1787 (2)

MOTTO: Virtue, liberty, and independence

TREE: Hemlock

FLOWER: Mountain laurel

BIRD: Ruffed grouse

NICKNAME: Keystone State

FAMOUS PENNSYLVANIAN: Taylor Swift, singer and songwriter

guess what? Founder William Penn wanted to name the state New Wales or Sylvania, Latin for "place in the woods." King Charles II, who wanted to name it in honor of Penn's father, chose a compromise and granted a charter for Pennsylvania, which literally means "Penn's Woodlands."

Harrisburg

Philadelphia

Ruffed grouse

RHODE ISLAND

CAPITAL: Providence

LARGEST CITY: Providence

POSTAL CODE: RI

LAND AREA: 1,045 square miles (2,707 sq km)

POPULATION (2009): 1,053,209

ENTERED UNION (RANK): May 29, 1790 (13)

MOTTO: Hope

TREE: Red maple

FLOWER: Violet

BIRD: Rhode Island red hen

NICKNAME: Ocean State

FAMOUS RHODE ISLANDER: George M. Cohan, composer of "Yankee Doodle Dandy" and "You're a Grand Old Flag"

guess what? *Rhode Island was the first colony to declare independence from the British Empire in 1776. The state celebrates its own Independence Day two months before the rest of the country, on May 4.*

Providence

George M. Cohan

SOUTH CAROLINA

CAPITAL: Columbia

LARGEST CITY: Columbia

POSTAL CODE: SC

LAND AREA: 30,111 square miles (77,987 sq km)

POPULATION (2009): 4,561,242

ENTERED UNION (RANK): May 23, 1788 (8)

MOTTOES: *Animis opibusque parati* (Prepared in mind and resources); *Dum spiro spero.* (While I breathe, I hope.)

TREE: Palmetto

FLOWER: Yellow jessamine

BIRD: Carolina wren

NICKNAME: Palmetto State

FAMOUS SOUTH CAROLINIAN: Jesse Jackson, civil rights leader

guess what? *The American Civil War began when Confederate soldiers attacked Fort Sumter in Charleston, South Carolina, on April 12, 1861.*

Columbia

Jesse Jackson

SOUTH DAKOTA

CAPITAL: Pierre

LARGEST CITY: Sioux Falls

POSTAL CODE: SD

LAND AREA: 75,898 square miles (196,575 sq km)

POPULATION (2009): 812,383

ENTERED UNION (RANK): November 2, 1889 (40)

MOTTO: Under God the people rule.

TREE: Black Hills spruce

FLOWER: Pasqueflower

BIRD: Ring-necked pheasant

NICKNAMES: Mount Rushmore State, Coyote State

FAMOUS SOUTH DAKOTAN: Crazy Horse, Sioux chief

guess what? Badlands, South Dakota, is sometimes referred to as "the playground of the dinosaurs," because of the diversity of fossils that have been found there. Scientists working in Badlands National Park have unearthed a camel the size of a dog, a three-toed horse, and a saber-toothed cat.

Pierre

Sioux Falls

Badlands National Park

TENNESSEE

CAPITAL: Nashville

LARGEST CITY: Memphis

POSTAL CODE: TN

LAND AREA: 41,220 square miles (106,760 sq km)

POPULATION (2009): 6,296,254

ENTERED UNION (RANK): June 1, 1796 (16)

MOTTO: Agriculture and commerce

TREE: Tulip poplar

FLOWER: Iris

BIRD: Mockingbird

NICKNAME: Volunteer State

FAMOUS TENNESSEAN: Miley Cyrus, singer and actress

guess what? President Andrew Jackson named Memphis, Tennessee, after the city of Memphis in Egypt, an important administrative and religious city in ancient times.

Nashville

Memphis

Miley Cyrus

TEXAS

CAPITAL: Austin

LARGEST CITY: Houston

POSTAL CODE: TX

LAND AREA: 261,914 square miles (678,357 sq km)

POPULATION (2009): 24,782,302

ENTERED UNION (RANK): December 29, 1845 (28)

MOTTO: Friendship

TREE: Pecan

FLOWER: Texas bluebonnet

BIRD: Mockingbird

NICKNAME: Lone Star State

FAMOUS TEXAN: Sandra Day O'Connor, first woman U.S. Supreme Court Justice

guess what? *Texas has an official state bread. Pan de campo, which means "camp bread" and is often called cowboy bread, is a simple baking-powder bread. It was a staple food for early settlers in the state.*

Pecan grove

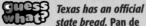

Austin ✪ Houston

UTAH

CAPITAL: Salt Lake City

LARGEST CITY: Salt Lake City

POSTAL CODE: UT

LAND AREA: 82,168 square miles (212,815 sq km)

POPULATION (2009): 2,784,572

ENTERED UNION (RANK): January 4, 1896 (45)

MOTTO: Industry

TREE: Blue spruce

FLOWER: Sego lily

BIRD: California gull

NICKNAME: Beehive State

FAMOUS UTAHN: Philo T. Farnsworth, inventor of the television

guess what? *Since 1959, Utah's state emblem has been the beehive. It is meant to symbolize thrift and industry.*

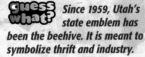

Sego lily

Salt Lake City

VERMONT

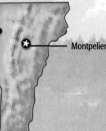

CAPITAL: Montpelier

LARGEST CITY: Burlington

POSTAL CODE: VT

LAND AREA: 9,249 square miles (23,956 sq km)

POPULATION (2009): 621,760

ENTERED UNION (RANK): March 4, 1791 (14)

MOTTO: Vermont: freedom and unity

TREE: Sugar maple

FLOWER: Red clover

BIRD: Hermit thrush

NICKNAME: Green Mountain State

FAMOUS VERMONTER: Joseph Smith, founder of the Mormon Church

guess what? *Vermont is the only state in New England that does not border the Atlantic Ocean.*

Burlington

Montpelier

Red clover

VIRGINIA

CAPITAL: Richmond

LARGEST CITY: Virginia Beach

POSTAL CODE: VA

LAND AREA: 39,598 square miles (102,559 sq km)

POPULATION (2009): 7,882,590

ENTERED UNION (RANK): June 25, 1788 (10)

MOTTO: *Sic semper tyrannis* (Thus always to tyrants)

TREE: Flowering dogwood

FLOWER: American dogwood

BIRD: Cardinal

NICKNAMES: The Old Dominion, Mother of Presidents

FAMOUS VIRGINIANS: Meriwether Lewis and William Clark, American explorers

guess what? *The surrenders that ended both the Revolutionary War and the Civil War took place in Virginia.*

Richmond

Virginia Beach

On behalf of the South, Robert E. Lee (right) surrendered to northern general Ulysses S. Grant at Appomattox Court House in Virginia, ending the U.S. Civil War.

WASHINGTON

CAPITAL: Olympia

LARGEST CITY: Seattle

POSTAL CODE: WA

LAND AREA: 66,582 square miles (172,447 sq km)

POPULATION (2009): 6,664,195

ENTERED UNION (RANK): November 11, 1889 (42)

MOTTO: *Al-ki* (an Indian word meaning "into the future")

TREE: Western hemlock

FLOWER: Coast rhododendron

BIRD: Willow goldfinch

NICKNAME: Evergreen State

FAMOUS WASHINGTONIAN: Bob Barker, game show host

guess what? *Washington grows more apples than any other state in the union.*

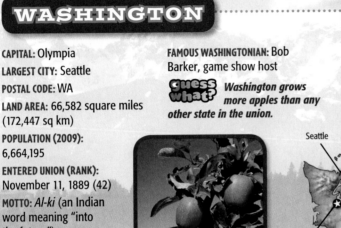

Apple orchard in Washington

Seattle

Olympia

WEST VIRGINIA

CAPITAL: Charleston

LARGEST CITY: Charleston

POSTAL CODE: WV

LAND AREA: 24,087 square miles (62,385 sq km)

POPULATION (2009): 1,819,777

ENTERED UNION (RANK): June 20, 1863 (35)

MOTTO: *Montani semper liberi.* (Mountaineers are always free.)

TREE: Sugar maple

FLOWER: Rhododendron

BIRD: Cardinal

NICKNAME: Mountain State

FAMOUS WEST VIRGINIAN: Mary Lou Retton, Olympic gymnast and winner of a gold medal in 1984

guess what? *The area now known as West Virginia split from the state of Virginia at the beginning of the Civil War. Virginia decided to leave the union, and West Virginia remained.*

Charleston

Rhododendron

WISCONSIN

WISCONSIN
1848

CAPITAL: Madison

LARGEST CITY: Milwaukee

POSTAL CODE: WI

LAND AREA: 54,314 square miles (140,673 sq km)

POPULATION (2009): 5,654,774

ENTERED UNION (RANK): May 29, 1848 (30)

MOTTO: Forward

TREE: Sugar maple

FLOWER: Wood violet

BIRD: American robin

NICKNAMES: Badger State, Dairy State

FAMOUS WISCONSINITE: Frank Lloyd Wright, architect

 The state dance of Wisconsin is the polka, which reflects the strong Czech-Polish and German heritage found in the state.

Madison

Milwaukee
Madison

WYOMING

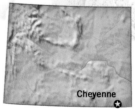

CAPITAL: Cheyenne

LARGEST CITY: Cheyenne

POSTAL CODE: WY

LAND AREA: 97,105 square miles (251,502 sq km)

POPULATION (2009): 544,270

ENTERED UNION (RANK): July 10, 1890 (44)

MOTTO: Equal rights

TREE: Plains cottonwood

FLOWER: Indian paintbrush

BIRD: Meadowlark

NICKNAMES: Big Wyoming, Equality State, Cowboy State

FAMOUS WYOMINGITE: Jackson Pollock, artist

 Wyoming is known as the Equality State because it was the first state in the union to extend the right to vote to women.

Cheyenne

Sego Indian

WASHINGTON, D.C.

The District of Columbia, which covers the same area as the city of Washington, is the capital of the United States. The district's history began in 1790 when Congress took charge of organizing a new site for the country's capital. George Washington chose the spot, on the Potomac River, midway between the northern and southern states. The seat of government was transferred from Philadelphia, Pennsylvania, to Washington, D.C., on December 1, 1800, and President John Adams became the first resident of the White House.

LAND AREA: 68.25 square miles (177 sq km)

POPULATION (2009): 599,657

MOTTO: *Justitia omnibus* (Justice for all)

TREE: Scarlet oak

FLOWER: American beauty rose

BIRD: Wood thrush

FAMOUS WASHINGTONIAN: Duke Ellington, jazz musician, composer

Completed in 2004, the World War II Memorial honors the 16 million Americans who served in the Second World War.

Many landmarks and memorials found in Washington, D.C., are monuments to people and events in U.S. history. Other impressive buildings are still used by government officials today. Here are a few Washington standouts.

The largest library in the world, the Library of Congress, is located in Washington, D.C. This building contains 650 miles (1,046 km) of bookshelves—if stretched from end to end, they would reach from D.C. to New York City and back again and then some!

The Jefferson Memorial honors Thomas Jefferson, the nation's third President and one of the main authors of the Declaration of Independence. Modeled after the Pantheon in Rome, it was commissioned by Congress in 1934.

The Washington Monument is 555 feet (169 m) tall. Built between 1848 and 1884, it honors President George Washington.

The Vietnam Veterans Memorial features a wall with the names of more than 58,000 Americans who died in the Vietnam War.

United States

231

PUERTO RICO

Located in the Caribbean Sea, Puerto Rico is about 1,000 miles (1,609 km) southeast of Miami, Florida. A U.S. possession since 1898, it consists of the island of Puerto Rico plus the adjacent islets of Vieques, Culebra, and Mona. Both Spanish and English are spoken there.

CAPITAL: San Juan

LARGEST CITY: San Juan

LAND AREA: 3,459 square miles (8,959 sq km)

POPULATION (2009): 3,967,288

MOTTO: *Joannes est nomen eius.* (John is his name.)

TREE: Ceiba (silk-cotton)

FLOWER: Maga (Puerto Rican hibiscus)

BIRD: Reinita (stripe-headed tanager)

FAMOUS PUERTO RICAN: Jorge Posada, baseball player

San Juan

OTHER U.S. TERRITORIES

Here are the four other U.S. territories.

AMERICAN SAMOA, a group of islands located in the South Pacific, is located about halfway between Hawaii and New Zealand. It has a land area of 77 square miles (200 sq km) and a population of approximately 65,628.

St. Thomas

GUAM, located in the North Pacific Ocean, was ceded to the United States from Spain in 1898. It has a land area of 209 square miles (541 sq km) and a population of approximately 178,430.

U.S. VIRGIN ISLANDS, which include St. Croix, St. Thomas, St. John, and many other islands, are located in the Caribbean Sea, east of Puerto Rico. Together they have a land area of 136 square miles (351 sq km) and a population of approximately 109,825.

THE NORTHERN MARIANA ISLANDS are located in the North Pacific Ocean. They have a land area of 176 square miles (456 sq km) and a population of approximately 88,662.

A Summer Road Trip

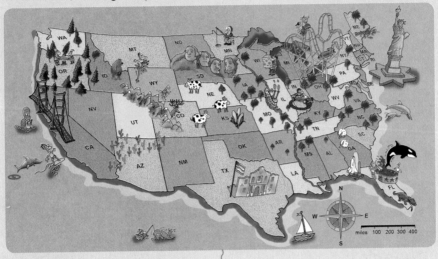

This summer, the King family hit the road. Study the map and answer the questions.*

TIME FOR KIDS GAME

1. The Kings live in Kansas. They drove to Texas. Which state did they drive through?

   _____

2. In which direction did they travel?

   _____

3. Next year they want to visit California. In which direction will they drive?

   _____

   *We left out Alaska and Hawaii. The Kings didn't go there.

Use the letters from the red blanks to solve our riddle.

1. Babe Ruth was born in Maryland's largest city, _ _ _ _ _ _ _ _ _.

2. New Orleans is the capital of

   _ _ _ _ _ _ _ _ _.

3. This state borders Utah to the south.

   _ _ _ _ _ _

RIDDLE: How do bees get to school?
ANSWER: On the school _ _ _ z!

Answers on page 245.

MYSTERY PERSON

Clue 1: I was born on August 1, 1779. I was a lawyer, but I wrote poetry as a hobby.

Clue 2: On September 14, 1814, I wrote an important poem about the U.S. flag.

Clue 3: The words of my poem became the lyrics of "The Star-Spangled Banner." In 1931, Congress officially named the song the national anthem.

Who am I? _____

Answer on page 245.

TOP 10 — Largest U.S. Cities by Population

	CITY	POPULATION
1	New York, NY	8,363,710
2	Los Angeles, CA	3,833,995
3	Chicago, IL	2,853,114
4	Houston, TX	2,242,193
5	Phoenix, AZ	1,567,924
6	Philadelphia, PA	1,447,395
7	San Antonio, TX	1,351,305
8	Dallas, TX	1,279,910
9	San Diego, CA	1,279,329
10	San Jose, CA	948,279

Source: U.S. Census Bureau

United States

233

Seattle
Tacoma
Olympia
Spokane
Portland
Washington
Salem
Eugene
Oregon
Boise
Idaho
PACIFIC
OCEAN
N
W   E
S
California
Reno
Santa Rosa Sacramento
San Francisco Carson City
Modesto
San Jose
Fresno
Nevada
Yosemite
National
Park
Death
Valley
Las Vegas
Los Angeles
Escondido
San Diego
Great Falls
Montana
Helena
Billings
R o c k y
Yellowstone
National
Park
Wyoming
Great
Salt
Lake
Salt Lake City
Utah
M o u n t a i n s
Grand
Canyon
Flagstaff
Phoenix
Arizona
Tucson
Missouri River
Bismarck
Pierre
Rapid City
Cheyenne
Denver
Colorado Springs
Colorado
Pueblo
Santa Fe
Albuquerque
New Mexico
El Paso
G r e a t   P l a i n s
Amarillo
Lubbock
Abilene
Texas

Kauai
Oahu   Hawaii
Honolulu   Maui
Hawaii
PACIFIC
OCEAN

ARCTIC OCEAN
RUSSIA
Alaska
CANADA
Anchorage
Juneau
BERING
SEA
Aleutian Islands
MEXICO
Laredo

0 mi.   300 mi.   600 mi.

0 km   400 km   800 km

PACIFIC OCEAN

234

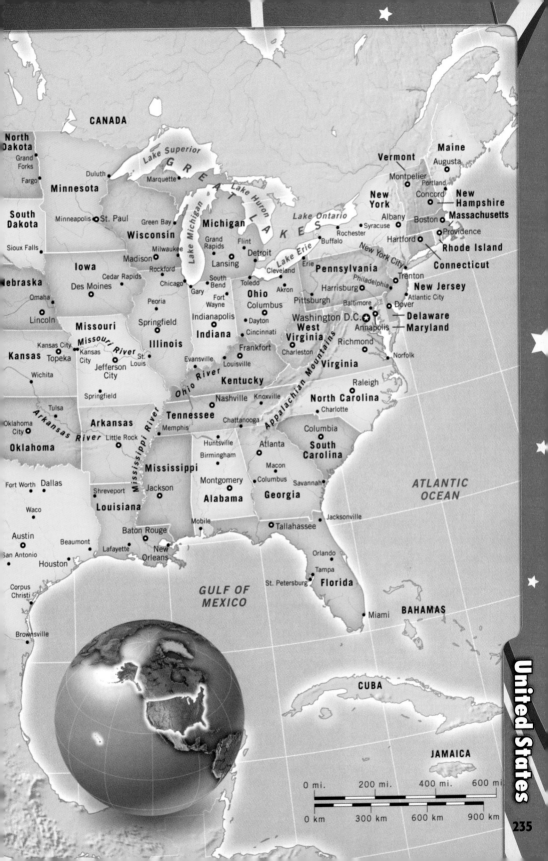

CANADA

North Dakota
• Grand Forks
• Fargo

Minnesota
• Duluth
• Marquette

South Dakota
• Sioux Falls
Minneapolis • • St. Paul

Wisconsin
• Green Bay
• Madison
• Milwaukee
• Rockford

Iowa
• Cedar Rapids
• Des Moines

Nebraska
• Omaha
• Lincoln

G R E A T   L A K E S

Lake Superior

Lake Michigan

Lake Huron

Michigan
• Grand Rapids
• Flint
• Detroit
• Lansing
• South Bend
• Fort Wayne

• Chicago
• Gary
• Peoria

Illinois
• Springfield
Evansville •

Missouri
Missouri River
Kansas City •
• Kansas City
• Jefferson City
• Springfield

Kansas
• Topeka
• Wichita

St. Louis •

Indiana
• Indianapolis
• Columbus
Ohio
• Dayton
• Cincinnati

Akron •

Cleveland •

Toledo •

Lake Erie

Erie •

Pennsylvania
• Harrisburg
• Pittsburgh

West Virginia
• Charleston

Kentucky
• Frankfort
• Louisville
Nashville •
Knoxville •

Ohio River

Lake Ontario

Rochester •
Buffalo •

Syracuse •

New York
• Albany

Vermont
• Montpelier

Maine
• Augusta
Portland •
Concord •
New Hampshire
Boston •
Massachusetts
• Providence
Hartford •
Rhode Island
Trenton •
Connecticut
New York City
New Jersey
• Atlantic City

Philadelphia •
Baltimore •
Dover •
Delaware
Washington D.C. ⊙
Annapolis •
Maryland

Richmond •
Virginia
Norfolk •

Raleigh •
North Carolina
• Charlotte

Appalachian Mountains

Tennessee
Chattanooga •
Memphis •

Arkansas
• Little Rock
Tulsa •
Oklahoma City •

Arkansas River

Oklahoma

Mississippi River

Columbia
South Carolina

Mississippi
• Jackson
Shreveport •
Huntsville •
Birmingham •
Alabama
Montgomery •
Macon •
Columbus •
Georgia
Atlanta •
Savannah •
Jacksonville •

Fort Worth • Dallas •
Waco •
Austin •
San Antonio •
Houston •

Louisiana
Baton Rouge •
Lafayette •
New Orleans •
Mobile •
Beaumont •

Corpus Christi •

Brownsville •

GULF OF MEXICO

Tallahassee •

Orlando •
Tampa •
St. Petersburg •
Florida
Miami •

ATLANTIC OCEAN

BAHAMAS

CUBA

JAMAICA

0 mi.   200 mi.   400 mi.   600 mi.

0 km   300 km   600 km   900 km

Volunteering
LEND A HAND!

Before setting out to be a volunteer, think about the cause that you would like to help most. Here are a few that might interest you.

EDUCATION

You might be able to help students from other countries speak better English. If you are good at math, tutor a younger child who is having trouble with the subject. Check with a teacher to find the best use for your time and talents.

ELDERLY PEOPLE

Elderly people—whether they live alone or in group homes—can often feel lonely. A visit from a young person like you can go far toward comforting them or helping them accomplish small tasks. You might call an assisted living community to see if they need young volunteers to help out or just to hang out, play cards, and share stories.

ANIMALS

If you love animals, donate your time to a local animal shelter or pet rescue group. You and your family might even be able to foster a pet.

KIDS AND ADULTS WITH ILLNESSES

Many hospitals and clinics have opportunities for those who want to help out. You might sit with sick children and talk with them, play with them, or read to them. You could also help serve meals, make beds, and deliver gifts to patients. Call your local health care center to find out about volunteering opportunities for students your age.

THE ENVIRONMENT

There are countless ways you can help the environment on your own or as a group. Organize a recycling drive, have a contest to see which street in your town can recycle the most trash, or start a gardening club at school. Volunteer at a nearby state or national park, or organize a tree-planting day throughout your community.

HOMELESSNESS AND HUNGER

Volunteer at a shelter, soup kitchen, or for a religious group that works with people who have no place to live or who need assistance to feed their families. Gather a group and organize a canned-food or warm-clothing drive.

MUSIC

Do you enjoy singing or playing an instrument? Look for a choir or another group that performs for nursing homes, hospitals, or community centers.

LITERACY

Share your passion for books with others. Libraries and schools welcome volunteers to read stories to younger children, and librarians always need help organizing and reshelving books!

SPORTS

If you like running, swimming, or even just walking, consider participating in a race for a cause such as cancer, AIDS, or multiple sclerosis. If you don't want to race, you can distribute water and cheer on others.

Kids Make a Difference

Here are just a few of the organizations founded by young people that are having a big impact on people close to home and around the world.

Craig Kielburger, of Toronto, Canada, was only 12 years old in 1995 when he heard about a 12-year-old boy in Pakistan who had probably been murdered for speaking out against child labor. Craig was so moved by the boy's heart-wrenching story that he organized a small group and began collecting signatures and giving speeches in schools about child labor. His organization, **Free The Children,** aims to free children from poverty, especially through education. Free The Children has built more than 500 schools in Asia, Africa, and Latin America. **freethechildren.com**

After watching a video about the millions of children in Africa who had lost their parents to AIDS, Austin Gutwein wanted to help. On World AIDS Day in 2004, he grabbed a basketball and shot 2,057 free throws—one for each child that would be orphaned that day. He raised nearly $3,000. Since then, Austin's foundation, **Hoops of Hope,** has grown into the largest basket shoot-a-thon in the world. The organization has raised more than $1.8 million, and has helped provide food, clothing, medicine, shelter, and educational opportunities to children affected by AIDS. **hoopsofhope.org**

TOP 5 U.S. States for Volunteering

More than 60 million Americans gave their time in 2007. In which states are volunteers most likely to give more than 100 hours?

1. **Utah**	44% of volunteers
2. **Nebraska**	40% of volunteers
3. **Minnesota**	40% of volunteers
4. **Alaska**	39% of volunteers
5. **Montana**	38% of volunteers

SOURCE: CORPORATION FOR NATIONAL AND COMMUNITY SERVICE

At 7 years old, Zach Bonner set out to help homeless and disadvantaged kids living in the United States, and he did it one wagonful of donations at a time. **The Little Red Wagon Foundation** is a non-profit organization that collects funds and supplies for needy children, including those affected by hurricanes. To raise awareness of the nation's 1.3 million homeless youths, Zach has completed two 280-mile (450-km) walks and a 650-mile (1,046-km) walk from his home in Florida to Washington, D.C. He has also thrown holiday parties for children displaced by hurricane Katrina. "Kids are the next generation," says Zach. "It doesn't matter how old or how young you are. You can make a difference." **littleredwagonfoundation.com**

going green

Every year in late April, people across the country celebrate Earth Day by volunteering their time or raising money to help protect and improve the environment. Are you one of them? Talk to your family to find an Earth-conscious way to spend the day.

Weather

WILD WEATHER

Good weather is a balance between cold and hot, wet and dry, and calm and wild. When the weather hits extremes in temperature, precipitation, or wind speeds, land is damaged and people suffer.

▲ Droughts can lead to dry, cracked earth.

DROUGHTS

A drought is an unusually long period of insufficient rain or snowfall. Droughts can last for years, though most last only a few weeks or months. Warm-weather droughts affect agriculture immediately and can lead to large crop losses. Cold-weather droughts, however, cause trouble the following spring, when rivers, streams, and the ground fail to fill with water from melting snow and ice.

▲ Hurricane Katrina hit the Mississippi coast in 2005, destroying many homes.

TROPICAL STORMS

These storms have winds stronger than 75 miles (120 km) per hour. They're called **hurricanes** when they form in the northern Atlantic Ocean and the northeastern or southern Pacific Ocean, **typhoons** when they develop over the northwestern Pacific, and **cyclones** when they form over the Indian Ocean. No matter what they're called, they can cause serious harm.

Hurricanes are created when tropical winds gather moisture as they pass over water that is at least 80°F (27°C). The winds of a hurricane rotate around an eye, or center. Within the eye of the storm, the weather is calm. It can even be sunny. Outside the eye, however, the warm ocean waters give energy to the storm, causing swirling wind and pounding rain. Hurricanes are strongest when they're over water, but they can remain fierce after reaching land, which is where they do the most damage. They are measured in categories, ranging from a Category 1, which has winds from 74 to 95 miles (119 to 153 km) per hour, to Category 5, which has winds greater than 155 miles (250 km) per hour.

▲ The eye of a hurricane

TIME FOR KIDS GAME

BRRRRRRR!

In many parts of the United States, the weather can be frightful in the wintertime. Is it snowy and cold where you live? Look at the five-day forecast for Chillytown, USA. Then answer the questions about what kind of weather folks there can expect.

Monday	Tuesday
High 30 Low 22	High 35 Low 30

TORNADOES

Tornadoes are fast-spinning columns of air that reach the ground. They can reach speeds of 300 miles (483 km) per hour. They generally form out of giant storms that occur when warm, moist air on the ground rushes upward and smacks into cooler, drier air. This colder air causes the warm air to cool down. As the warm air cools, the moisture in it condenses and forms huge thunderclouds. The thunderclouds pull up warm air from the ground, which causes air to swirl around. It is this process that creates the distinct funnel shape of a tornado.

Some tornadoes measure only a few feet in diameter. Others are much wider—up to a mile (1.6 km) in diameter. Some build up quickly and disappear. Others move across the land at 30 to 70 miles (48 to 113 km) per hour, sometimes for hundreds of miles. The winds that make up a tornado can be strong enough to pick up cars, trees, homes, and anything else in their path.

▲ Most tornadoes are visible as funnel-shaped clouds.

FLOODS

Floods are a danger to people and property. Just 6 inches (15 cm) of rushing water can knock a person down. Floods are usually caused by rivers or lakes overflowing their banks or by surges of ocean water during periods of heavy rainfall. The Galveston Flood of 1900, in Texas, was caused by a hurricane surge and took the lives of more than 5,000 people. Other floods are caused by failures of engineering. For example, the 1899 deadly Johnstown Flood began when a dam collapsed.

The term *flash flood* refers to a particularly dangerous type of flood that takes place very quickly and without warning. They generally occur when the water in streams or rivers in low-lying areas come up over their banks.

A large vehicle, such as a school bus, will begin to float in as little as 2 feet (61 cm) of water.

▲ Severe storms in Fargo, North Dakota, led to terrible flooding in 2009.

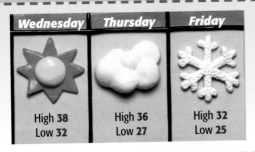

Wednesday	Thursday	Friday
High **38** Low **32**	High **36** Low **27**	High **32** Low **25**

1. Which day will be the warmest?

2. When might you wear snow boots?

3. Which day has the biggest difference between high and low temperatures?

Answer on page 245.

Weather

What's Next?

going green

E. coli up close

Fuel from Bacteria?

Ever heard of E. coli? Short for *Escherichia coli*, it is a type of bacteria that usually lives inside the intestines of humans and some animals. Most strains are harmless, but some can cause outbreaks of disease. For many people, the name only comes up when there is a story about food poisoning in the news.

But some scientists at Texas A&M University have been investigating the bacteria as a possible energy source. They've found out that, with a little chemical engineering, E. coli produces a great deal of hydrogen. Unlike fossil fuels such as coal and oil, hydrogen is a clean, renewable source of fuel. Today, hydrogen can be removed from water through a process of separating the elements that make up water. It is an expensive method that uses a lot of energy. But one day, bacteria could be a renewable source of clean energy.

Color-Changing Tiles

A group of recent graduates of the Massachusetts Institute of Technology has come up with a simple plan to save on energy use: Replace roof tiles. Different colored roofs absorb sunlight and heat differently. When the sun beats down on a black roof, the roof absorbs the heat and warms the home. White roof tiles, on the other hand, reflect up to 80% of sunlight, keeping homes cooler. To help homeowners keep heating and cooling costs down, the scientists are developing tiles that turn white on hot days (to help cool a home) and black on cold days (to help warm a home). The tiles are still being tested, but they are one great idea for a green future.

A researcher blows hot air onto a color-changing tile. As the tile warms up, it turns white.

Living Architecture

Eco-friendly buildings are becoming even greener! The Edith Green/ Wendell Wyatt Federal Building in Portland, Oregon, is planning a serious renovation. Architects will cover one side of the building with plant life. This 250-foot-tall (76 m) vertical garden would help provide shade in the summer to keep air-conditioning costs down. In the winter, the sunlight can stream in and help warm the building.

BREAKTHROUGHS IN BODY AND HEALTH

Good News for Diabetics

Diabetes is a disease that affects how a person's body absorbs sugar from food. Diabetics take insulin shots because insulin helps them absorb the sugars, or glucose, they need to get energy. Without the insulin, glucose can build up in the blood and make them dangerously ill.

A professor at the University of Western Ontario has developed a new way to monitor blood-sugar levels without drawing blood. He has created a contact lens that can detect the amount of glucose in a person's tears. It changes color according to the wearer's blood-sugar levels. Diabetics may soon have a new, pain-free way to keep an eye on their health!

Modern-Day Mind Reader

Neuroscientists (scientists who study the brain) have made it possible to read people's minds. In a recent experiment, a test subject hooked up to a computer watched as technicians flashed letters onto the screen, one at a time. When the subject saw the letter he wanted, the computer detected a change in his brain waves and chose the letter. It was a slow process, but the subject was able to create short messages using nothing but his mind. Another set of scientists in Germany actually created a brain-wave–operated pinball game. A person wearing a special helmet could play the game with no hands.

Scientists Spot the Regrowth Gene

Some animals, such as newts, sponges, and flatworms, have the ability to regrow damaged tissue. People do not currently have the ability, but scientists may have stumbled onto the secret to regrowing tissue in humans.

New research suggests that a gene called p21 prevents your body from being able to quickly grow new tissue. Scientists have found ways to interfere with certain genes, and some believe that if they can keep the p21 gene from working properly, humans might be able to regrow tissue like newts do. This would allow humans to heal without scarring. In tests on lab mice, scientists pierced the ears of mice whose p21 gene was "switched off." Within weeks, the holes had closed completely, without even leaving a scar! Because of their success with early experiments, researchers are hopeful. But they will continue testing to make sure that interfering with p21 won't cause other problems.

While humans will probably never be able to regrow a lost arm or leg, the ability to heal more quickly and without scarring could drastically change the future of medicine.

> If a newt loses a limb, it is able to regrow the missing part.

guess what?

Scientists in Spain have discovered a way to implant tiny silicon chips into living cells. These cells can be used as sensors to monitor microscopic activities. They could be used to detect early symptoms of diseases, deliver medicine to certain unhealthy cells, or even repair cell damage.

What's Next?

Faster than a Speeding Bullet!

China already has some of the fastest trains in the world, and an even faster one is on the way. The proposed high-speed rail link will travel an average of 217 miles (350 km) per hour. It will link Wuhan in Central China to Guangzhou in the south, cutting travel time from six hours down to two hours and 45 minutes. Now engineers have plans to extend the rail system all the way to London, England, by 2020! The new stretch of railway would pass through a total of 19 countries, linking London to Beijing, the capital of China. It would carry passengers 5,033 miles (8,100 km) in just two days! Today, that trip takes at least seven days by train. China has offered to pick up the expensive tab for this massive rail line in exchange for natural resources, like lithium, timber, oil, and gas, from the partnering nations.

Waterless Washing Machines

Many everyday activities—from taking showers to watering plants—use up water. Washing clothes is one of the biggest water-wasters, and many consumers are on the lookout for ways to conserve. A company called Xeros has developed reusable nylon beads that can be used to clean clothing with nothing more than a cup (.2 L) of water and a drop of detergent. Compared with the 41 gallons (155 L) of water used by the average washer, one cup is a big improvement. This new invention could drastically reduce the amount of water used in homes and Laundromats.

Pay by Phone

Cell phones are used for a lot more than making phone calls. They are also used to take pictures, play games and music, surf the Web, view interactive maps, and much, much more. Soon, many people will be using their phones to make purchases. Personal account information will be stored on a tiny card inside the phone. Instead of pulling out cash or a credit or debit card, a user will simply hold his or her phone up to a particular machine to make a payment.

The SideTap is one brand of mobile payment card that is being introduced in 2010.

ENTERTAINMENT OUTLOOK

To create a 3-D image, two projectors are used to shoot images from slightly different angles. In a 3-D recording, your eyes are seeing doubles of everything on the screen. The special glasses force your eyes to put the images together—which creates the illusion of depth.

Coming Soon to Theaters

- *Cars 2*
- *Cats & Dogs: The Revenge of Kitty Galore*
- *Despicable Me*
- *Gulliver's Travels*
- *Harry Potter and the Deathly Hallows: Part I*
- *Harry Potter and the Deathly Hallows: Part II*
- *Kung Fu Panda: The Kaboom of Doom*
- *Pirates of the Caribbean: On Stranger Tides*
- *Ramona and Beezus*
- *Stretch Armstrong*
- *Tangled*
- *The Adventures of Tintin*
- *The Chronicles of Narnia: The Voyage of the Dawn Treader*
- *The Sorcerer's Apprentice*
- *The Twilight Saga: Breaking Dawn*
- *Transformers 3*
- *Yogi Bear*

3-D TV in Your Living Room

Early 3-D (three-dimensional) movies, like *Creature from the Black Lagoon*, amazed audiences in the 1950s. But digital 3-D technology has come a long way from the days of wearing red-and-blue-tinted cardboard glasses. Recently, films from *Avatar* and *Alice in Wonderland* to *Jonas Brothers: The 3D Concert Experience* have used cutting-edge technology on the big screen. What's next for 3-D?

TVs that are equipped to beam 3-D images straight into your home are already on the market. In March 2010, Panasonic announced it had sold its very first 3-D home-entertainment system. It comes with one pair of special "3-D active shutter lens eyewear," and sells extra pairs for $149.95 each. With a price tag of almost $3,000, these deluxe devices probably won't be replacing standard TVs any time soon, but the idea of playing video games in 3-D may attract many buyers in the near future.

guess what? *Not everyone can see in 3-D. According to a recent study, 5 to 10% of Americans suffer from something called "stereo blindness." When shown a 3-D image, they will either see it in two dimensions or suffer from headaches and eye fatigue.*

Stay tuned! Rupert Grint, Emma Watson, and Daniel Radcliffe will be back for the final two installments of the Harry Potter saga.

Answers

Page 25:
SOUTH AFRICAN WILDLIFE
1. Five: Namibia, Botswana, Zimbabwe, Mozambique, Swaziland
2. Southwest
3. Lesotho
4. Manyeleti Game Reserve
5. Itala Game Reserve and Willem Pretorius Game Reserve

Page 27:
MYSTERY PERSON: Claude Monet

Page 31:
BODY BASICS
A. Heart
B. Lungs
C. Muscles
D. Brain
E. Bones

Page 33:
MYSTERY PERSON: Bram Stoker

Page 41:
LANTERN LOOK-ALIKES
1 and 3
2 and 5
4 and 6

MYSTERY PERSON: Julius Caesar

Page 83:
MYSTERY PERSON: Mary Robinson

Page 97:
MYSTERY PERSON: John Muir

Page 101:
AN AMAZING HARVEST

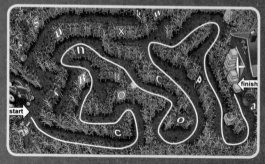

Page 103:
REBUSES
1. Sandbox
2. Pretty please
3. Double trouble
4. Forgive and forget
5. Jack in the box
6. Broken promises

PICTURE PUZZLE

Page 108:
MYSTERY PERSON: Marco Polo

GLOBAL WORD SEARCH

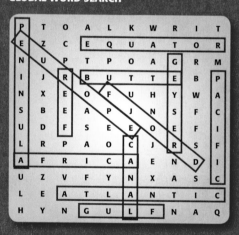

Page 129:
MYSTERY PERSON: Thomas Jefferson

Page 135:
MYSTERY PERSON: Queen Elizabeth I

244

Page 139:
KING'S DREAM

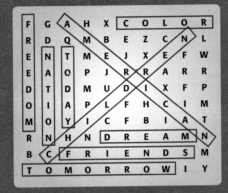

```
F G A H X C O L O R
R D Q M B E Z C N L
E N T M E J X E F W
E A O P J R R A R R
D T D M U D I X F P
O I A P L F H C I M
M O Y I C F B I A T
R N H N D R E A M N
B C F R I E N D S M
T O M O R R O W I Y
```

Page 143:
MYSTERY PERSON: George Eastman

Page 145:
MYSTERY PERSON: Sequoyah

Page 149:
HOLIDAY GIVING
There are many answers to this game. As long as the total cost of your four gifts is less than $50, you've won. See how many different sets of presents you can buy and still stay within your budget of $50!

Page 155:
MYSTERY PERSON: Julie Andrews

Page 161:
MYSTERY PERSON: Louis Armstrong

Page 171:
MYSTERY PERSON: William Henry Harrison

Page 179:
INSECTS IN THE GARDEN

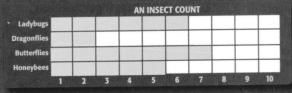

Page 187:
MYSTERY PERSON: Robert Goddard

Page 205:
SUPER SPORTS GRAPH

Bonus Questions: 2, 21

Page 205:
MYSTERY PERSON: Bonnie Blair

Page 233:
A SUMMER ROAD TRIP
1. Oklahoma
2. South
3. West

U.S. RIDDLE
1. Baltimore
2. Louisiana
3. Arizona
Riddle Answer: On the school buzz!

MYSTERY PERSON: Francis Scott Key

Page 239:
1. Wednesday
2. Monday or Friday
3. Thursday

Index

Photo Credits

FRONT COVER: Shutterstock.com (butterfly, bamboo, tiger, Big Ben); AP Photo/Amr Nabil (Tut); Warwick Innovative Manufacturing Research Centre (WIMRC), part of Warwick University (WorldFirst F3 race car); AP Photo/Brian Zak/Sipa Press (Swift); AP Photo/Mark Duncan (James).

BACK COVER: Shutterstock.com (girl with laptop, globe, Venice, girl on bike, tornado); AP Photo/Kyodo (White).

CONTENTS: 1: Shutterstock.com (scuba diver, ice skater, building); Courtesy Hirotaka Sato and Michael M. Maharbiz (cyborg beetle). 3: AP Photo/J. Scott Applewhite (Obama); Photo by Larry Madin/Woods Hole Oceanographic Institution (sea cucumber); Shutterstock.com (dog and cat, paint, yoga girl, gargoyle, candy canes); Courtesy Dutton Children's Books/Penguin Young Readers Group (*Paper Towns*); by Christopher Paolini, Jacket Art ©2003 by John Jude Palencar (*Eragon*); ©iStockphoto/PhotographerOlympus (column). 4: Shutterstock.com (laptop, girl with cell phone, building, greenhouse, farmer); AP Photo/Mark Davis/PictureGroup (Dance Crew); AP Photo/ Paul Sakuma (*Super Mario Bros.*). 5: Shutterstock.com (sailboats); Courtesy Speaker.gov (Pelosi); Shutterstock.com (tablet); Courtesy Shawn Kelly (electric eye); Library of Congress, Prints and Photographs Division (Sequoyah); Illustration for TIME For Kids by Jannie Ho (Holiday Giving). 6: AP Photo/Matt Sayles (Lautner); AP Photo by Scott Gries/PictureGroup (Beyoncé); Library of Congress, Prints and Photographs Division (Lincoln and son); Shutterstock.com (periodic table, mushroom, Jupiter); NASA (space food). 7: Fred Vuich/Sports Illustrated (del Potro); Heinz Kluetmeier/Sports Illustrated (Yu-Na); Library of Congress, Prints and Photographs Division (Geronimo); Photo Courtesy Free The Children (boy with lamb); Illustration for TIME For Kids by Amy Vangsgard (Brrrrrr!); Shutterstock.com (girl with magnifying glass).

WHAT'S IN THE NEWS?: 8–15: Shutterstock.com (border, paper). 8: AP Photo/Gerald Herbert (Haiti); AP Photo/David Lillo (Chile cars); AP Photo (Chile buildings). 9: AP Photo/Wong Maye-E (Iran); AP Photo/Steve Helber (Somali pirates); AP Photo/Susan Walsh (Obama). 10: AP Photo/M. Spencer Green (job fair); Photo Courtesy of U.S. Army (troops); Shutterstock.com (cable car). 11: Official White House Photo by Pete Souza (Sotomayor); AP Photo/ J. Scott Applewhite (Obama). 12: AP Photo/Damian Dovarganes (clunkers). 12: Imaginechina via AP Images (H1N1); AP Photo/Amr Nabil (King Tut). 13: NASA (moon); AP Photo/Mark Lennihan (Kindle); AP Photo/Paul Sakuma (Jobs); AP Photo/Jae C. Hong (backpack). 14: AP Photo/Matt Sayles (Swift); AP Photo/ Chris Pizzello (Glee); AP Photo/L.Martinez/JPegFoto (Gaga); AP Photo/Kilchiro Sato (Winfrey). 15: AP Photo/Lefteris Pitarakis (*Twilight* actors); AP Photo/Ben Liebenberg (Brees); Kyodo/AP Images (White, Yankees).

ANIMALS: 16: Shutterstock.com (border, background); Photo by Larry Madin/Woods Hole Oceanographic Institution (sea cucumber); Photo by Woods Hole Oceanographic Institution (Nereus); David Shale (octopod). 17: ©2006 Graffiti Sky Photography/Image from Bigstock.com (squirrel in tree); Shutterstock.com (porcupine, chipmunk, squirrel, King Philip, spaghetti, sturgeon). 18: Shutterstock.com (clown fish, newt, crocodile, parakeet, kangaroo, chimpanzee); AFP/Getty Images/Kenting National Park Headquarters (strawberry crab). 19: Shutterstock.com (sponge, jellyfish, worms, snail, bee, ants); ©Johnandersonphoto/Dreamstime.com (brittle star). 20–21: Shutterstock.com (all). 22: Ryan Hagerty/U.S. Fish and Wildlife Service (ferret); M. R. Matchett/U.S. Fish and Wildlife Service (USFWS member); Shutterstock.com (saber-toothed tiger); ©2008 interactimages/Image from Bigstock.com (dodo). 23: Mary Plage/Getty Images (rhino); Shutterstock.com (gorilla, walrus, penguin, tiger). 24: Shutterstock.com (all). 25: U.S. Fish and Wildlife Service (zookeeper); Jean Wisenbaugh for TIME For Kids (game); ©iStockphoto/brightstorm (dolphin trainer).

ART: 26: Shutterstock.com (background, paint smears, trees, aquarium); ©iStockphoto/Ekaterina Roma (color wheel). 27: ©Bridgeman Art Library, London/SuperStock (*The Last Supper*); Shutterstock.com (paintbrushes, palette); Public Domain (Monet).

BODY AND HEALTH: 28–30: Shutterstock.com (all). 31: ©iStockphoto.com/johnwoodcock (heart); ©iStockphoto.com/romandekan (circulatory system); Illustrations by Sharon and Joel Harris for TIME For Kids (Body Basics).

BOOKS AND LITERATURE: 32: Shutterstock.com (background); Random House/Wendy Lamb Books (*When You Reach Me*); Random House Children's Books/Delacorte Books for Young Readers (*Going Bovine*); Random House Children's Books/Knopf Books for Young Readers (*Return to Sender*); Shutterstock.com (reader); Copyright © 2009 Tanya Lee Stone, reproduced by permission of the publisher, Candlewick Press, Inc., Somerville, MA (*Almost Astronauts*); Copyright © 2009 by Matt Phelan, reproduced by permission of the publisher, Candlewick Press, Inc., Somerville, MA (*The Storm in the Barn*). 33: Dutton Children's Books/Penguin Young Readers Group (*Paper Towns*); Random House/Schwartz & Wade (*The Lincolns*); by Christopher Paolini, Jacket Art ©2003 by John Jude Palencar (*Eragon*); Random House Children's Books/Laurel Leaf (*In the Forests of the Night*); *Swordbird* by Nancy Yi Fan,

Cover Courtesy HarperCollins (*Swordbird*); Hulton Archive/Getty Images (Bram Stoker); Shutterstock.com (Dracula).

BUILDINGS AND ARCHITECTURE: 34: Shutterstock.com (all). 35: Shutterstock.com (White House, Duomo, St. Peter's Basilica, Empire State building, Doric column); ©iStockphoto.com/PhotographerOlympus (Ionic, Corinthian columns). 36–37: Shutterstock.com (all).

CALENDARS AND HOLIDAYS: 38–40: Shutterstock.com (background). 41: ©iStockphoto.com/cthoman (dancing bird); Shutterstock.com (boy); Illustration for TIME For Kids by Paul Tong (Lantern Look-Alikes); New York Public Library, Astor, Lennox, and Tilden Foundations (Caesar).

COMPUTERS AND COMMUNICATIONS: 42: Shutterstock.com (border, background); AP Photo/Peter Dejong (online reporter); AP Photo/Hasan Sarbakhshian (protester). 43: AP Photo/Koji Sasahara (Stone); AP Photo/Jason DeCrow (Berners-Lee, Fallon). 44: Shutterstock.com (background); TIME For Kids (www.timeforkids.com). 45: Courtesy of Reading is Fundamental (girl); Shutterstock.com (girl with laptop); Sports Illustrated Kids (www.sikids.com). 46: Shutterstock.com (all). 47: NASA (astronauts); Shutterstock.com (girl's head, boy's head, basketball star); Warner Bros/The Kobal Collection (*Where the Wild Things Are*); 20th Century Fox Film Corporation/The Kobal Collection (*Night at the Museum 2*). 48: Shutterstock.com (background, palm tree, phone); AP Photo/John Miller (cactus). 49: FEMA News Photo (satellite phone); Shutterstock.com (Space Needle, girls, boy).

COUNTRIES: 50: Shutterstock.com (border, background); ©iStockphoto.com/FrankvandenBergh (Wamala King's tombs); Shutterstock.com (Avila, Pueblo). 53–55: Shutterstock.com (all). 64: ©iStockphoto.com/seregeti130 (hoatzin). 68: Shutterstock.com (baobab). 70: Photos.com (dodo). 71–79: Shutterstock.com (all). 81: ©iStockphoto.com/Laser143 (crane). 83: UN Photo/Paulo Rilgueiras (Mary Robinson). 84: ©iStockphoto.com/essxboy (map); Shutterstock.com (Big Ben, Eiffel Tower, Chichen Itza, Machu Picchu); ©iStockphoto.com (Christ the Redeemer). 85: Shutterstock.com (all).

DANCE: 86: Shutterstock.com (background, break dancing, rumba, waltz); Just One Productions/The Kobal Collection/Raschke-Robinson, Claudia (*Mad Hot Ballroom*); Tiger Aspect Pics/The Kobal Collection/Keyte, Giles (*Billy Elliot*); 87: Adam Larkey/©ABC/Getty Images (*Dancing with the Stars*); AP Photo/Vince Bucci/PictureGroup (We Are Heroes); AP Photo/Mark Davis/PictureGroup (season 4 contestants).

ENERGY AND THE ENVIRONMENT: 88: Shutterstock.com (border, background, Lake Mead); AP Photo/Rick Rycroft (farmers). 89–90: Shutterstock.com (all). 91: Shutterstock.com (red pepper, pollution, oil); U.S. Fish and Wildlife Services/public domain (ducks in oil). 92: Shutterstock.com (all). 93: Shutterstock.com (geothermal field, house, fan, boy); NASA (hydrogen). 94–95: Shutterstock.com (all). 96: AP Photo/Oregon State University/Elizabeth Gates (dead zone); NASA (phytoplankton); AP Photo/University of North Carolina at Chapel Hill/Hans Paerl (Pamlico Sound); Shutterstock.com (trash bag). 97: Ocean Conservancy's International Coastal Cleanup, Samantha Reinders/Aurora (Coast Cleanup); Library of Congress, Prints and Photographs Division (Muir); Shutterstock.com (mouse).

FOOD AND NUTRITION: 100: Shutterstock.com (backgrounds); Official White House Photo by Samantha Appleton (kitchen, Obama); Library of Congress, Prints and Photographs Division (Roosevelt). 99: U.S. Department of Agriculture (food pyramid); Shutterstock.com (kids, apple, avocado). 100–101: Shutterstock.com (all); Illustration for TIME For Kids by Steve Skelton (An Amazing Harvest).

GAMES: 102: Shutterstock.com (background, kids); Shea Walsh/AP Images for Nintendo (Wii Fit); AP Photo/ Paul Sakuma (*Super Mario Bros.*); AP Photo/Katie Collins/PA Wire (Wii controller). 103: ©Mreco99/Dreamstime.com (Scrabble® tiles).

GEOGRAPHY: 105: Shutterstock.com (border, background, Ang Thong, atoll, map, butte); Photos.com (Grand Canyon). 106–107: Shutterstock.com (background, all). 108: ©iStockphoto.com/Hulton Archive (Marco Polo); Shutterstock.com (camels).

GOVERNMENT AND LAW: 122: ©iStockphoto.com/gavni (border); Library of Congress, Prints and Photographs Division (background, Declaration of Independence, Madison, Constitutional Convention). 123–24: Shutterstock.com (all). 125: Courtesy Speaker.gov (Pelosi); Department of Defense/Mike Kaplan (Biden). 126: Official White House Photo by Chuck Kennedy (Obama signing, meeting); Official Presidential Portrait/public domain (Obama); Official Vice Presidential Portrait/public domain (Biden). 127: Official White House Photo by Chuck Kennedy (Cabinet). 128: AP Photo/Charles Dharapak (Justices); Library of Congress, Prints and Photographs Division (Story); Shutterstock.com (gavel). 129: Official White House Photo by Pete Souza (Sotomayor); Photos.com (Jefferson).